CAMBRIDGE STUDIES IN PHILOSOPHY

Moral legislation

T0382617

Moral legislation

A LEGAL-POLITICAL MODEL FOR INDIRECT CONSEQUENTIALIST REASONING

Conrad D. Johnson

University of Maryland

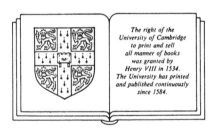

The right of the
University of Cambridge
to print and sell
all manner of books
was granted by
Henry VIII in 1534.
The University has printed
and published continuously
since 1584.

Cambridge University Press

Cambridge
New York   Port Chester   Melbourne   Sydney

CAMBRIDGE UNIVERSITY PRESS
Cambridge, New York, Melbourne, Madrid, Cape Town, Singapore, São Paulo, Delhi

Cambridge University Press
The Edinburgh Building, Cambridge CB2 8RU, UK

Published in the United States of America by Cambridge University Press, New York

www.cambridge.org
Information on this title: www.cambridge.org/9780521102421

© Cambridge University Press 1991

First published 1991
This digitally printed version 2009

A catalogue record for this publication is available from the British Library

Library of Congress Cataloguing in Publication data
Johnson, Conrad D.
Moral legislation : a legal-political model for indirect
consequentialist reasoning / Conrad D. Johnson
p.   cm – (Cambridge studies in philosophy)
Includes bibliographical references and index.
ISBN 0-521-39224-1
1. Consequentialism (Ethics)   2. Law and ethics.   I. Title.
II. Series.
BJ1031.J64   1990
171′.5–dc20   90–39746
                                CIP

ISBN 978-0-521-39224-2 hardback
ISBN 978-0-521-10242-1 paperback

To the memory of my father and mother
Conrad C. Johnson
and
Catherine M. Johnson

Another man, or perhaps the same man (it's no matter) says, that there are certain practices conformable, and others repugnant, to the Fitness of Things; and then he tells you, at his leisure, what practices are conformable and what repugnant: just as he happens to like a practice or dislike it.

The mischief common to all these ways of thinking and arguing (which, in truth, as we have seen, are but one and the same method, couched in different forms of words) is serving as a cloke, and pretence, and aliment, to despotism: if not a despotism in practice, a despotism however in disposition: which is but too apt, when pretence and power offer, to show itself in practice.

Jeremy Bentham

We entirely repudiated a personal liability on us to obey general rules. We claimed the right to judge every individual case on its merits, and the wisdom, experience and self-control to do so successfully. This was a very important part of our faith, violently and aggressively held, and for the outer world, it was our most obvious and dangerous characteristic. We repudiated entirely customary morals, conventions and traditional wisdom. We were, that is to say, in the strict sense of the term, immoralists. The consequences of being found out had, of course, to be considered for what they were worth. But we recognized no moral obligation on us, no inner sanction, to conform or to obey. Before heaven we claimed to be our own judge in our own case.

John Maynard Keynes

Contents

Preface

The particular version of indirect consequentialism defended in this book represents the most recent stage in a rather long period of thinking about morality and its legal analogues. It may make no sense to attempt to mark the beginning of such a long evolution, but I am tempted to do so anyway. It seems that it all began in my first year in graduate school, when I ran across a comment of H. L. A. Hart's on Hare's characterization of morality, saying that it represented "an excessively Protestant approach," taking morality "as *primarily* a matter of the application to conduct of those ultimate principles which the individual accepts or to which he commits himself for the conduct of his life."[1] This remark intrigued me, partly because it seemed to contain a very important kernel of truth usually missed by contemporary moral philosophy; but also partly because it was not clear how the idea of a social rule could be incorporated into moral theory in any nontrivial way without endangering the autonomy of critical moral thinking. I was impressed also with G. E. M. Anscombe's remark – itself an echo of J. S. Mill, among others – that the concepts of guilt and sin and injustice are at bottom juridical notions depending for their full-blooded sense on the idea of law. That at least the core of morality could be likened to law would seem to be an antidote for that (act) consequentialism through which, as Anscombe put it, "the kind of consideration which would formerly have been regarded as a temptation, the kind of consideration urged upon men by wives and flattering friends, was given a status by moral philosophers in their theories."[2] Yet, once we remember how bad existing social rules can be, it is not obvious how we can make use of this idea.

Reading the great legal philosophers, as well as those moral philosophers influenced by legal ideas, ranging from St. Thomas Aqui-

1 Hart, 1958, p. 100.
2 Anscombe, 1958, p. 225.

nas to Hume, Kant, and John Stuart Mill, my thinking has thus been influenced – some will no doubt think overly so – by seeing the ways in which moral reasoning has benefited, and might be made more consciously and explicitly to benefit, from ideas that are at root essentially legal in character. Thinking of the probable charge that morality is not like law, that it is a mistake to allow moral theory to be guided by legal analogies, I take comfort in the fact that many classic conceptions of morality have been modeled in significant ways on legal ideas.

It is of course impossible to mention all the people whose encouragement or intellectual influence somehow figure into this book. Indeed, the identities of some of these people remain unknown to me. Perhaps they will read this resulting work and recognize their influence in what I have written. Among the many to whom I know I am indebted in some way or other, the following deserve special mention: Richard Brandt, whose empirical, utilitarian approach to morality, and whose philosophical advice over the years have exercised a considerable influence on my thinking; Stephen Darwall, who has, on and off over the years, been a stimulating partner in philosophical conversation on these topics, and who suggested the title of the book to me (I must, however, accept full responsibility for the subtitle); and Michael Slote, who read and helpfully commented upon earlier versions of the present work.

Thanks are due to the Graduate Research Board of the University of Maryland for providing me on more than one occasion with the time off from teaching to enable more intensive work on this book. I must also note here my appreciation of the helpfulness and intelligent professionalism of my editor, Terence Moore, and his assistant, Nick Alpers. Finally, the painstaking care and sensible advice of my copy editor, Herbert Gilbert, saved me from the consequences of some unexamined habits common to professional philosophers.

Conrad D. Johnson

1

Introduction

This essay is an attempt to buttress the case for a consequentialist moral theory. In doing so, it addresses an important and recurrent difficulty confronting consequentialism: the problem of providing a rationale for the moral prohibitions that, in our commonsense thinking, we take seriously. The kinds of prohibitions I have in mind include those – like the prohibitions on lying, stealing, and killing – that sometimes constrain one to do or avoid certain actions even when compliance with the prohibition would produce less overall good than some other action available to the agent. Consequentialism in its broadest conception I take to be the view that the ultimate, foundational criterion of the rightness of actions refers to consequences. From that broad conception, we can follow some of the more familiar divisions among types of consequentialism. Act consequentialism proposes that an act is right if and only if it would have the overall best, or equally best, consequences of any alternative open to the agent. It is thus a direct form of consequentialism because the overall consequences of each action are directly relevant to its rightness or wrongness.

The fundamental appeal of consequentialism as a moral theory no doubt owes to its use of a widely shared and plausible idea: that if the rightness of actions is to be explained at all, it must be in terms of good consequences that are brought into being by those actions. We often have conflicting intuitions about what is right, and we sometimes recognize that our ideas about the right thing to do need correction or adaptation. It seems that the most plausible common currency by which we can resolve conflicting intuitions and correct our moral opinions is that of the goodness of consequences – that the concept of right should rest squarely on the concept of the good.

Important as these advantages of consequentialism may be, it nevertheless confronts some well-known difficulties. Applied thoroughly and consistently, it has often been said, consequentialism would in a number of areas come into radical conflict with our commonsense moral views. For consequentialism seems ineluctably to bring a maximizing doctrine with it; that is, if overall good results is the ultimate determinant of the right, then it can never be wrong to do that which maximizes overall good. Indeed, some have maintained that this maximizing doctrine has such intuitive appeal that it constitutes the main reason why utilitarian moral theory continues to exercise such a hold on the philosophical imagination, in spite of the abundant criticisms that have been made of it.[1] Yet this maximizing feature of utilitarianism is most troublesome in many contexts precisely because it conflicts with what we take to be some of our most compelling moral reasons. For the idea that maximization is always permissible (or perhaps required) means that we may or must do what brings about the best consequences even if doing so would involve lying, cheating, killing the innocent, or anything else that goes against some of our most deeply held common-sense convictions.

These implications, I take it, constitute difficulties for consequentialism. But in calling them such, I do not presuppose that common-sense convictions *must as such* be accommodated within any adequate moral theory.[2] Nor am I suggesting that the guiding idea behind the development of an adequate moral theory is to reach a kind of reflective equilibrium between theory and commonsense convictions. However, consequentialists do need to take account of commonsense convictions in the following way at least. It is reasonable even for a thoroughgoing consequentialist to afford some presumption in favor of commonsense morality on the ground that, given certain normal background conditions at least, a deeply entrenched and long held article of commonsense morality would probably not survive long if its existence did not do some good, or perhaps maintain some valued stability in the circumstances. Still, nothing of importance for our purposes depends on this being the case. What is important about the difficulties is that they may, I contend, constitute unnecessary obstacles to the philosophical acceptance of consequentialism, for they arise from a

---

1 Scheffler regards this maximizing feature not only as inherent in utilitarianism, but as that feature of utilitarianism which gives it its great and persistent appeal. See Scheffler, 1982, p. 4; and 1988, p. 1.
2 Michael Slote stressed the importance of making this point clear at this juncture.

misconception about the ways in which rational agents are to take account of consequences in their thinking and action.

Those who wish to defend a form of consequentialism that avoids these difficulties often turn to forms of indirect consequentialism. Indirect consequentialisms use some intermediate concept standing between the appraisal of actions and the appraisals of consequences. One such proposal would have us evaluate the rightness of an action by reference to what a properly motivated person would do, defining a properly motivated person as one whose motives lead to the best overall long-term results of any set of motives possible, say, for that person. Another type of indirect consequentialist proposal is the much more familiar category of rule-consequentialist theories. They hold that the rightness of actions is to be determined by reference to rules which must in turn be justified by reference to *their* consequences. Once we use such an intermediate concept, it is no longer so easy to argue that an act of lying or of killing the innocent would be permitted. Thus it seems quite unlikely that a general rule permitting actions of this kind would itself be utilitarianly justified.

It is significant that indirect consequentialisms typically retain some version of a maximizing doctrine. The difference, of course, is that the idea of maximization is shifted to another level. Thus rule consequentialists typically claim that, although the maximization requirement is not to be applied to individual acts, it is to be applied to the rules by which those acts are to be judged: An act is right if and only if it conforms to the utilitarianly best rule.

But this shift from the idea of maximization at the level of individual acts to that of maximization at the level of rules has served to trade one set of problems for another. I think it is fair to say that in recent years the preponderance of philosophical opinion about rule consequentialism has been unfavorable to it. To most philosophers it has seemed to be an unstable and unmotivated compromise between consequentialism, which holds that the morally right is a function solely of the good (usually understood as the good consequences of actions), and deontology, which denies this. For if a rule requires an action that does not maximize overall good, then, even if the rule is wholly justified in terms of the good it brings about, the question can always be raised why one ought to comply with the rule. Many would hold that, by hypothesis, there

3

is no satisfactory answer *in terms of the bringing about of good* that can be given. Another problem arises even more directly from shifting the applicability of the maximizing doctrine from acts to rules. The most likely objection to this move is that existing rules and practices are usually less than the best and cannot be changed by one person. In what sense, then, does maximization have any place in a theory that might require me to act in accordance with a rule when (i) the act does not itself maximize, and (ii) the rule in accordance with which I am acting is also not the best?

A central object of this essay will be to state, and in part to restate, a case for rule consequentialism that escapes the most important of the traditional objections to it, including the objection that there is no satisfactory reason for complying with a justified rule in cases in which compliance will not maximize overall good. It will be no part of my proposal to suggest that the rightness and wrongness of actions is in all circumstances to be referred to rules; nor that the concept of right can only be meaningfully used in moral judgments when some rule is being presupposed. The main idea is rather that, in some, though surely not all, spheres of behavior, it is highly desirable for us to abdicate our title always to act to produce the best overall results, and that it is rational for us to recognize utilitarianly justified rules as preempting – that is, partially replacing – the reasons for maximizing that we individually have. But this abdication of individual title does not entail giving up collective responsibility to maximize, and it is in their function in promoting collective maximization that social rules and practices find their justification.

When we conceive of the responsibility to maximize as a collective concern that properly focuses on social rules and practices, we can recognize at once the limitations and obstacles that we face as moral agents. Improving social institutions is obviously not a matter of simply imagining what the best would be like, and then acting straightway as the best institutions would require. It is mostly a matter of public criticism of institutions, of persuasion, of setting good examples, and of using public instrumentalities like the law, to bring about changes in the complex set of attitudes and expectations of which social institutions consist. Thus the most reasonable application for the maximization doctrine at the level of evaluating and changing social institutions is to think of it as re-

4

quiring us to act (i) in ways that will change those institutions for the better, but (ii) in a way that is respectful of one's responsibility to do one's part under justified, even if imperfect, social rules and practices.

To think of moral rules as social rules or practices that function as public and right-defining standards is, of course, not the only way in which philosophers in the utilitarian tradition have conceived of rules, though it is at least close to the way in which John Rawls once conceived of them."[3] Other philosophers do think that there is a place for rules in moral thinking, though the rules as they conceive of them are rules of a very different sort: They do not have any right-defining function. Thus one may acknowledge the usefulness of rules of thumb in giving the individual some general indication as to what is right or wrong on some independent criterion. And one may likewise acknowledge that rules can be used simply as summaries of what has been found to be right or wrong on some independent criterion ("As a rule, it has almost always turned out to be wrong to do X."). And recently, at least one writer has suggested that one can conceive of moral rules as strategies that it is rational for the individual to adopt for the more effective pursuit of the good.[4] A strategy, unlike a summary rule, can provide one with rather stringent reasons for doing certain things that seem not to be recommended from the standpoint of simple maximization. For example, Smith, knowing of his weakness for rationalization, and hence mistake, when faced with the temptation to do X, might be rational in adopting the strategy of refusing all temptations to do X. Like rules of thumb and summary rules, rules conceived as strategies never replace or supplement the independent criterion which alone gives the meaning of "right action": that an act is right if and only if it produces the overall best consequences of any alternative available to the agent. I shall argue that, important as these devices are as aids in doing the right thing, they do not reach far enough. They are insufficient primarily because they do not provide us with an adequate basis for mutual trust, nor for engaging

---

3 "Two Concepts of Rules," in Bayles, 1968, p. 59. As will become clear, some of my ideas about the proper function of rules derive from Rawls, though there are important differences. I leave my account of these differences for Chapter 9.

4 Berger, 1984.

in collective moral debate, mutual evaluation, and the exercise of influence on one another's behavior in accordance with standards that are public and knowable to all.

Central to this argument is the idea of the good of mutual trust, a good that is in many areas undercut by the use of individual strategies of doing good. What is required is a mutual resolution or willingness – like a Humean convention in the sense that it characteristically does not arise from any act or promise – to adhere to rules that limit individual discretion to maximize. The good to which this resolution gives rise derives only partially from the fact that, by and large, it leads to acts that have good consequences. No doubt it is the tendency to think of all good consequences as somehow reducible to the good consequences of behavior that has been the major source of the conviction that rule utilitarianisms, in their most usual form, are unstable and must collapse into act utilitarianism. There are other kinds of good consequences than those traceable to acts or even, speaking more generally still, behavior: There is, for example, the good that derives from the general knowledge that one lives among people who, following justified rules, have forsworn individual maximization; they are people of virtuous character and not just people of correct action.

That people are of virtuous character in this sense might be understood to mean nothing more than that they have been so socialized, trained, or even brainwashed that they do not even think in terms of doing the most overall good; instead, one might understand this to mean that they have been developed to think in ways that will lead others to trust them, and that is all we need to achieve the good of trust. But on this conception of trust there is still an important component of the good that is missing. For we want to live among people who do the right thing autonomously and with full information about what is right. Though it might even be possible, however doubtful, to force on people the requisite false ideas and beliefs to get them to behave in beneficial ways, and even to develop general confidence that they will behave in beneficial ways, it is far better if this confidence is based on the mutual recognition that others are disposed to do the right because it is right. Relationships between people are both more stable and intrinsically better when mutual respect is based on autonomous individual recognition of the right than when it is based on ignorance, brainwashing, or other forms of diminished opportunity to use

6

one's moral capacities. I shall argue that this feature of the good tells against those proposals that would drive a wedge between the objectively right and that which is supposed to be a reason for action.

Some forms of rule utilitarianism propose that the rules binding on us are those rules that would, if accepted, be the best possible. And this might seem to be the only plausible course open for any kind of utilitarianism that takes the notion of maximization seriously, even if maximization is an idea to be applied to rules rather than to acts. Surely, the thought runs, virtually any prevailing moral rule, not to mention whole moral codes, are utilitarianly defective in some way or other, and it just seems wholly unmotivated to link the rightness of acts to any rule that is less than the best. Against this familiar line of thought, I shall argue that generally accepted rules do have some priority over ideal rules that are not generally accepted. (How much priority, and in what circumstances they have priority, are questions to be dealt with later.) This priority is itself based on the idea of maximizing good, and is not, as some might think, (inexplicably) divorced from it: For the point of having rules – that everyone abdicates title to engage in unlimited individual maximization – would be defeated if it were left to the discretion of each to determine which rules would lead to the best results if generally accepted.

All of this leads to a final introductory remark, one especially apropos of this book's title. When some of the most important moral rules are conceived, as they are in this book, to be social rather than personal, this raises an important new question: What are the processes by which such rules are brought into existence, changed, or eliminated? What processes constitute the analogues in morality to the familiar processes of legislation and creative interpretation in law? My answer to this – developed in Chapter 8 – is roughly that we use whatever resources are available and reasonable in light of the overall spirit of the enterprise, the main object being to get general acceptance of justified, and, where possible, improved, moral rules. Sometimes we can coordinate our acceptance of a justified rule around the persuasive leadership of some individual, precisely because of the salience of that person. More often, perhaps, we look to the coordinating effect of the legal institutions of our society, allowing the debates and decisions that take place in and around both legislatures and courts to serve as the hitching posts for our common moral views. In this way, moral legislation often rides piggyback on legal legislation. None of this, I shall argue, need be thought to endanger the independence and autonomy of moral thinking; nor does it entail thinking of those with the power to enact laws as also having the authority, by virtue of their position, to "enact" valid moral rules.

2

The primary principle: Doing good

2.1. INTRODUCTION

My purpose is to motivate and sketch a teleological conception of morality, one on which rules and practices have an important function in defining the right, while the rules and practices themselves are ultimately to be evaluated and justified by considerations of the good they produce. On a teleological conception as I shall understand it, the ultimate good or goods are not themselves to be explained by reference to what is right or obligatory: We are not to explain the goodness of a state of affairs by referring to some obligation to bring it about; instead, we are to explain obligations by reference to the good. This is one natural meaning of the familiar utilitarian notion of the priority of the good over the right. These ideas are by themselves nothing new. Together they comprise the central features of what has usually been called "rule utilitarianism," of which many versions have been proposed. But the view for which I shall argue – the moral legislation model (MLM) – differs from most other recently proposed rule utilitarianisms in at least one major respect: It uses the notion of a collective rule or practice of a social group, thus conceiving of some of our most important rule-based moral judgments as relative, either to rules that already exist in a particular group, or to rules that, it is implied, ought to exist.

My object is to make such a view as this plausible, defending it at least against the most serious objections likely to be raised against it. Later I shall explain part of the motivation for defending a form of rule utilitarianism that conceives of right-defining rules and practices as those of actual communities, and then raises the kinds of questions just mentioned. In later chapters, I turn to some theoretical issues drawn from recent philosophical debate about con-

9

sequentialism, and I discuss the ways in which the MLM compares to several other consequentialist theories.

Our attention will be focused mainly on the theory of the right. But we need at least a sketch of a theory of the good. If we think of social practices as playing an important role in defining the right, and if social practices themselves are to be evaluated, and accepted or rejected, in accordance with the good that they promote or fail to promote, then we need some idea of what the good is.

A pluralistic concept of the good, viewing a number of things as intrinsically good, is more defensible than a concept on which all goods are reduced to one intrinsic good, like pleasure or happiness. It would be difficult to reduce the value of knowledge to the pleasure it produces, which is often lacking. And it would be a mistake to reduce the value of friendship to the pleasure that it often brings. Various things, then, are good: beauty, friendship, loyalty to a worthy cause, complex goal-oriented activity, and individual autonomy. In accounting for these goods, it is helpful to distinguish between those things which owe their importance to the structure of a particular person's desires from those that owe their importance to the fact that they are good to everyone. And we can distinguish these two from those things that owe their importance to what might be called a "species ideal."[1] For example, that human beings are different from other animals in having moral capacities, like the capacity to understand moral concepts, to have a developed conscience, and to exercise and act upon autonomous moral judgment, is an important fact giving rise to an ideal regarding their good: It is one of our ends to be in a position to exercise these capacities, and the opportunity to develop and exercise them is itself a good that is distinguishable from the goods we may or may not achieve through their exercise.

The idea that the satisfaction of desires is an important part of the good is central to, and indeed a starting point of, a proper account of the good. Yet some desires are more important than others, and can be thought of as the foundation for interests, some

1 In this I follow Griffin, 1986, p. 56. Griffin calls these "desire" accounts, "objective" accounts, and "perfectionist" accounts, respectively.

of which are in turn to be given more weight than others. Thus to say that an individual has an interest in something is to say that the individual has a stake in that thing.[2] Though the interests that we have are connected to the desires that we have or ought rationally to have, to have an interest in X is not to be equated with having a desire for it. Some desires may be too fleeting or impulsive on which to base an interest, and sometimes we have interests in things for which we have no actual desire, as when our information is mistaken or when our desires are not realistic or rational. In determining what is an individual's good, it is important that we not simply take that individual's desires as we find them; it is necessary to use the concept of an informed desire. This is not, however, a matter of all or nothing, forcing us either to take an individual's desires exactly as we find them, or, at the opposite extreme, requiring that each desire be fully informed if it is to count as a foundation of that person's good.[3]

We can distinguish between those of an individual's interests that are necessary means to many other goals, and those that are presumably less important because they do not serve as the means to so many other ends. In moving thus toward a greater element of objectivity that is available when we develop an account of an individual's interests, we consider how that individual's desires fit into an overall structure.[4] Then certain desires begin to emerge as foundations, not only for individual interests, but for universal interests. For example, health and vigor, the absence of absorbing pain, and the integrity and normal functioning of one's body, constitute interests that are of central enough importance to count as primary goods or welfare interests.[5] It is natural for our purposes to think of an individual's good, or well-being, as constituted by the harmonious advancement of that individual's interests, where the relative importance of an interest to the individual's good is a matter of the centrality of that interest as necessary means to the advancement of other interests. Thus one's interest in having a house at the beach is less important than one's interest in health, the latter being necessary to the realization of so many goods,

2 I draw this idea of the totality of one's interests, as well as the concept of an interest, from Feinberg, 1984, p. 34.
3 Griffin, 1986, pp. 33–4.
4 Griffin, 1986, p. 34.
5 Rawls, 1971, p. 62; Feinberg, 1984, p. 37.

including using and enjoying a house at the beach. The importance and centrality of X's interest in having or realizing something is relevant, both to another person's decisions on such questions as what resources to provide to X, and to X's own decisions about what desires and interests to acquire, reduce, or eliminate in X's own portfolio. So X's preoccupation with achieving some relatively unimportant goal might be ruinous to X's health, undercutting thereby the chances for X to realize so many other goals.

Such comparisons of interests with one another are intrapersonal comparisons. But we can extend the idea of the relative centrality of interests to some interpersonal cases as well. Thus, in adopting an impersonal standpoint, weighing the good of X's health against the good of Y's being honored at a banquet, X's health will count for much more. Assuming that other things are roughly equal (for example, that Y's being so honored is not somehow necessary to Y's health), the very impersonality of the evaluation would be called into question by any other conclusion about the respective importance of these interests of X and Y. This kind of interpersonal judgment about interests thus uses an objective criterion, at least in that its correctness is independent of X's and Y's tastes and overall interests. Though X might intensely want his favored outcome, the intensity of the preference is overridden by the nature of X's interest, and by X's reasons for having that interest.[6]

Where goods must be traded off against one another, they can be given different weights, some even lexical priority. This I take to be at least a theoretical possibility, though it is difficult to think of many situations in which an argument for a lexical priority, strict as that kind of priority is, could be mounted. It is implausible to some, including myself, to think (as Rawls does) that no amount of equal political liberty, however small, could reasonably be traded away for any amount of increased social wealth, however great. But at the same time, we can allow for the possibility that lexical priorities are in some cases rationally defensible. For example, in

6 This notion of objectivity of a criterion is borrowed from Scanlon, 1975, p. 658. As Scanlon puts it, "The fact that someone would be willing to forego a decent diet in order to build a monument to his god does not mean that his claim on others for aid in his project has the same strength as a claim for aid in obtaining enough to eat, even assuming that the sacrifices required of others would be the same." Scanlon, 1975, pp. 659–60.

some societies, something close to a lexical preference of one good over another might be held by virtually everyone.

Sometimes, though not often, we may find ourselves in the position of having to compare the good produced by one society's moral code to that of another. Our comparisons are usually not like this, of course; they are usually of a much more local sort, as when we ask whether one of our own practices has become burdensome and pointless. But when we do make intercultural comparisons of moral institutions, the advancement and protection of the more central interests constitutes the most natural starting point. Those interests are the ones which all persons are presumed to have, whatever their society or condition or other interests. So, when comparing the moral code of some other society to that of our own, it is reasonable to ask whether some practice they value serves well, in their circumstances, to advance an interest that we can understand as central and universal, even though we may advance or protect that interest in a quite different way.

This brief account of the good has focused mainly on interests, giving special place to welfare interests. The account could be further elaborated, and in quite different ways, each of which would be consistent with the sketch. It might be filled out by adding certain intrinsic goods. And, as already mentioned, one might move toward a particular conception of distribution by attaching some weight, or even lexical priority, to some resulting distribution of resources. On one such conception of the good, an equal distribution of certain things, such as liberty, opportunities, or wealth, would itself be a good. Of two distributions that are equally good in other respects, the equal distribution would be better.[7]

Before proceeding further, it is necessary to look a bit more closely at the notion of the good of individual autonomy. This is particularly important because of the role that notion will play in part of the argument of this book. Among the different things that can be meant by individual autonomy are the following:[8] the *capacity* to govern oneself, the *actual condition* of self-government, the *ideal of character,* and the *sovereign authority* to govern oneself. The notion

7 For a fuller discussion of "pluralistic lexical consequentialism," see Scheffler, 1982; and Scanlon, 1976.
8 Here I follow, in part, a very helpful discussion in Feinberg, 1986, ch. 18. See also G. Dworkin, 1988.

of self-government, of course, covers a pretty broad territory, including even the relatively unimportant aspects of one's life. The kind of self-government that especially interests us here is that of governing oneself by moral requirements. Applied specifically to moral self-government, then, the capacity that interests us is really that set of capacities which we have to grasp moral concepts, and sometimes to form new ones; to understand and apply facts to the making of moral judgments; and to participate with others in the process of moral deliberation and, as I prefer to characterize it, in the process of moral legislation. These are not the only moral capacities, of course; the focus here is primarily directed to the more or less cognitive capacities, for they are our chief concern under the heading of moral self-government.

This capacity of moral self-government then constitutes the basis for the claim that the exercise of this capacity, that is to say, the actual condition of moral self-government, is a good of major importance. It likewise provides the basis for the ideal of character associated with moral autonomy, a kind of species ideal, one might say: It is good both that people exercise moral autonomy, and that they develop toward the ideal qualities of character associated with the condition of autonomy. Now, among other things, moral autonomy as a condition involves engaging in moral deliberation with others as well as moral reflection on one's own; not being deprived by others or oneself of access to facts and information that is relevant to making moral judgments and decisions; and, above all, not being deprived, by others or by oneself, of knowledge of the general concepts of the objectively right and wrong. One cannot exercise moral self-government when one has been systematically deceived about the ultimate criteria of right and wrong, having been led to think that X is right if and only if X is F, when in reality, X is right if and only if X is O. In the sense of a character-ideal, the morally autonomous person will generally strive to be in possession of the moral reasons that justify his or her actions, though that need not involve being obsessed with the moral dimensions of one's situation; one will refuse to accept the pronouncements of other people on moral questions; and generally, one will be unwilling to follow prevailing moral opinion without deeper verification of its correctness.

It is especially important to the explanation of the MLM that we distinguish autonomy in the sense of sovereign moral authority from the three meanings we have just examined. To have moral autonomy in the sense of sovereign moral authority is, on one conception, to have certain *rights,* corresponding to which other people have certain duties. It implies that I have a certain sphere of thought, decision, and action, interference with which would be wrong. It may also imply something that might best be conceptualized as a set of Hohfeldian immunities, at least in the sense that no other person or group can impose on me their moral principles or conception of the right.[9] We must be careful to notice that this sense of autonomy belongs therefore to the theory of the right and not properly to the theory of the good. On the MLM, we are not entitled to appeal, in our attempts to show that moral autonomy is a good thing, and that lack of it, or violation of it, is bad, to the idea that violation of autonomy would be wrong. To do so would be to smuggle into the putatively teleological theory some prior and unargued for ideas about right and wrong. What does properly belong to our account of the good at this stage of the argument, therefore, are the concepts of autonomy as capacity, condition, and ideal of character. Whether individuals have a moral right to such things as privacy, and freedom of opinion and action, or whether the prevailing moral views of other persons and groups lack the normative capacity to impose moral duties on one, are questions that must be answered by appeal to the concept of the good, rather than answered independently of it.

2.3. GOODS DERIVING FROM SOCIAL UNION

We must now turn to some aspects of the good that are necessarily linked to cooperation with others and, more specifically, to membership in a community governed by collective moral rules. We can begin with something like Rawls's distinction between a social union and a private society. A social union is a group of people, located in the same geographical area or scattered, and existing either simultaneously or over an extended period of time, all of whom share certain final ends, and who value their common institutions both because those institutions serve to promote the good,

9 Hare's (1963, pp. 1–3) notion of the moral agent's freedom – presumably deriving from the very concept of morality – from any individual's or group's power morally to bind him to a principle, simply by virtue of their opinion, would seem to be an example.

15

and because they are, among the various possible institutions, those that are in fact accepted. In short, they regard adherence to the requirements of those institutions as important in itself, and not simply as that which accidentally turns out to coincide with the requirements of some independent criterion like, say, that requiring that each act maximize overall good. By contrast, a private society is one in which individuals have their own private ends which may or may not be competing, but which are not complementary; and institutions are not regarded as important in themselves, the activity of engaging in them not being thought a good but if anything a burden.[10] Now, it is clear that a social union has many advantages over a private society in promoting the good. Applied especially to a social union that includes moral standards that are public and applicable to all, there are several important features: (i) Individuals derive satisfaction from participating in a cooperative enterprise in which their own good is, in significant part, identified with that of others and of the community. When this enterprise is that of governing their conduct by moral standards, shared moral standards constitute the focus of this identification in the sense that everyone knows that those standards are public, as is moral discussion and debate, and so these belong to all as a kind of common property. (ii) Guided by a common goal, a social union is different from a private society in that members can cooperate among themselves in the interpretation of this goal, and in adopting subgoals. In this they are capable both of realizing their autonomy as individuals, and of a kind of collectively autonomous action. For they have opportunity, with others, to know what moral standards require, and thus they have the opportunity to do the right with the recognition that it is right and to be responsible, under normal conditions, for having done wrong. They can also join with others as equal agents of interpretation and construction of these standards. (iii) A social union reflects, and reinforces, a sense of mutual trust and acknowledgement of equality, facilitating further cooperation and diminishing the need for coercion – most especially, legal sanctions – as a means of producing that cooperation. This is so because everyone knows the terms of their relationship to others as a community: They know that, in certain important areas of interaction,

10 Rawls, 1971, p. 522. The idea of social union I develop here is inspired by Rawls and also by J. S. Mill. See Mill's *Utilitarianism*, ch. 3.

16

their conduct is governed by rules understood to apply to all. (iv) Finally, stable cooperation is itself the means to a broad range of external goods achievable only by joint efforts.

To avoid misunderstandings, a remark on the concept of equality is in order. I shall later argue for the claim that social moral rules are to be understood as public and equally applicable to all. This idea of the equal applicability of rules to all persons within some understood group thus belongs to the framework within which we are to conceive of moral rules, to evaluate them, and to argue about them. Now, this framework notion of the equal applicability of rules may seem to be unmotivated, at least from a consequentialist point of view. Thus it might seem to belong to a nonconsequentialist, even Kantian, conception of morality to insist that moral rules must apply equally to all, and that exceptions should be included within the understanding of what the rule is, rather than made ad hoc outside it.

Though there is much to be said for the view that equal application of moral rules belongs to the very concept of morality, it is even more important that we not forget the many connections between equal treatment under rules, and the good of social union. It greatly undermines the possibility of social union when announced, public rules are not respected in the distribution of burdens and benefits, whether punishment, taxes, honors, or offices. To apply rules in a consistently *in*consistent way is reasonably taken as an expression of unequal respect for members of the group to which the rules apply. To apply rules in a wholly capricious way may be reasonably taken as a sign of lack of respect for all members of the group. Moral rules, of course, are not applied in the same way that legal rules are. There is no set of moral officials, who use systematic procedures to decide whether individuals are blameworthy or not. But at the same time, there are similarities that are not to be overlooked. We all apply moral rules in deciding whether we ourselves ought or ought not to pursue some course of action; whether we ought to feel guilty about an action of ours, and whether it would be appropriate and fair to blame another person. In this way, moral rules too can be ignored or misapplied. The

17

unequal or capricious application of moral rules – whether in assigning praise and blame, in giving advice, or just in expressing something about a person's moral standing – can reasonably be taken as an expression of disrespect for some or all. If I hold most other people to strict moral standards about truth-telling, promise-keeping, and sexual behavior, but ignore these same standards when judging my own (say) racial group, and when challenged I indicate that the inconsistency does not worry me at all and that I feel no need whatever to provide further justifying reasons for this, then my judgments will likely and reasonably be taken as manifesting unequal respect. Now, this expression of unequal respect is both intrinsically bad and, more importantly, bad because of the deterioration of social unity it leads to. In circumstances in which people can engage in moral reflection and debate – one in which there is a tendency to look for the underlying reasons for differences in role – expressions of unequal respect will lead to mutual estrangement, resentment, and anger. For such expressions involve elements of condescension and contempt.[11] They represent offensive attitudes that are in fact likely to be returned with interest added.

In this way, we can regard the idea of equality as a marvelous, elegantly simple – indeed, ingenious – *device* for solving a large set of difficult social problems of attitude and perception: For example, we want to communicate, as clearly as possible to two children, that there is not a trace of love or preference for one over the other; so we have one cut the cake and the other take first choice. And, as moral and political philosophers have long recognized, inequality at one level may raise an especially strong demand for the idea of equality at a deeper level. Thus a manager recognizes the need to pay some employees more than others, give bigger raises to some than to others; so she establishes public criteria, backed by a rationale that all can understand as reasonable, for making these decisions and then she adheres to these criteria in a very visible way. Her deeper recognition of the equal standing of her employees is signaled in the use of a rationale that can be accepted by all as a reasonable basis for determining salaries and raises. In the first of these two examples, one or both of the children may become envious of the other, resentful toward a third-party cake cutter, or

11 My development of this idea, which has many antecedents, is most immediately influenced by Williams, 1967.

both envious and resentful if the division of the cake is seen as reflecting a personal preference. In the second example, the same danger exists, except that there are now great costs, in the form of diminished productivity, attached to equality in the sense of strictly equal distribution of proceeds from the enterprise. Because the sources of envy and resentment run too deep to eradicate from the human constitution, the solution is to shift their focus in productive ways. In both cases, the institutional form that the idea of equality is to take is dictated by broad considerations of costs versus benefits, maximizing productivity with minimum resentment and envy.[12]

That the idea of equality serves these purposes helps also to explain why it does not apply, or apply with the same force, in many situations. While two employees working under the same manager will be prepared to rivet their attention on even minute differences in their raises, those same two employees working for different managers will not be able to find the same focus for resentment. In all likelihood there will then be no one person to whose judgments any invidious comparison, or any comparison at all, of these two employees could be attributed.[13] And where a free market exists, the possibilities of finding a target for potential resentment become even more limited. If X's lesser share owes to the sum total of many individual decisions, none of which had X's share as their intended object, X's chances of finding a plausible target for resentment will also be greatly diminished. Where there is no natural target of resentment in the first place, there is less need for the special devices of universally applicable criteria and rules.

2.5. THE DISCRETION ENJOYED BY THE UNATTACHED MORAL AGENT

Now let us return to the individual's problem of how to do the right thing by doing good. It is useful to begin with an abstraction: that of a moral agent who has no special connection to any society's code, and for whom there is no existing moral code which carries

---

12 The idea that envy is potentially very dangerous to society, and yet both absolutely necessary to social control and ineradicable from human nature, is defended by Schoeck, 1987.
13 I made this kind of point some years ago in connection with the idea of equity in the distribution of welfare benefits. See Johnson, 1981.

any special obligation. This individual is not bound, in any special way that others are not, to comply with the rules or practices of any group. To fix ideas further, let us suppose that such a moral agent is bound only by the universally valid requirement of doing good and avoiding evil. This principle – "promote good and avoid evil" – would seem to be the natural guide, beginning as we do with a broadly consequentialist conception of the right. (In the pages to follow, I will sometimes refer to this principle simply as the "primary principle," distinguishing it thereby from collective rules that, I shall argue, can preempt reasoning based on the primary principle.)

We should note also that the principle of doing good and avoiding evil is consistent with act consequentialism, the doctrine which says that the right act in any given situation is that which will produce the best overall results, judged from an impersonal standpoint which gives equal weight to the interests of every person. However, while the principle of doing good and avoiding evil is consistent with act consequentialism, it does not entail it. For act consequentialism explicitly links the rightness of particular actions in each case to what will be optimific, and the injunction to do good and avoid evil does not entail this. One reason for this is that being called upon to do good and avoid evil is not by itself to be provided with a clear dividing line between doing enough and not doing enough to be "doing good." This invites a distinction between optimizing, satisficing, and scalar principles.[14] A scalar principle or theory is one that makes only comparative judgments of better or worse among acts or motives; it does not by itself establish a dividing line between sufficiently good, and insufficiently good. Combined with a theory of the good, the principle that one is to do good and avoid evil would yield at most a scalar principle.

Another reason why act consequentialism is not entailed by the principle is that one might do good simply by developing traits and dispositions to do what has as a matter of fact the best consequences. This would not necessitate producing, or aiming at the production of, the overall best outcome for each act. So something like motive utilitarianism would be one way of understanding the injunction to do good and avoid evil. Motive utilitarianism calls for the individual to "have the most useful among the patterns of

14 Slote, 1985a, chs. 3 and 5.

motivation that are causally possible for human beings."[15] To do good would then be to act in conformity with these traits and dispositions.

Though act consequentialism may not be entailed by the principle of doing good, some would nevertheless maintain that it is entailed by that principle when we add certain plausible assumptions belonging to our very notion of practical rationality. For example, Scheffler says that: "[G]iven only the innocent-sounding assumption that good is morally preferable to evil, it seems to embody the principle that we should maximize the desirable and minimize the undesirable, and that principle seems to be one of the main elements of our conception of practical rationality."[16] Whether (i) maximization and/or (ii) *act* consequentialism is entailed by the principle of doing good and avoiding evil, combined perhaps with some other plausible premises, is a controversy I shall try to avoid here. Let us then provisionally assume, for the sake of argument, that the moral agent who is to do good and avoid evil must, to the extent possible, maximize the overall good.

If moral agents, then, are bound only by the requirement to maximize overall good, they have moral discretion to kill, to lie, or to steal (or to do anything else) *so long as it maximizes overall good*. To be sure, they do *not* have moral discretion to do other than maximize overall good, but they do have discretion to do anything *else*. Given only the principle that one is to do good and avoid evil, we remain without any account of *agent-centered restrictions,*[17] – prohibitions on one's doing certain things; prohibitions which hold whether or not doing those things would produce the most good overall. Such restrictions are agent-centered in that an injunction not to do X is an injunction not to *do* X; and that is different from an injunction to bring about some impersonally desirable state of affairs, like that in which *people in general* do not do X. As one writer puts it, "A *prima facie* injunction to keep promises is a *prima facie* injunction to keep *one's* promises, not to bring about the intrinsically good state of affairs of people keeping their promises."[18]

15 The definition of motive utilitarianism is from Adams, 1976, p. 470.
16 Scheffler, 1988, p. 1.
17 Otherwise referred to as "agent-relative constraints." The notion is Scheffler's. See his 1982, pp. 2–5; also 1988, pp. 4–5.
18 Darwall, 1986, p. 293.

If agent-centered, or deontological, restrictions are a necessary part of any adequate moral conception, we must either show how such restrictions are rational within a broadly consequentialist conception, or we must abandon consequentialism. I shall attempt to show that deontological restrictions are rational within a consequentialist conception. In particular, I shall argue that, in order that good be maximized, the moral agent must take a collective point of view, giving up some discretion, and acknowledging some such restrictions on individual maximization.

First, however, we should recognize some of the devices that a moral agent might rationally use as a way of fulfilling the requirement to do good and avoid evil. These, I shall argue, may serve as weak limits on the agent's discretion, but the limits will be insufficient to count as the deontological constraints of morality. Most important for consequentialism, they will be insufficient to avoid certain evils such as the mutual mistrust and abuse of discretion that results from the general perception, both that discretion may be abused, and that there is only limited collective influence that can be exercised to limit the abuses.

One device by which the moral agent may limit his or her own discretion is that of developing suitable dispositions and traits of character. So it may well be rational, in following the injunction to do good and avoid evil, among other things to develop in oneself a desire to help others, to develop loyalty and devotion to some particular other persons, an aversion to killing, lying, and stealing.[19] It can be counterproductive constantly to *aim* at doing the most good, regularly trying to think of how best to promote impersonal good in the world; hence one might do more good in the long run by thinking of wife and children first, thus being able to take pleasure in helping these particular persons just for their own sakes. And a deep aversion to killing, lying, and stealing will reduce the likelihood of doing wrong out of temptation, self-deception, or some kind of mistake.

Another device available to the moral agent is to adopt certain strategies with regard to some kinds of decision and action.[20] If one tends, owing to deficiencies of information, or of weakness, to do the wrong thing, in the sense of producing less than the best overall

19 See Railton, 1984.
20 See Berger, 1984.

22

result available, it can then be rational to adopt a strategy of not doing certain things except under certain conditions. It might be rational for me to adopt the strategy of never making serious decisions under stress, or never breaking a promise where it is in my interest to do so, even though it might really seem to be the optimific thing to do. If I tend to make the wrong decisions under stress, or if I have a tendency to break promises all too easily where I see something in it for me, these strategies might be advisable. Having adopted a strategy of flatly refusing to break a promise whenever my reasons have to do with self-interest, I would no doubt still make some mistakes, but fewer than if I followed no such strategy.

3

The advantages of collective strategies

3.1. EXPLAINING THE PRIORITY OF RULES OVER ACTS

To many friends and foes of consequentialism, it has seemed obvious that our appraisal of consequences must ultimately be of the consequences of acts. Here we must mark well the qualifier 'ultimately'. Even unsophisticated consequentialists know that we attribute consequences to lots of things in the world other than acts, and that the appraisal of these consequences matters to the application of consequentialist theory: States of mind, desires and aversions, traits of character, rules, and even a public atmosphere of trust, or distrust, are just some of the things that can lead to good or ill. Yet the most common approach is to think of the value of their consequences wholly in terms of the consequences of the acts to which they somehow lead, directly or indirectly. The utility of everything is "cashable in terms of the effects of acts," as Williams has stated the underlying view.[1]

Of course, someone might object here that it is implausible to attribute consequences to the particular acts of particular individuals where the effects are small, or when some good result has been brought about only by the joint action of a large group. For it seems that each person's action made only a negligible contribution, and could be ignored. But as Parfit has convincingly argued, we cannot ignore small effects, nor small chances of effects. Further, it makes sense to attribute a share of the total good thus brought into being to each of the various members of a group whose joint action was necessary to that result.[2]

Once we have accepted the view that the utility of a rule is wholly

1 Smart and Williams, 1973, pp. 119–20. Williams calls this the "act-adequacy" premise.
2 "Five Mistakes in Moral Mathematics," in Parfit, 1984, ch. 3,

cashable in terms of the consequences of acts, we have taken a giant step toward the conclusion that the rightness of acts is logically prior to the desirability of rules. For if our concern is to see that the good be maximized, and all good consequences are ultimately explainable as the consequences of acts, rules can only serve a secondary role. Rules might serve to help fallible humans avoid mistakes, or to form admittedly imperfect ideas about patterns of rightness. In these ways, then, they might serve either as useful guides to action, or as retrospective summaries. But it is the result that counts. If all good results are traceable to acts, or may in more complex cases be plausibly divided among individual acts via some conception of sharing the total, then rules can only serve secondarily as means to bringing about the best behavior. Rules are the instruments which should be dispensed with when they get in the way of bringing about a good-maximizing set of actions.

It is important to notice that this picture is not significantly altered when we take account of what philosophers have in recent years called the "acceptance utility" of rules. The acceptance utility of a set of rules is usually defined as "the value of the effects of the general acceptance of the set of rules".[3] Discussions then usually add the observation that the acceptance utility and the utility from actual conformity to a rule may be different. Anyone who has deliberated about whether to teach a child a simple, flat prohibition or a complex and subtle rule, hedged with many qualifications, can be expected to know this. Because of human fallibility, we may make fewer mistakes when teaching and using simple rules than if we used complex rules that would be best for creatures of vastly greater capacities of perception and self-control. But it is clear from the way in which these accounts are spelled out that even acceptance utility is again ultimately to be cashed out in terms of the acts and their consequences to which the acceptance of a rule or rules leads.[4]

3.2. WHAT IS MISSING FROM THIS PICTURE?

This picture, I shall contend, is mistaken. To measure the utility of rules solely in terms of the utility of acts and their consequences

3 Lyons, 1965, p. 140.
4 Williams, 1973, p. 122: "[T]he utility of *acts* that follow on the obtaining of a rule is not to be equated with the utility of *acts* that consist in obeying the rule." [emphases added] This is also very much the tenor of Brandt's discussion. See Brandt, 1963.

25

is to miss one of the most compelling and distinctive elements of rule utilitarianism. There can be a surplus utility attributable to the general acceptance of a rule, and this utility cannot, in any natural and plausible way, be attributed to, or even divided among, particular acts. Indeed, it is the recognition of this "surplus causal effect" – to use Williams's words – which constitutes a key to understanding what once seemed intuitively clear but then doubtful: that indirect consequentialism does not collapse into direct consequentialism. The existence of justified social rules provides a most fundamental component of the good of any society. This good is the mutual trust and security deriving from a general commitment to those rules, from the public knowledge that there is such a general commitment, as well as from the knowledge that being true to the commitment is rational on the part of each individual. The view that this good can only be obtained through the general acceptance of social rules, and that this good cannot be cashed out in terms of the consequences of acts, I shall now attempt to explain.

3.3. HUME'S CONCEPTION OF JUSTICE AND THE "SURPLUS CAUSAL EFFECT" OF RULES

Among the most prominent classic conceptions of morality, it now seems to me, David Hume's conception of justice most clearly contains the outlines of a correct and deep understanding of the role of social rules and conventions. We can learn a great deal by rereading Hume on this subject, and in the following I shall give special attention to some often ignored features of Hume's views. But there is, it seems to me, another, more direct avenue to the conclusions Hume reached, and it is arguably the avenue that Hume himself took. This avenue opens up if we think of some of the core rules of social morality on a legal model, and as having some of the functions that legal rules have. There is probably more than coincidence in the fact that Hume's discussion of the value of adhering to a system of conventional rules takes place within his inquiry into the origins of justice, arguably the most juridical of the virtues.[5]

5 Hume, *A Treatise of Human Nature*, edited by L. A. Selby-Bigge (Oxford, 1888), bk. 3, pt. 2. The view that some of Hume's most important contributions are also his most overlooked – that is, those in legal philosophy – is to be found in "The Legal and Political Philosophy of David Hume." Hayek, 1967.

In a community governed by law, the existence of a rule of property, of criminal law, or of contracts serves – in addition to the well-known function of inducing people to behave or not to behave in certain ways – to provide people with a sense of mutually acknowledged commitment upon which trust and the confident planning of lives can be based. The ordinary citizen can know that he or she will run afoul of the law only for behavior within a certain well-defined sphere; that contracts of certain kinds, entered into in certain ways will be enforced, and that one who obtains property in certain specified ways will enjoy a certain package of liberties, powers and rights with respect to that property. Everyone in such a society – officials and ordinary citizens alike – understand this, and know and acknowledge the limits placed on each other's actions.

Hume's discussion of justice makes clear that he thinks of its rules as having *both* the function of securing certain patterns of behavior, *and* – what is, if anything, more important – of providing the bases of mutual trust:

I observe, that it will be for my interest to leave another in the possession of his goods, *provided* he will act in the same manner with regard to me. He is sensible of a like interest in the regulation of his conduct. When this common sense of interest is mutually express'd, and is known to both, it produces a suitable resolution and behavior. And this may properly enough be call'd a convention or agreement betwixt us, tho' without the interposition of a promise.[6]

And again:

[W]hatever may be the consequence of any single act of justice, perform'd by a single person, yet the whole system of actions, concurr'd in by the whole society, is infinitely advantageous to the whole, and to every part. . . . Every member of society is sensible of this interest: Every one expresses this sense to his fellows, along with the resolution he has taken of squaring his actions by it, on condition that others will do the same.[7]

We should notice first that Hume speaks of "suitable resolution" and "behavior", and of the "resolution" each has taken, and the mutually shared "sense" of concurrence. From this, it is clear that Hume is talking about much more than the use of convention to coordinate behavior, though his famous example of the two men

6 Hume, 1888, p. 490.
7 Ibid., p. 498.

pulling the oars of a boat is concerned primarily with the coordination of actual behavior, and this is admittedly one important function of convention. Those who think of the function of coordinating behavior as Hume's central point about conventional moral rules have only half digested his message.

If justice provides the foundation for some of the most fundamental of goods, including above all mutual trust, then our next question must be how to obtain this good. The first thing to recognize is that it simply does not make sense to think of this good as reducible to the good consequences of acts, individually or collectively. Clearly this good has an important connection to acts, for if people's behavior did not in general conform to their supposed "resolution," no one could reasonably believe that the rules were really "concurr'd in by the whole society." In addition, a central aim of such a resolution is obviously to direct behavior. Were there no behavior even potentially in prospect, there would be little point of having any such resolution in the first place. But that is not to admit that the good of mutual trust is to be reduced to that of acts. The most obvious reason for this is that the good of trust emerges as soon as there is a credible general resolution to follow the rules, and before any occasion for just or unjust behavior arises. If I live among just people, I can have a sense of confidence and well-being from the mere fact that I know that I am among just people. I can know that they will not treat me unjustly even if it turns out that they have no occasion to treat me at all, one way or the other.

A second reason for this is that the good of mutual trust may fail to exist even when everyone's behavior is in outwardly strict conformity to the demands of justice. If each knows that everyone does the just thing – or better: fails to do anything that is unjust – only because of fear of punishment, then there would be no solid basis for mutual trust. Much the same point holds of people whose behavior is in outward conformity to the demands of justice only because they are deluded, irrational, or simply too ignorant to spot opportunities. We can distinguish here two kinds of trust, each marked in English by a locution proper to it: (i) "I trust that you (he) will not do X." (ii) "I trust you (him) not to do X." The first is open, to a degree that (ii) is not, to the possibility that it is fear, ignorance, or manipulation that insures the not-doing of X. The kind of trust that is most valuable, both intrinsically and instrumentally, is that of free and autonomous persons trusting each other, rather than that of individuals trusting that others will not do certain things.

Finally, we should pay attention to a peculiar feature of Hume's concept of conventional rules which makes it conceptually difficult for individuals bound by them to link the good of rules to particular acts. What the rules call upon all individuals to do is to exclude certain considerations that would normally be relevant. As Hume puts it, "When a man of merit, of a beneficent disposition, restores a great fortune to a miser, or a seditious bigot, he has acted justly and laudably, but the public is a real sufferer."[8] It might seem that Hume's man of merit *could* be engaged in a kind of utilitarian weighing, deciding in the end that he can do greater good in the long run by restoring this miser's fortune, even if the miser will make no good use of it. In this decision, it seems, he would take into account the effects for public trust. But this utilitarian weighing is not open to the man of merit. What justice requires is, putting it plainly and simply, that the fact of the man's bigotry or miserhood be excluded from consideration. The legal analogue of this is the literal exclusion of certain evidence from being introduced into the proceedings. The miser's fortune is to be restored even if he could be deprived of it with no ill effects for mutual trust in the community. Thus we have the conceptual difficulty inherent in attempting to carry out the program of justice by linking particular acts to the production or diminution of the collective good of trust: What ultimately produces this collective good is the public knowledge that each has resolved to follow the rules on condition that others do so too, and that this resolution is individually rational and individually binding. In the context, this resolve is, among other things, the resolve to exclude certain otherwise relevant considerations in deciding the rightful ownership of property. So to engage in the usual weighing of utilitarian considerations just is the sort of thing inconsistent with this resolve. This is not to say that an unjust act must always have bad effects for mutual trust; for it may not, as when done in full secrecy. The problem is instead a matter of a the practical inconsistency of project: The program that does the good involves the resolve to exclude, and if adherence to such resolve were individually irrational (which common sense tells us it is not), this would quickly become recognized, and the good

8 Ibid., p. 497.

of mutual trust would be unachievable. It should be clear, then, that this argument does not proceed by tracing a causal connection between an action and a state of affairs.

3.4. PRAISING AND BLAMING

One of the chief advantages of publicly understood collective strategies can be seen if we consider their role in praising and blaming. Utilitarians since Sidgwick have often emphasized the distinction between the utility of an action, and the utility of praising or blaming it. Smart says that "neglect of this distinction is one of the commonest causes of fallacious refutations of act-utilitarianism."[9] His point, of course, is that it might not be worthwhile to blame an agent for an action that is wrong because of its bad consequences, and, conversely, it might be worthwhile to blame an agent for an action that is not wrong. Indeed, from a utilitarian standpoint, there would seem to be no necessary connection at all between the appropriateness of blaming (or praising) an agent and the wrongness (or rightness) of the action. Smart holds that, for the act utilitarian, "the notion of *the* responsibility is a piece of metaphysical nonsense and should be replaced by 'Whom would it be useful to blame?' "[10]

To the contrary, I suggest that one of the most important reasons why right-defining rules are sometimes necessary is precisely because praising and blaming are such an integral part of the process of moral judgment and discussion. There are sometimes powerful utilitarian reasons for tying blame closely to the doing of wrong as defined by rules. (This is not, however, to say that blame is to be made a function of wrongdoing only. For the degree of blameworthiness is no doubt also to be made a function of the agent's mental stance toward the wrongdoing.)

What is the utilitarian point of linking blame to wrongdoing as defined by rules? The promulgation and enforcement of laws provides one of the best illustrations of the usefulness of right-defining rules. Smart's suggestion – that the notion of responsibility should be treated as a piece of metaphysical nonsense and replaced with the simple question, "Whom would it be useful to blame?" – would lead to much the same kind of disaster as the analogous policy of

9 Smart and Williams, 1973, pp. 55–6.
10 Ibid., p. 54.

30

replacing the notion of legal responsibility with the idea of whom it would be useful to punish. For it is important to people, living in community with others, to know what they need to do in order to be in good standing with others, and to be confident that they have done their duty and that they therefore can rightly claim that they are not to be blamed or criticized. If legal penalties were applied on Smart's principle of direct case-by-case usefulness, the uncertainty, fear, and confusion would reach deeply into all aspects of life. If moral blame were in all departments of life to be applied on this principle, it would be hard for anyone to escape the sense that they too could be called to task, even publicly excoriated, merely for being the unfortunate though useful causal link in some utilitarian program of educating the masses. Though you may have done your duty to your family and children as any reasonable person would understand it, if people are already inclined to believe otherwise, it might be useful to hold you up as an object of moral reprobation, so that others may be taught a stern lesson. And there would be a standing tendency for the use of this act-utilitarian principle to become public. Either the process of defending acts of blaming would have to be greatly diminished, or that process as practiced would have to rely heavily on bad arguments, manufactured evidence, and false beliefs. If the former, then at the very least an important component of the good of social union would have been lost; at the worst, people would tend to regard the lack of moral discussion as confirming their worst suspicions about the functions of blame and punishment, and about the willingness of other people to use them as manipulative tools to advance the good. But given the fact that people do by and large want to get to the bottom of the reasons why they are being blamed, they will tend to uncover the artificiality of the arguments being used to justify the sanctions against them. And, contrary to the purposes of applying blame on the act-utilitarian principle, the result will not be to advance the good.

One might be tempted to reply at this point that the disutility of this debilitating public sense of uncertainty would soon make the application of sanctions inappropriate even on Smart's act-utilitarian principle. Then, in all but the most extraordinary situation in which the full facts can be kept from public view, the act-utilitarian principle would call for blame only when something was done that was generally believed to be wrong.

But this reply would miss an important point about the concept of right-defining rules and their utilitarian function. What is needed is the *public knowledge* that blame will be linked to wrongdoing as defined by an understood standard. Smart's act-utilitarian standard would be insufficient for the purpose of reducing mistrust and promoting social union, because it would remain, or tend to become, public knowledge that you could be held blameworthy without wrongdoing whenever the opportunity to do good thereby arose. That this opportunity would not be likely to arise very often is just not relevant to the fact that the act-utilitarian standard would be understood to express the terms of people's relationships to one another. This fact alone would pollute the atmosphere of cooperation, on which so much that is good depends.

What is often needed, therefore, is something approximating a collective understanding, first about what is to count as morally wrong behavior, and secondly that blame, when otherwise appropriate, will be directed toward people for the wrongs they have committed, and not simply for the good that a particular instance of blame might do. Right-defining rules serve precisely these utilitarian functions. They constitute public, authoritative standards by reference to which persons are blamed or defended against blame for actions that are wrong according to those standards. They are rules that it would be rational for enlightened benevolent persons to accept as right-defining, and then, in individual instances, to respect because of the good they do as a systematic, long-term, collective strategy understood to apply equally to all.

3.5. COLLECTIVE STRATEGIES

In the last chapter, we briefly considered some devices an individual might use as strategies of doing good and avoiding evil. Both of the devices mentioned there – individual traits of character and individual strategies – have the same sort of limitation. Neither provides any single, public standard that is meant to apply to everyone, or even meant to apply to everyone within some group or community. Because of this, I suggest, their usefulness, though genuine, is limited in certain crucial respects. Such devices are of necessity individualized, tailored to the individual's situation, and to the individual's proclivities, weaknesses, and strengths. Without quite specific information about a person's characteristics and situation, it is hard to know whether that person has done wrong because of following the wrong strategies or in spite of having followed the right strategies; because of having an inappropriate set of desires and aversions, or in spite of having the best feasible for them. These individualized devices must, as a practical matter, be left largely to the private judgment of the individual. They do not enable sufficient collective supervision and guidance of individual behavior, and in some spheres this is essential.

Collective supervision and guidance of behavior is different from self-supervision and guidance in requiring that the behavior of so many separate individuals be evaluated, judged, and sometimes blamed, criticized, held up as a worthy or base example by others. Now, most of these others cannot be expected to know or find out about the characteristics and histories of the individuals being judged. When each is guided only by the primary principle of doing good and avoiding evil, combined with whatever strategies and dispositions that person judges to be the rational means to this end, there are several sources of uncertainty. First, there are the usual difficulties in determining with some precision which actions are right and which are wrong according to the primary principle. As is the case when applying an act-consequentialist principle, it may be very difficult to determine in practice just whether X's act A did have objectively the best overall results of those available. (Or, on a subjective version of act consequentialism, the question would be whether, given X's information, X could reasonably believe that A would have the best overall results.) Then there is uncertainty about the motives of others. If X's act A was wrong, does this reflect insufficient motivation on X's part to do the right? In order to determine this, we need to know more about the various strategies X has adopted and dispositions X has chosen to develop. Were these decisions themselves rational means to doing good and avoiding evil? What personal strengths and weaknesses was X trying to deal with in developing these strategies and dispositions? If X claims that he did this wrong only because he was "led to it" by character traits that, for him anyway, are the best possible, then, unless we have special information about X, we remain uncertain whether this is true, and whether X is strongly motivated to do the right, or merely weak and all too ready with an excuse. Finally, this uncertainty about what others are doing, and whether they have chosen a reasonable and permissible way of doing good, extends to one's own actions. Not knowing whether others are abusing their discretion as moral agents, one may be uncertain about the permissibility of one's own actions. But one may be rightly reluctant to take a measure of discretion that others have not yet taken for themselves. Doing so is likely to increase mistrust.[11]

A uniform, public standard, understood to apply to all, and employing more useful descriptions than the injunction to do whatever has the best results overall, would go a long way toward reducing these uncertainties. Such a public standard would greatly simplify inquiries; at its simplest, there would be a public rule forbidding acts that fall under a certain description. If lying is forbidden, and X's act A correctly falls under that description, then X has done wrong. And, in determining whether X is sufficiently strongly motivated to do the right, we also have a more restricted and manageable inquiry: We need to know whether X was sufficiently concerned to avoid *lying*.

The condition of destructive mistrust can be analogized to the situation of neighbors, each of whom has self-interested reasons for encroaching on the other's land. If the border between them is either objectively unclear and ill-defined, or in practice difficult to ascertain and reach public agreement about, mistrust will tend to grow. For it is not merely a matter of being able to prove violations in a public forum. It is also a matter of each being able to communicate to the other, convincingly through actions, that he or she has good intentions, and is sufficiently motivated to do the right. Such is in large part the function of clear public boundaries, whether in law, politics, or morality.[12]

Examples of mistrust abound in those areas of human behavior where individuals' interests are in clear conflict, and there are strong temptations to act at the expense of others' interests. The taking of human life, appropriating valued but scarce goods, and taking advantage of another in a competition are all examples. It is therefore important in each of these areas that there be a clear public criterion distinguishing between right and wrong behavior. What

---

11 Scanlon makes a similar point about mistrust, arguing that rules assigning rights serve to "ensure an equitable distribution of a form of control over outcomes." Scanlon, 1978.

12 On the role of public boundaries in law and political conflict, see Schelling, 1960, especially ch. 3, and Fuller, "Human Interaction and the Law," in Winston, 1981.

boundary happens to exist may, within some range of possibilities anyway, be of less importance than the fact that there is such a boundary.

It is now important to distinguish these points from some related though different ideas in the literature of rule utilitarianism. For example, one familiar idea is that individuals need rules in order to reduce the likelihood of mistakes. And the idea that clear, simple, and teachable moral rules are more desirable from a utilitarian point of view than vague or complex rules is also familiar.[13] But the view I argue for here goes beyond these well-known observations. The most important difference is the emphasis on the idea that rules are to be taken quite literally to be collective, right-defining strategies rather than individual rules of thumb, individual strategies, or hypothetical ideal rules. Rules of thumb provide the moral agent with usually reliable guides to right action, but one who uses them must frequently check to see whether they yield the correct answer in particular applications, and they must often be revised; they do not define the right, but yield more or less reliable guides to it. Individual strategies properly vary from one person to another. It is implausible to suppose that some one strategy, whether with regard to investments, the drinking of alcohol, or the doing of the optimific thing, will turn out to be the most rational strategy for each person to adopt as his or her own individual strategy. But, as I shall argue later, philosophers have typically ignored this, supposing themselves to be discussing personal moral rules and principles even while assuming uncritically that these will somehow turn out to be the same for everybody. That some moral rules and principles are valid for everyone, at least over a wide range of community or group, is a phenomenological fact that we can all recognize, though one that is hard to account for when we take moral standards to be personal and individual.

A rule which would not be chosen by each person as that person's best individual strategy for doing good might well be a rational choice from a collective point of view, being a strategy for doing good that is understood to constrain everyone's actions equally. A strategy that is rational from a collective point of view may require that it have preemptive force, being understood to provide individual moral agents with reasons for action that supersede and

13 Brandt, 1963, 1979; also Hare, 1981.

exclude some of the reasons that they would ordinarily have, and without regard to certain characteristics of particular individuals and particular situations. For example, suppose that Robin is an unusual person in an unusual situation. He is both profoundly altruistic, and uninterested in acquiring wealth for himself. Robin has the chance to take money from the account of a wealthy person, with negligible prospect of being discovered, giving it to the needy. Suppose that, everything considered, including the (negligible) effects on Robin himself, this action would do the most good of those available to Robin. If this action also does not contravene any individual strategy that Robin has adopted or ought to adopt, say, to refuse all such temptations because of the likelihood of mistaken judgment, then Robin has reason to do it, and no reason to exclude these considerations in its favor. But if there exists a moral rule, conceived as a collective strategy for doing good, and forbidding the taking of another's legitimate holdings even in circumstances like those described, then Robin's reasons in favor of the taking would be preempted. That is to say, the existence of the rule would provide a second-order reason for excluding certain considerations. In this sense, the rule provides a first-order reason for action that is protected by a second-order reason.[14]

Though some contemporary defenses of rule utilitarianism do put emphasis on the importance of moral rules as public rules that are simple, teachable, and, by implication, applicable to all, this has been combined with the idea that the right is defined by hypothetical ideal rules rather than by actually accepted rules.[15] In Chapter 9, I shall discuss in detail a proposal of this kind. However, if we conceive of the value and importance of rules in terms of their usefulness in maintaining collective supervision and influence over individual behavior, then we have grounds for according priority to actually accepted rules. For the purpose of having a clear, public standard against which to judge behavior is largely defeated if the right is defined as that which is permitted, or required, by an ideal rule, or a rule that would be accepted under certain ideal conditions. If this formula is to be used by moral agents as their decision procedure, it will be surrounded by much the same

14 The concept of a protected, or preemptive, reason is explained and discussed by Raz, 1975, 1979.
15 Brandt 1963, 1979, is the best example. The definition of "morally right" is in 1979, pp. 193–5.

36

uncertainties as surround the principle of doing good and avoiding evil. Determining whether an action is right or wrong, or praiseworthy or blameworthy, though in principle still possible, would be much more difficult.

3.6. SOME PRELIMINARY DEFINITIONS

In this section, my aim is to summarize, and briefly explain the role of some of the central ideas of the MLM. I shall seek to do this as briefly as possible, leaving the further elaboration of the ideas for later chapters, particularly for the discussion on their application in practical reasoning.

Let us first attempt to get a clearer conception of what it is for a rule to be accepted. We can say that:

(a) A rule is *generally accepted* in some group G if:

  (i) behavior of members of G generally conforms to R;
  (ii) members of G generally regard R as supplying a good reason for conforming to the requirements of R; and
  (iii) members of G generally regard R as supplying such good reasons for everyone in G.[16]

[Applying this in the obvious way to the individual case, we can say that R is accepted by X if X's behavior conforms to R, X regards R as supplying a good reason for conforming to the requirements of R, and X regards R as supplying such good reasons for everyone in G.] The third feature is especially important in distinguishing collective rules or strategies from overlapping individual strategies. Where a collective rule is accepted, individuals regard one another as appropriately held to the same rule, and this will typically appear in the form of a critical attitude that they take toward the nonconforming behavior of others in the group. For example, it would not count as a generally accepted rule in this sense if there were only generally converging opinions about the undesirability of drinking alcoholic beverages, each person thinking it bad for his or her part only. But if each person regards the nondrinking of alcohol as a standard of behavior to which everyone

---

16 On the concept of the acceptance of a social rule, see Hart, 1961, pp. 54–5; and Brandt, 1979, pp. 164–76. My account follows Hart's more closely than Brandt's, which focuses more specifically on the psychological properties of the individual's acceptance of moral rules.

can legitimately be held, then the prohibition against drinking alcohol counts as a generally accepted rule.

(b) A rule *R* is *justified* for *G* if the general acceptance of *R* in *G* produces greater overall good than that which would be produced if members of *G* governed their actions in that sphere by use of the primary principle, along with appropriate individual strategies, and without use of any collective rule like *R*. (Call this latter state of affairs the utilitarian state of nature.) For example, it might well do the most good if, with respect to the giving of gifts to others, every person were left to be guided by the principles of doing the most overall good. Perhaps individuals, by and large, have the most reliable information and impulses. In that case, no rule other than the primary principle would be justified. But the situation might be otherwise. It might produce more good if there were a generally accepted rule that each must give a certain portion of one's income to certain groups or organizations that would otherwise tend to be undersupported. Such a rule would then be justified, though there might be other, quite different rules that would also be justified. One initial question about this notion of a rule's being justified arises because justification would seem to be relative to the background against which the rule is assessed. For example, suppose that the institution of chivalry is justified given a moral code that provides for significant sexual inequalities. A code of chivalry serves, say, to soften the otherwise harsh treatment that women would receive. But this is consistent with the chivalric code's *not* being justified given a background of equality between the sexes. It seems natural to conclude that chivalry is justified against a certain background moral code only if that background code is itself justified. So if some feature of justification depends on the assumption that some larger code is in existence, we need to push our inquiry a step further back, making an assessment of that larger code.

This concept of justification serves to set a lower limit. It is obviously not a standard for picking out ideal rules. But the concept is not ad hoc, and is well motivated by the idea of maximizing overall good. If we as a group can do better by cooperation, then we each have compelling reason to join in an available cooperative scheme.[17] One's having a reason to accept a justified and generally

---

17 That one has reason to do good through joint efforts, where such efforts are available, has been amply discussed by Parfit 1984; and Regan, 1980.

accepted rule is therefore a special instance of having reason to join a cooperative good-doing scheme. In many situations, of course, there may be no rule that is generally accepted. This may be because of confusion or disagreement about what that rule ought to be.

(c) So we can say that there is *potential general acceptance* of a rule *R* when members of *G* could, through efforts to persuade others and set an example, bring about, or make substantially more probable, the actual general acceptance of *R*. Members of *G* then have reason to make efforts to bring about the general acceptance of *R*. This too is an instance of the reason we have under the primary principle to set up, where feasible, cooperative good-doing schemes.

(d) *Group G*, for purposes of the idea of potential general acceptance of *R*, is defined by a variety of sociological, psychological, and natural factors. Thus whether *X* is a member of *G* depends on whether *X* is regarded by others as a member, whether *X* takes himself or herself to be a member, and whether, as a consequence, *X* influences, and *X* is influenced by, these others. In some cases, individuals are "members of a group" only in the weak sense that they all recognize their mutual willingness to engage in joint action to achieve some goal. In others, individuals are members in the much stronger sense that they consciously identify themselves with the group, and with its collective achievements. This vagueness about the concepts of group and group membership is not, I suggest, as serious as it may seem. One reason for this is that an individual's obligation to comply with a generally accepted rule does not even arise unless the general acceptance of that rule is better than if people were, in that area of behavior, to be guided by the primary principle. Another reason is that whether I am, or ought to regard myself as, a member of *G* is often answerable by appeal to the primary principle. Thus I am often not in a position to do good by conforming to some group's rule because of physical distance from them, or because my compliance with the rule is not expected by them, or would be rejected, or would not even make sense in the circumstances. So as not to delay the discussion when other more immediate matters are at hand, I shall put off saying more about this until Chapter 7.

(e) *The preemptive status of justified rules.* It is now necessary to explain a notion that will be used in many places as the investigation develops – the notion of a rule preempting the primary principle.

The primary principle, on one interpretation often favored by consequentialists, requires that one do that which promotes the greatest overall good. This idea requires that states of affairs be evaluated and compared from an impersonal perspective in the sense that one's own life, happiness or suffering, well-being or ill-being is not to be counted as more or less important simply by virtue of the fact that it is one's own rather than someone else's. Thus if human suffering is intrinsically evil, a state of affairs in which three people suffer is, other things being equal, worse than one in which one person suffers. If the telling of a lie is intrinsically bad, then, other things again being equal, the state of affairs in which ten lies are told is worse than one in which two lies are told, and so on. The primary principle requires us to weigh good against bad, and it allows no good or bad consequences to be excluded from the weighing, since all are relevant. So a rule R preempts the primary principle if R provides a reason that is both a reason for acting in some way and a reason, backed by a rationale, for excluding some range of reasons that would otherwise need to be weighed in the balance if the primary principle were unpreempted. In short, R provides a protected reason for action.[18] The ideas of rationale and range need special emphasis here because of the inveterate tendency to misunderstand what an exclusionary reason amounts to, and so to think that to have an exclusionary reason is to be in some state of moral or other blindness or ineffability. I shall return to this issue later. For now it is important to remember that rules exclude reasons of some kinds and within certain limits, and a full understanding of a justified rule involves having some conception of how to find and interpret these limits.

A command issued by, and within the scope of, legitimate authority supplies one with a protected reason. Similarly, the fact that one has made a promise to do X serves both as a reason for doing X and as a reason for excluding some range of reasons that would normally count against doing X; for example, that it would be a minor inconvenience. In many cases, of course, the existence of a preempting rule will make no difference to the practical conclusion one reaches. For a full weighing of all of the ordinarily relevant considerations would lead to the same result; for example, the promise ought to be kept because that would do the most good all

18 Raz, 1975; and 1979, ch. 1.

things considered, or that one ought anyway, on ordinary grounds, do what the legitimate authority has commanded one to do. But the force of a protected reason is different, since it excludes certain considerations from the outset. The range of reasons excluded in this way need not be extensive. It suffices to count as an exclusionary reason that some such range be excluded. Normally, as I have said, the existence of a rule brings with it some conception of the sorts of reasons it is the point of the rule to exclude, as well as of the categories of reason that remain untouched by it. We all recognize that a promise to water a friend's houseplants while she is out of town excludes considerations of minor inconvenience, but does not – indeed, does not from the outset – exclude considerations about the lives that could be saved by going instead on an emergency rescue mission.

3.7. AN EXAMPLE

It will help in focusing these ideas if we consider an example drawn from Brandt, which has now become a significant part of the literature of utilitarian debate:

Suppose that, in wartime England, people are requested, as a measure essential for the war effort, to conserve electricity and gas by having a maximum temperature of 50 degrees F. in their homes. A utilitarian Frenchman living in England at the time, however, argues as follows: 'All the good moral British obviously will pay scrupulous attention to conforming with this request. The war effort is sure not to suffer from a shortage of electricity and gas. Now, it will make no difference to the war effort whether I personally use a bit more gas, but it will make a great deal of difference to my comfort. So, since the public welfare will be maximized by my using gas to keep the temperature up to 70 degrees F. in my home, it is my duty to use the gas.'[19]

A rule setting a 50-degree maximum on individual house temperatures serves here to preempt the usual weighing of impersonal utilities. Using the primary principle directly in the usual way, the utilitarian Frenchman's reasoning would be correct: His greater comfort would indeed outweigh the negligible cost to the war effort, which has, we assume, already reached the threshold of success through the efforts of the others anyway. The history of

19 Brandt, 1959, pp. 389–90. This example is quoted and discussed in Bales, 1971, pp. 259–65; and in Smart and Williams, 1973, p. 57.

the rule was probably something like this: The overwhelming bulk of the public recognized the need to save fuel, and so there was potential general acceptance of some rule like the 50-degree rule that eventually got implemented. It could have been a 51- or 49-degree rule, though in these matters the advantages of clarity and the appearance of nonarbitrariness would seem to be on the side of the 50-degree rule. Any of several of these rules would be justified, for the general acceptance of any of them would constitute a considerable improvement over the situation in which everyone is left to a general weighing of impersonal utilities. In all but unusual situations, it would be unwise to the point of madness to announce, "We leave it to everyone to make his or her own conscientious decision, deciding, after weighing the needs of the nation against one's own needs, and the likely behavior of others, how much fuel to use." And in the circumstances, it is fairly clear what the relevant group is: It is the British, as well as other residents of the country who are in a position to make their contribution to the war effort by observing the rule. Now, even from this description of the situation, we all know that the rule is supposed to exclude, among other things, *just* the sort of reason that the utilitarian Frenchman is trying to use: that the good to him produced from violation of the rule would outweigh the total disutility it would produce. It is not that this is false; nor that it would otherwise be irrelevant. Rather, it is excluded.

As I suggested earlier, the idea that rules may serve a useful purpose in coordinating the actions of people in groups is in itself nothing new to utilitarian debate. But this still leaves us with a number of questions if any case for the priority of rules is to be made out. In the following, I shall use the foregoing example in structuring and then answering the following questions, among others: (1) Why is the general acceptance of rule R a better state of affairs than that in which it is not accepted? (2) Why ought I to join in accepting R when R is already generally accepted in G? (3) Having accepted R, why ought I then to recognize R as providing preemptive reasons for action – why not just act individually to maximize good? (4) If I have not actually accepted R, then why, and under what conditions, ought I to recognize R as providing such preemptive reasons as if I had actually accepted R?

Relying on our earlier examination of the advantages of collective strategies, the answer to (1) can now be briefly summarized. There is the value of coordination, of course. We need to get a large group of people to end their confusion about what to do, and coordinate around some systematic plan for saving fuel. This rule is a plausible part of such a plan, and perhaps the only one that is public and salient enough to succeed. But the avoidance of a disastrous shortage of fuel is just the most obvious component. Availability of a publicly known standard by which individuals can evaluate and influence the behavior of others is another. In order to avert mistrust, uncertainty, and suspicion, we need to know definitively and publicly what counts as doing one's part and what doesn't. This is especially important where there are well-known reasons of self-interest for not doing one's part. In such cases we need to be able to limit inquiries and cut reasoning and reason-giving, if not rationalization, short. So the rule is not to be evaluated merely as a guide or goad to action that has completely fulfilled its role if the fuel shortage has been averted. It is to be viewed as a standard which is applicable to all even though it may have become clear that enough people will in fact comply to avert the shortage.

3.8. WHY OUGHT I TO ACCEPT *R*?

My reasons for accepting *R*, where it is already generally accepted, can be explained in a familiar act-utilitarian way. *R* is justified, so its general acceptance is better than the utilitarian state of nature. And the general acceptance of *R* constitutes a good-doing scheme in which I ought to participate. Notice here that the kind of good-doing scheme it is – in particular, the fact that its good emerges in large part from the general concurrence, or Humean "resolution" and not merely from the actual securing of coordination to produce the right behavior – begins to play an important role. For if part of the enterprise is the building of mutual trust and enabling of social supervision and control, my acceptance of *R* is very important. That the enterprise is of this kind tends to block my objection that the others are already complying, and the job will get done without me. To be sure, this factor, while important, is just one of many that needs to be weighed in the scales; and it may sometimes be outweighed. For example, if it is clear to everyone that the fuel-saving project will get done anyway, and that I belong to some well-defined and limited group – say, people with serious and publicly obvious health problems – who could make better use of the fuel and are unlikely by the nature of their situation to be faking, then it is unlikely that even my public refusal to subscribe will diminish trust or confidence in individual resolve.

The role of conventional rules in providing the bases for mutual trust, supervision, and control highlights the importance of accepting a generally accepted justified rule even when a better rule could be imagined. The utilitarian Frenchman might believe, correctly, let us suppose, that a different rule – say, allowing a maximum of 52 degrees instead of 50 degrees – would be the best rule, given the real nature of the shortage and of the debilitating sacrifices required by the existing rule. Thus, suppose that a sufficient amount of fuel will be saved if a large percentage, but less than 100 percent, follow the rule. A few people could heat their homes normally with no interference in the war effort. Discussing Brandt's example, Smart suggests that a *mixed strategy* might be possible; that is, one in which each person gives himself a certain but very small probability p of not obeying the government's request. This might be accomplished if each person throws dice, say, and disobeys the government's request if and only if he gets a certain number of successive sixes.[20] If p is determined properly, and everyone follows the procedure, the result might be even better than if everyone obeys the government's request without exception. To be sure, this would not amount to what Smart calls an "all or none" version of rule utilitarianism,[21] since a few would end up heating their homes normally while most others would comply with the request. Call the rule corresponding to this procedure R_2. R_2 might very well be justified if it were an understood and generally accepted public rule. It might even be better than the unadorned R. The fact that R_2 contains a dice-throwing procedure, and has the result that some people will be allowed to heat their homes normally while others make sacrifices, does not automatically disqualify it. But the mere fact that R_2 would hypotheti-

20 Smart and Williams, 1973, p. 59.
21 Ibid., p. 62.

44

cally be better than R does not by itself provide someone with good reason for accepting it, and even less for proceeding to decide their own case using it. For again, a significant component of the good of justified rules derives precisely from their being, in Hume's phrase, "concurr'd in by the whole". If it were rational for individuals to give no priority to an existing rule over a somewhat better hypothetical rule, then such concurrence would in most cases be simply unachievable.

3.9. WHEN DOES ABSENCE OF AN ACTUAL COMMITMENT MAKE A DIFFERENCE?

There would seem to be an important difference between cases in which one has made a conscious commitment to a joint project for advancing some optional good and those in which one has made no such commitment. This raises a problem that has a close analogue in the theory of political obligation. If actual commitment to a generally accepted rule is a necessary condition for having preemptive reasons to comply with the rule, then it will no doubt turn out that very few people have such preemptive reasons. Yet if the mere existence of a project for doing some good or other in the world is sufficient, then one's obligations to comply with the requirements of good-doing projects will multiply beyond reason.

Although there are some rules that are actually accepted by everyone within a small group, such actual agreement is rare. So if I have not actually accepted R, then why, and under what conditions, do I have reason to recognize R as providing preemptive reasons anyway? Though there needs to be some account of conditions sufficient to give rise to obligation without actual acceptance, there is likely to be more than one such set of conditions. So the task of setting forth sufficient *and* necessary conditions for obligation would be too ambitious a task to embark on here.

The following kind of argument does, however, provide one plausible approach to answering the question by providing one set of sufficient conditions. The steps of such an argument, applied to our problem, would take this general form:

45

(i) *P* is a member of a group *G*, each of whom is in a position to make a contribution to an indispensable good by participating in the acceptance of some justified rule like *R*.

(ii) *R* is generally accepted in *G*.

(iii) Because of *P*'s general duty to do good, *P* could not reasonably reject *R*.

(iv) Therefore, *P* ought to recognize the preemptive reasons that *R* provides (i.e., *P* ought to reason as if *P* had accepted *R*).

Though this kind of argument has many antecedents,[22] the version here takes individuals as rationally guided by reasons of impersonal good rather than self-interest. Thus individuals are not represented as contractors, each of whom is in a position to veto the terms of a contract; rather, they are each guided by the primary principle, and recognize that they are in a position to fulfill its requirements by complying with the provisions of an ongoing project. A further difference is that the notion of public rules that are equally applicable to all has its place here not because it is the outcome or presupposition of a contract, but because of the good that results from having such rules, like the good of uniformity and reliability of application, of impersonality, and of the sense of equal treatment.

Reasonable persons recognize a distinction between indispensable and optional goods, and recognize that an objection to participation in a project providing indispensable goods is less likely to be reasonable than an objection to one providing only optional goods. Thus, if (i) is true, (iii) will probably also be true. In addition, objecting to *R* merely on grounds that others already accept *R* and thus that they insure that the indispensable good is provided would be to raise an unreasonable objection. Another way of understanding the point is that if such an objection could not reasonably be made publicly from a position of equality with others, it does not constitute a reasonable objection in light of one's duty under the primary principle. The fact that others are already doing their part in the necessary scheme is typically not the basis for a reasonable objection.

The good realized by the general acceptance of R must be an indispensable good, something that is central to any rational person's conception of the good. By contrast, if the general acceptance of R advances only goods that are optional or discre-

---

22 Rawls, 1971; Scanlon, 1982; Brandt, 1979; and Kavka, 1986. My use of the idea adopts Scanlon's notion of what no one "could reasonably reject."

tionary, then, other things being equal, it will be likely that one could reasonably reject *R*. Private clubs and associations employ rules for the governance of their members, typically to advance goods that are optional. Advancing the cause of chess or tennis or philosophy may be a good thing; but it would be difficult to believe that every person, as part of his or her duty to do good in the world, must contribute to their advancement. A person could therefore raise a reasonable objection to the joint acceptance of such a rule. Only in rare situations would such an objection not be reasonable.

The utilitarian Frenchman in Brandt's example is in a position to contribute to an essential good, and in this is no different from the others in the imagined group. There is as close a commonsense causal connection between his fuel-using behavior and fuel supplies in England as there is between the fuel-using behavior of any of the British living there and those same fuel supplies. Moreover, this connection has nothing to do with his being a Frenchman. This might appear to be a trivial point. But being a Frenchman might in some circumstances be relevant. For example, if British solidarity and pride is a good to which the actions of the British can naturally contribute, it may also be one to which a Frenchman is ill-positioned to contribute. Rules requiring all to engage in actions showing pride in being British would undoubtedly not obligate this Frenchman, if for no other reason than because ought implies can.

A local association levying dues for philosophy lectures or music in public places would not be providing an essential good, and thus not a part of the good that all persons have a duty to promote, even if they are well-positioned to do so. So a consequence of this is that it makes sense to think of individuals as having an obligation to do their part in schemes to provide these sorts of discretionary benefits only if they have actually consented to the scheme, have actually accepted the benefits for themselves, or have in some way made an active commitment to the particular project. Only in one of these, or closely analogous, ways would one naturally come to be included within the scope of others' reasonable expectations. And only then would one's actions and stance toward the others have the potential for contributing to, or diminishing, the good of mutual trust in the advancement of a good-doing scheme.

47

We come now to what for many will be the most important question. It is one thing, an act utilitarian will be quick to point out, to demonstrate that it is best very openly to subscribe to a generally accepted rule; but it is quite another to demonstrate that one must actually recognize the exclusionary reasons it purports to provide, especially when the usual weighing of good against bad would favor noncompliance. If it is best overall to subscribe to the rule, then so be it; but then it may also be best overall to violate it when the occasion arises. To exclude any normally relevant consideration in this weighing would be irrational.

To answer this, I shall distinguish between two different points of view with respect to the doing of good, that of individual rationality, and that of collective rationality.

(a) *The point of view of individual rationality.* Taking this perspective, *I* do what will maximize good without necessarily taking account of what *we* ought to do to maximize good. Thus whether I ought to water the garden or weed it might depend upon whether you will weed the garden or water it. But from the perspective of what we ought to do, it might be clear that I ought to water it while you weed it, rather than the other way around.[23] The perspective of individual rationality focuses simply on what I ought to do for my part, given the surrounding circumstances, including the actions of other people. As such, it does not employ any collective perspective about how a group of people ought to act, nor how they ought to resolve to act. From the point of view of individual rationality, our appraisal of actions hinges solely on the appraisal of individual acts and *those consequences that can plausibly be attributed to those acts.* Here we must recall our earlier examination of the surplus causal effect of rules. These effects are a consequence, not of any act or collection of acts; nor are these effects distributable through any plausible method of division among the acts of individuals. As we have seen, they are as much the consequence of public knowledge that there exists a generally prevailing rational and consistent resolve to respect the rules. So from the point of

23 This way of distinguishing between the two questions, as well as the example, are taken from Postow, 1977.

view of individual rationality, as I argued earlier, these good effects slip through the net. From this point of view, they are not taken into account in deciding what one ought to do.

(b) *The point of view of collective rationality.* From the collective point of view, one does need to ask what we as a group ought to resolve and do in order to produce the best results. From this perspective we seek to provide the devices, typically, rules applying to all, that will enable the collectively best result to be achieved. As a first approximation, we might say that in any situation, a group of one or more persons ought to follow a course or courses of action that would produce the most good possible in that situation.[24] This is plausible enough in the abstract, but it will certainly not do as an action guide for individuals. It is addressed to the group, and one often has no knowledge of, or control over, the behavior of others, which must be accepted as given. If you are already watering the garden, it will not make sense for me to water it too. In this utilitarian state of nature, we need some device which will serve to coordinate our actions and – if the argument so far about the importance of public, right-defining rules is correct – provide a kind of publicly understood, specific definition of the right thing for each of us to do. This definition, as I have already suggested, will need to be constructed partly as a solution to the needs for uniformity and fairness of social control, especially where the discretion afforded individuals in the utilitarian state of nature would be a source of general distrust. It will not suffice either to adopt the ideal-rule utilitarian approach, saying that each member of a group ought to follow those rules that would produce the best results if followed by all. For there may be incompatible sets of rules that are tied for first place and, anyway, others may in fact not be doing their part according to these ideal rules. If the behavior of others conforms to nonideal rules, it may actually be self-frustrating to act on ideal rules.[25] On the other hand, if justified, though imperfect, rules are generally accepted, it would not be a rational strategy simply to give up, risking a return to the utilitarian state of nature. Their general acceptance provides one with an opportunity to participate in a practice that constitutes an improvement over the utilitarian state of nature. Now, when one

24 Ibid., p. 51.
25 For this point, as well as an interesting proposed proof that there is no unique set of rules that satisfies a universal *conformity* test, see Sobel, 1987, p. 279.

participates in the observance of a rule or practice, a good-doing moral agent takes a point of view that is impersonal in a special way. One views oneself as one would any arbitrarily chosen person in the group, so that the rules that are to apply to one's own behavior are the same as those that are understood to apply to any person in the group. The collectively rational plan of action distributes rational plans over individuals in the group, but it is not the case that the attribution of the beneficial consequences of that plan distribute without remainder over the individual actions done in furtherance of the plan. It makes sense, from the collective point of view, to attribute the good that slipped through the net when we took the point of view of individual rationality to this universalized rational resolve. One recognizes that, from the point of view of collective rationality one has no reason to except oneself from the application of the rules, because the whole project would not succeed if one retained the right to except oneself, continuing to make decisions on their usual merits in a utilitarian state of nature. There may, however, be reasons for the rules themselves publicly to include exceptions for persons in situations like one's own. Taking the collective point of view, one understands that the whole point of such a scheme is to restrict the moral liberty of all under public rules, and thus to except oneself from their application to one's own case is to miss the point, involving oneself in a kind of practical inconsistency.

This distinction between the points of view of individual and collective rationality resembles each of two distinctions defended by Rawls in a well-known article: that between justifying a practice and justifying an action falling under it, and that between the separate offices of legislator and judge.[26] These are distinctions that we have no difficulty understanding in everyday contexts. Thus if, after recognizing that it would be best for me to water the garden and for you to weed, and that it would also be best if neither of us is to yield to the temptation to encroach on the other's job, you and I agree to divide our labors in this way, then we can separately take the collective point of view, doing our separate jobs as designated, and simply abjuring the usual reasons one might have for making encroachments on the other's job. Our further reasons for

26 Rawls, 1955, in Bayles, 1968. On several points, however, I believe that Rawls's account is either in error or in need of supplementation. I shall have more to say about this in Chapter 9.

abjuring our usual reasons for encroachment have to do with the collective, impersonal good of having the garden properly cared for, to be sure; but they may also include reasons of expressing mutual respect, and indicating a mutual willingness to stay out of each other's way.

This account of the points of view of individual and collective rationality must raise for many readers serious questions of the following kind: Given that we can consider an action from one point of view, does that preclude the other point of view? Can these two standpoints on rationality be kept hermetically sealed off from one another? And if they can, does that not reintroduce the old problems of moral schizophrenia that have so plagued the history of rule-utilitarian accounts?

I shall attempt to answer these questions in the next chapter. Briefly, I shall claim that the moral rules of a reflective society of rule utilitarians are to be interpreted by them in the light of a rationale, and that it is the rationale that guides the individual in determining whether the point of view of collective rationality is appropriate, or if direct individual maximization is the indicated course. In this way, we avoid falling into the grip of moral schizophrenia.

3.11. RECONCILING MAXIMIZING RATIONALITY WITH AGENT-CENTERED RESTRICTIONS

Our thinking about moral reasons seems to lead directly to puzzles when we attempt to reconcile two ideas: On the one hand, we are properly concerned about what happens, and we want it to turn out for the best. Thinking of a natural disaster, we acknowledge that it is better if only a few people die than if many thousands do, or that only one or two, rather than hundreds, suffer. And very commonly we think it our duty to do what we can to bring about the best outcomes. This concern is neutral from one agent to another, because the goodness or badness of a state of affairs is independent of perspective. But on the other hand, commonsense morality tells us separately as individuals that we may not do certain things, even if we thereby produce the best outcome available to us. "How," Nagel asks, "can there be a reason not to twist someone's arm which is not equally a reason to prevent his arm from being twisted by someone else?"[27] Nagel's point is that the reason for not twisting a child's arm (in order to gain access to his family's house in a desperate emergency) is a reason for me to avoid doing something; it is not equally a reason for me to prevent something from happening (a child's arm being twisted by someone or other). This is strange, because the reason to avoid twisting the child's arm has to do with that evil happening, and, so far as that is concerned, it is hard to see why it should matter whether I am considering doing it, or I simply have the chance to prevent someone else from doing it. The reason one has for not twisting the child's arm is thus an agent-centered restriction (ACR), one centered on agents and what they do rather than on the states of affairs that they bring about.

Samuel Scheffler has claimed that attempts to provide a rationale for ACRs within a consequentialist moral theory run into the following general problem.[28] If some restriction R – forbidding one, say, to murder – is to be based on agent-neutral reasons, as consequentialism would surely seem to require, then R will not turn out to be properly agent-centered, as our intuitions would suggest. Thus suppose that I am confronted with a choice either to violate R, bringing about some disvalue N_1, or not to violate R, bringing about some greater disvalue of the same kind, $N_1 + N_2$. For example, suppose that I must choose between killing an innocent person or, as a consequence of inaction, allowing five other innocent persons to be killed. Whatever it is that is objectionable about such killing, the thought runs, it will presumably be outweighed by the greater disvalue of not killing. But R disallows this kind of weighing. It directs one not to kill, period. In short, even if we grant the most wide-ranging possibilities for a theory of the good, it seems impossible to derive ACRs from wholly neutral, or impersonal, consequentialist considerations. If the action is wrong, it must be because of some characteristic of the action or of what it brings about. But if that is so, then it is hard to imagine how a usual weighing of goods against evils can rationally be avoided. And if that is so, there is no exclusion, no restriction at all.

One familiar consequentialist proposal about such restrictions as R is that they are based on considerations about the mistakes that

27 Thomas Nagel, 1986, p. 178.
28 Scheffler, 1982.

people are likely to make if they have the moral authority to weigh lives against one another and to kill one to save more. This is one interpretation that has been put on the consequentialist's concern about mistrust.[29] We quite understandably fear for the consequences if everyone were to regard himself as having the moral authority to kill in order to produce the best available state of affairs.

This rationale, however, is not quite satisfying as it stands. The problem arises partly from the kind of concern that the term "mistrust" is supposed to mark. For if mistrust is to be cashed out in terms of the dangers of mistake, that concern, though real, does not apply to everyone equally. Some people are much more likely to make mistakes than others. Why not think of constraints on killing as having varying force, stringent for some, weak for others, and virtually nonexistent for a few? Again we encounter the familiar shortfall of argument: What needs to be explained are restrictions that, if they apply to anyone, apply to everyone; but the preferred rationale suggests no more than restrictions that apply with varying force across a group of agents. Indeed, we can imagine that a machine, which Scheffler calls the "Infallible Optimizer," and which never made mistakes in its optimizing judgments, were also to make it causally impossible for humans to kill unless necessary to minimize total deaths. Scheffler observes that "Defenders of agent-centered restrictions will presumably feel a residual intuition that, even under circumstances such as these, it would be wrong to kill a person in order to minimize deaths."[30]

Of course, consequentialist defenders of ACRs, while feeling such a residual intuition, might come to the conclusion that such an intuition is, in a world with plenty of Infallible Optimizers anyway, irrational. Our own fear of being killed for such a purpose might be counterbalanced by the effect it would have in raising our own net chances for living a long life.[31]

I think that the consequentialist might have a plausible rationale for such an intuition. This rationale would be based on the value of trust and the ill effects of mistrust, though not, to be sure,

29 See Scheffler, 1982, p. 110; also Scanlon, 1978.
30 Scheffler, 1982, p. 111.
31 This possibility is mentioned by Scanlon, 1978, p. 109. Scanlon, however, is not thinking of such a scheme as guaranteed by the use of Infallible Optimizers. On the contrary, his point about mistrust seems mainly to be based on the idea that the decision-makers will be likely to make mistakes.

mistrust based on the fear of mistake; for we are here supposing the universal use of Infallible Optimizers. The rationale would proceed along the following lines. To have generally accepted restrictions on killings, even on those done for the purpose of preventing a larger number of killings, is collectively to express the terms of the relationship of human beings toward one another. It is not, therefore, simply a matter of minimizing the number of acts of killings; it is partly a matter of expressing, by public rules understood to apply to all, a form of human interrelationship. That interrelationship is one that involves equal restrictions on the moral authority of all. Even if everyone were equipped with an Infallible Optimizer, and could therefore make no mistake, we might reasonably be horrified by the knowledge that such killings were collectively licensed. So to prevent this, it is desirable to set equal restrictions that would be genuinely agent-oriented: In order to have and to express this form of human interrelationship, it would obviously not be enough merely to minimize killings overall; it must be the case that each is morally forbidden to kill, period. The reconciliation of consequentialism with ACRs would then be carried out, though partly by denying that it is end-result behavior of a certain kind that is the sole aim of the restriction.[32] The reason for setting restrictions has to do with providing the bases of trust, but not the kind of trust that can be explained purely in terms of eliminating mistakes. For what worries us, on this view, is not only that others might decide to kill us on the mistaken belief that it will do the most good overall; it worries us even more that individuals, armed with their trusty Optimizers, are given license, deliberately to sacrifice us (or others; it makes no great difference) on a cold though correct calculation of the overall good.

Why should this worry us? Does not such a worry virtually amount to a kind of superstition, or the introduction of a personal perspective that is inappropriate here? What is it about deliberate killing that makes it worse than accidental death? It would seem no worse for the victim, not, at least, if we assume that other things

32 This approach may fit what Scheffler has in mind when he says that "to show that agent-centred restrictions are compatible with maximizing rationality, therefore, one must agree that the behaviour they rule out is morally objectionable or undesirable, but deny that that very objectionableness constitutes the entire rationale for the restrictions." Scheffler, 1988, p. 257.

are equal.[33] The answer here must rest, I think, on facts about human psychology, in particular, on facts about how our feelings, reactions, and concept of self are affected by different understandings of our relationship to other people individually and collectively. Obviously, I can offer here no hard conclusions, but only informed intuitions about what is very probably the case. We take a strong interest in the terms of our relationship to others in society both because those terms reflect our value, as particular human beings, to others, and because our sense of closeness to others is inevitably affected by what we understand those terms to be. We seek fellowship with others. That is such a deeply characteristic fact of human nature that there is hardly any point in questioning whether the desire is rational or not. The perception that there is a generally recognized liberty to sacrifice anyone at the Optimizer's green light, and that everyone, indeed, especially the most moral people among your friends and fellows, will be prepared to sacrifice you when it blinks, will have deeply chilling effects, and is bound to have far-reaching consequences for cooperation generally. This is not to say that a particular instance of sacrifice will have this result. It may not. Nor is it to say that being killed deliberately is, in itself, worse than being killed accidentally. What is bad – very bad, I believe, if all its full effects were considered – is the sense, the understanding, that a deliberate killing, perhaps yet only a possibility, is fully permitted, and that one could not raise an objection to it, at least not an objection that would be publicly recognized as having any validity.

A public rule, indeed, is a collective expression in which everyone has a stake. It says something about what we think and what we authorize, and so we have an interest in *what* it says. For what we authorize may understandably excite pride in ourselves, fear of others, or self-loathing; it tells us and others something about who we are and what we stand for, and thus raises issues about our integrity as a people, nation, community, or family.[34] In a society

---

33 Nagel, 1986, p. 178: "After all, it is no worse *for the victim* to be killed or injured deliberately than accidentally, or as an unavoidable side effect of the dangerous rescue operation."
34 This notion of the effect of a rule as a collective authorization, along with the associated utility or disutility of expressive effects, constitutes one important difference between my use of the notion of mistrust, and Scanlon's (1978), though

permitting the use of Infallible Optimizers, everyone would potentially have a double stake: as potential agent, and as potential patient. As a potential agent, one's sympathy for the sacrificial victims will make it psychologically difficult to understand or to be part of such actions, even indirectly through participating in their collective licensing. As a potential patient, one might well prefer a shorter life expectancy with the knowledge that being deliberately sacrificed for the greater good is not only unlikely, but, above all, not collectively licensed. The atmosphere in such a society, the kind of mutual respect or lack thereof which prevails there, may be debilitating and damaging.

It is clearer now why the Infallible Optimizer is not enough, even though, ex hypotheses, it correctly informs us as to whether actions optimize. The trouble is that our Optimizer was designed only to take full account of all the consequences, for good or bad, of proposed actions. This, of course, it does flawlessly. For the reasons explained earlier in this chapter, the Optimizer is not capable of taking account of good or bad consequences that are not somehow traceable to actions. And no such device, unless it can also bring about major changes in human nature, can make people like the fact, or function well with the knowledge, that killing on its instructions is collectively licensed.

When we ask, what reason is there for me to recognize this ACR, forbidding me to kill though the consequences be for the best, we must take account of the restriction's full rationale. To ask this question in this context would be to take the point of view of individual rationality only, thus missing the point of the restriction. Among other things, its point is collectively to express the terms of human relationship *by* a restriction, the function of which is partially to *define* the right. Its point, therefore, is not to add yet another item to the individual's catalogue of evils to be weighed against goods, but collectively to do good and avoid evil through a right–defining rule which is then addressed equally to all, and is acknowledged by all. Given such a choice, I ought not to violate this ACR because it sets a standard of right behavior, preempting the usually relevant considerations about individual maximization. I am still concerned about maximization, but the concern has been

I can agree with most of what he says about the importance of limiting discretion for reasons of mistrust.

shifted to the collective level, where the focus is on the way in which right ought to be defined in the first place.

Respect for human life would seem to be something that can collectively be shown in different ways, and individuals as well as whole communities can reasonably differ about how it should be shown. Given the kind of rationale I have just proposed, it follows that moral prohibitions on killing might justifiably vary from one community to another. Different conceptions of self-defense – of the circumstances under which one may respond to aggression with aggression, and of how far one may go in those circumstances – would seem to be an example.[35] Thus on one conception, the use of deadly force in response to an attacker is only permissible if and to the extent that that response is necessary to saving one's own life. On another conception, one who attacks you has by that very fact violated your autonomy. One may then take steps to vindicate that autonomy, in effect "punishing" the attacker, even though it is not strictly necessary to protect oneself. Now, for the consequentialist anyway, one significant consideration in choosing among various conceptions of self-defense will be the ways in which a conception expresses the terms of human relationships in that community, and the effects that such an expression would have. Some people are greatly troubled by the thought of individuals having the discretion to use force, especially deadly force, simply to enforce their rights and vindicate their autonomy. Part of their concern, of course, may have to do with their judgment that ordinary people will make too many mistakes. But their concern may not be entirely reducible to this. For the conception of a society in which each person has the moral freedom to punish a violator of his or her autonomy is very different from the conception of a society in which the vindication of individual autonomy is left to the state. Certainly the "feel" of life in the one society would be different from that of life in the other. In the one case, I am confronted by so many individuals, each of whom is understood legitimately to wield significant power over others, including me. In the other, this power confronts me mostly in the form of the centralized power of the state.

A further point is that our lives are complicated by the fact that

35 A useful discussion of different models of self-defense is provided by Fletcher, 1978, pp. 855–75.

57

we belong simultaneously to different communities, and by the fact that new communities and memberships can and ought to be formed. I may belong to a community in which the prohibition against killing another person is a very strong one, a prohibition that very narrowly circumscribes the right of self-defense. I and members of my community might be horrified by the broad permissions to kill that exist in other communities and, indeed, that exist among the nations of the world, for example, in the form of the conventions governing killing in wartime. Our horror would then be a relevant factor in determining whether these laxer prohibitions are acceptable, though it would not be the only factor, and might indeed be a small one at that.[36]

Before concluding this chapter, we must take note of a possible objection. The notion of collectively expressing the terms of human interrelationship may to some readers sound perilously close to a Kantian one, thus threatening to vitiate the consequentialist character of the rationale for various ACRs. Thus one might object that to speak of "the terms" of our relationship to one another, and of "expressing" those terms, is to presuppose the validity of ACRs rather than to provide a consequentialist foundation for them. One who makes such claims, after all, seems to be expressing moral emotions based on moral judgments. And these moral judgments would themselves need to be accounted for without departure from consequentialism. Such an objection as this might appear to cut quite deeply if the way in which these notions are to figure in our thinking were misunderstood. In the next chapter I shall argue that these ideas do not rest on any covertly deontological view, like Kantianism. Moreover, they need not commit us to deontology even if the horror, suspicion, fear, and self-loathing, upon which the rationale for ACRs may rest, is itself commonly expressed and argued for in Kantian moral terms.

36 These comments arise from Michael Slote's questions about the status of conventions of war on my conception.

4

Relations between collective and individual rationality

It might be objected that the argument to this point rests at some crucial points on a nonconsequentialist, if not outright Kantian, foundation. The most prominent example of this, the objector will no doubt say, is the appeal that the argument makes to our moral emotions; in this case, that we would be horrified at the idea that certain things, like murdering in order to prevent more murdering, are collectively licensed. But as a moral emotion, the horror reaction, our objector tells us, is based on a moral judgment that certain things are just wrong, and wrong apart from their consequences. In short, this horror reaction is based on a deontological intuition, and it has no place in a moral theory that proposes to be consequentialist.

Nor, the objection might go on, is this the only place in which deontological intuitions are being smuggled into a putatively consequentialist account. Thus consider the earlier example of the utilitarian Frenchman in London during a wartime fuel emergency. If he judges that it would be best, all things considered, for him to break the rule about house temperature, our natural response is that his action is wrong because *unfair*. And judgments of unfairness, it might seem, are paradigmatic of the deontological. More generally, it might be claimed that the whole idea of collective rationality, with its conception of treating all equally, and thinking of oneself as any arbitrarily chosen member of the group to whom public rules apply, cannot be explained in consequentialist terms. The idea appeals to our moral intuitions because our moral intuitions contain an important deontological component.

59

Let us focus first on the example of the collective licensing of killing, and the horror reaction it would produce. Because consequentialist arguments are in significant part empirical, we must first allow that this claim might turn out to be false. Or possibly, though true for us now, it might turn out to be false for some society, perhaps in some other era. If the claim turns out to be false, that would raise serious questions about whether such an ACR on killing for the good of it is justified. In this case, such an ACR might have to be rejected as a relic of different times or of outright superstition.

With that preliminary qualification in mind, there nevertheless seem to be strong and overlooked reasons for thinking that the ACR is justified, partly because it provides us with a basis for trusting others who are prepared to accept justified rules, and for reducing fear and suspicion. Most importantly, however, the claim does not rest on any deontological intuition, covert or otherwise. Although it may be true that many people in fact do have a horror of killing or being deliberately killed, and that they typically express this horror in connection with a simple deontological moral judgment, this judgment itself need not be either true or justified on any deontological grounds if the horror is to be both rational and justified.

Indeed, many of our emotional reactions are like this. They are commonly associated with, or expressed by, a moral judgment, but their rationality does not require that they be based on that moral judgment. So even if the moral judgment plays a causal role in the reaction, that fact does not presuppose the truth of any particular moral theory. I may be horrified by theft, and my horror may in part be caused by my unremittingly Kantian ideas about property and theft. But it is still open to a Humean to contend that the wrongness of theft is actually based on psychological facts about mankind, like the fact that, as Hume puts it, "What has long lain under our eye, and has often been employ'd to our advantage, *that* we are always the most unwilling to part with".[1] Because we tend to become attached to those things we have held for a long time, that fact alone constitutes some basis, anyway, for a rule that validates first possession. It is a psychological fact that lends productive

---

1 Hume, *Treatise,* 1888, p. 503.

stability to a corresponding normative principle. Of course, I express my attachment to my property, as well as my sympathy for others who are likewise attached to their property, in my Kantian way. But, the Humean says, it is such deep and widespread feelings of attachment, not the moral theories in which they happen to be clothed, that provides the real justification for property.

It would seem that our feelings about being deliberately killed have just as solid a foundation. Our daily contact with one another makes it clear that we are concerned, from the most superficial to the deepest levels, with the intentions and attitudes that others have toward us. In particular, we are interested in the meanings of their actions: Does this person mean well or ill? Was my being bumped into intentional or accidental? (Physically, the bump itself could not have been more trivial; for that matter, it could just as well have been a pat on the back.) We understand the need to clear the air of these fears and suspicions by apologies and corrections. Most people, I think, would be more troubled by the thought that someone was seeking to kill them than by the thought that they might be killed accidentally, though they may know the likelihoods of these possibilities to be identical. This apparently works in the opposite direction too: I am at least more interested, and probably also more uplifted, by the fact that someone's action has my good as its direct target than by the fact that someone's action benefits me as a side effect.[2] In the former case, I may have a potential friend, admirer, or ally, and at the very minimum, someone who knows of my existence, and thinks favorably of me; whereas it is consistent with the latter that the agent does not even know I exist. In short, the more directly one becomes the target of another person's intentions, the more that person, and the direction of that person's intentions, gets magnified in one's thinking. Our tendencies to think in these ways hardly needs to be explained by reference

2 The idea of being the direct target of another's intentions was in part inspired by Warren Quinn's (1989) discussion of the doctrine of double effect. Quinn, however, says that that doctrine "gives each person some veto power over a certain kind of attempt to make the world a better place at his expense. This would be absurd if the entire point of morality were to maximize overall happiness or welfare." Quinn, 1989, p. 351. My whole point in the text, of course, is that this is not so absurd: to provide each person with such a veto power would be to provide collective backing for a deeply important sense of security and trust, counterbalancing a natural fear that we have of being targeted in certain ways in the intentional actions of others.

to deontological moral convictions. They are natural, no doubt, as much as our tendencies to cry or laugh. More than that, they are natural to anyone – which is here to say everyone who must live in society with others – whose interests depend crucially on the local climate of interaction and, in particular, on whether it is one of hostility or cooperation, coldness or warmth.

No doubt our concern is heightened when coldness toward individuals becomes elevated to the level of a generally accepted rule of proper behavior, rather than merely a common characteristic of so many separate individuals. It is one thing for an individual, or even group of individuals, to be fully prepared to sacrifice me, or anyone, for the greater good, and for me to know this. It represents an even more troubling expression of attitude toward individuals when the entire group in which we live accepts this as the universally applicable norm of behavior. Now, it becomes natural and reasonable for each of us to feel the potential for being ganged-up against; the suspicion and fear becomes magnified by seeing that one is confronted by a potential combination, and that anyone who would use you for the good now has the benefit of the eyes, ears, strength, and above all, quite literally the moral support of all the others. In general, it is the presence of other centers of consciousness; creatures who can develop conscious plans that are either adverse or favorable to us; who can make us the targets of those plans, and feel that they can even legitimately target us in their collective plans, which greatly magnifies the importance in our minds of the end results that they can bring about. Our tendencies are so deeply entrenched in us, in fact, so much a part of what it is to be human, that they can hardly be rejected as irrational. To do so would be like arguing that the human need for fellowship and love is irrational. However, these tendencies represent for us ends that we can adopt means to advance and protect, and the means we adopt can be either rational or irrational. Therefore, concern about these tendencies would seem to warrant the teaching and acceptance of certain moral rules, among them ACRs forbidding killing for the good of it. In teaching and accepting moral rules, we avail ourselves of a capacity that is also characteristically human, and which enables us to get the benefits of collective action and of a publicly known mutual resolve.

This conclusion might still seem strange, for something like the following reason. If we begin with the assumption that we are all bound by the primary principle of doing good, then for me to give such a prominent place to my fear of being killed at the Infallible Optimizer's green light would seem out of place. For the good that the primary principle requires us to do is impersonal good. No person's good is to count for any more or less than anyone else's. So perhaps I have this understandable fear of being killed for the good of it; but that might only show that I am not capable of living up to the requirements the primary principle places on me. Perhaps I could be excused from blame for rejecting its demands in this case; but that does not show that I have no objective duty. It shows only that I am too afraid to face up to it, even as others would be in the same situation.

This point has little force, though, when the dispositions and reactions getting in the way of direct pursuit of the good are themselves widespread and deeply seated. If I alone feared being the targeted victim of a good-doing plan, then it would be possible to view my fear as something that reflects on me rather than on what is objectively right, something for which I am perhaps to be excused because of my peculiar situation. As a characteristically human reaction, however, it is something that properly figures in a consequentialist picture of what we are to be collectively permitted to do. As such, the reaction belongs to our concept of the good. It would be otherwise if we were so constituted that it made no essential difference to us whether or not our being harmed figures directly in the plans of others.

A final remark now about the empirical spirit in which these observations are made. It requires no excursus into science fiction to imagine communities in which this fear of being deliberately killed for the good of it does not exist. Indeed, it is easy enough to imagine a community in which people so submerge their own identities and interests in those of the group that they would quite willingly sacrifice themselves for the greater good, their only concern being, perhaps, that no error was being made. In such a community, there would be one reason less for thinking of ACRs as desirable. That would still not be the end of the matter, to be sure; for we would still need to know more about this general willingness to sacrifice oneself: Is it consistent with full advancement of other interests? Does it provide the basis for human flourishing, or is this identification with others based on a deep misconception about them, serving simply to make it easier to accept being sacrificed by them? In this way, we are pushed back to questions about the concept of the good, and to empirical issues about how best to realize the good. But that is no doubt where the consequentialist must more often seek to push ethical debates.

4.3. FAIRNESS

An objector might also claim that the idea of an obligation to respect rules rests on deontological intuitions about fairness. If the rules require each to keep the heat below some preassigned level, non-compliance is of course unfair to the others, but that idea does not belong to consequentialist theory. Or an objector might argue in the alternative that if the reason for complying with rules like the fuel-saving rule is to do good, then this has nothing to do with fairness. The duty to do good, one might argue, is quite distinct from the duty of fairness, having nothing to do with the fair distribution of anything.[3] I suggest, however, that there is room for the notion of fairness here on at least two levels. First, the concept of the good that we bring about by our actions may itself be in some way distribution-sensitive, and this too provides room for talk of fairness. Thus suppose that a set of rules for fuel-saving serves very well to save fuel, but only at the expense of imposing especially heavy burdens on some people but relatively light burdens on others. Taking this additional, distribution-sensitive dimension of the good into account, the effective saving of fuel under these rules may turn out to be unjustified after all. Secondly, the very concept of being governed by restrictions that apply equally to all brings with it a place for the concept of fairness: It is unfair to apply the rules unequally, most obviously so when one makes an exception for oneself to advance one's own good. To do so is inconsistent with the enterprise, one that we suppose to be collectively rational. But this, I have argued, is at bottom a consequentialist enterprise, based on the idea that some collective goods, like that of mutual trust, cannot be achieved except through mutual commitment and equal application of the rules. That there is here

---

3 Simmons writes: "Our duties to promote happiness and to help those in need, for instance, are actuated by occasions for providing indispensable goods. But these duties have nothing to do with *fairness;* they rest on the moral importance of the goods provided (not on considerations of fair distribution)." Simmons, 1987, p. 272.

a legitimate concern about the distribution of something is clear: It is the distribution of individual discretion that we are concerned about. But the reason for limiting that discretion equally with respect to the using of fuel can, if I am right, be given a broadly consequentialist explanation.

4.4. EQUALITY BEFORE THE RULES

Then how can equality before the rules be so important to a consequentialist, anyway? Here again a critic might suspect that deontological intuitions are being smuggled in by way of the very idea of a collective enterprise, the rules of which apply equally to all. The idea of such an enterprise itself needs a clear, explicitly consequentialist justification.

We should first recall that equality before the rules allows both (i) that the rules may themselves contain public exceptions and conditions, and (ii) that rules are understood to have a scope which limits their applicability to a particular group. Thus the rules that we acknowledge as necessary to guide our behavior in our family, our small band, or troop are not understood to apply to others. It would be inappropriate, both in our view, and in the view of those others, to extend the application of the rules to them. So the idea of equality under the rules already contains important limits. It does not require that all people everywhere be bound by all the same rules; nor that the rules must be insensitive to the differences among people.

We should also recall the earlier point about the value of the idea of equality in some practical applications. The value of equal application of the rules rests in large part on our constant need to depersonalize many of our most important interactions with one another. We understandably fear that others may take advantage of us by making special exceptions for themselves. In much the same way, we fear that others may be singling us out because of hostility or envy, or that they may be ignoring us, not thinking of us as important enough to merit attention, perhaps not even as beings with intentions and plans, or not thinking of us at all. We attempt to explain decisions that are adverse or disappointing to others by noting that "this is nothing personal". If it were something personal, the people they affect would understandably be angered, and would no doubt aim their hostile attention personally at us. Yet punishments must be meted out, salaries must be assigned, tax burdens must be allocated, people must be hired, and duties must be imposed. All of these things must be done by real human beings, not machines or Infallible Optimizers acting on their own. The equal application of rules serves as one device to bring about these results while convincingly communicating that the aim was not the good or ill of any particular persons: No one was their target, even though many were unavoidably affected. Here again we must recall that it is not just the actions complying with the rules that produce good in the world; it is also the public understanding that there is a general acceptance of the rules and of their equal application. In this way, the individual can recognize his or her standing in the community. One knows how the group as a whole is collectively disposed to deal with individuals.

No doubt many today think first of the misuses to which these "depersonalizing" devices are put: They are sometimes used to provide people in power with hypocritical cover, and with a method of escaping responsibility. But we should not allow this fact to obscure the importance, indeed, the indispensability, of the device of rules and their equal applicability. What the equal application of rules provides is not, therefore, escape from moral responsibility either for actions or judgments; one is still accountable for the rightness of one's actions and the validity of one's judgments. But it does provide an all-important shift in the level on which this accounting takes place, moving it from the personal to the impersonal. If some rules or institutions are given to misuse, that may raise serious questions about the justifiability of those rules from the start.

4.5. DOES THE MLM INVOLVE MORAL SCHIZOPHRENIA?

Because the MLM uses a distinction between the points of view of collective and individual rationality, it is open to some of the same questions that have plagued rule-utilitarian accounts. When does one take the one point of view and when the other? What does one consult in deciding this – some third point of view? And when one takes the point of view of, say, collective rationality, does this exclude any and all thinking about individual maximization? To the extent that it does, what is this exclusion supposed to involve?

Does it involve remaining blind to, or ignorant of, the moral merits of individual cases?

Where the points of view lead to conflicting conclusions, we need guidance in avoiding a collision. Discussing a closely related problem, Nagel suggests three possibilities for dealing with conflicts between the impersonal point of view, in which our concern is with objective end results only, and the subjective point of view, from which ACRs apply. These possibilities are reduction, elimination, or annexation.[4] One reductionist possibility would be to hold that act-consequentialist reasons rarely or only in uninteresting situations conflict with ACRs anyway,[5] or that "objective" consequentialism is a view about what is objectively right rather than a view about what ought to guide our thinking and action, matters that may be best left to character traits, habits, or even superstition. Later in this book, I shall argue against this second reductionist line of thought. And as to the former, it would be complacent and dangerous to proceed on the hunch that it is right. Elimination would proceed by dismissing the subjective point of view, giving at most an explanation of how people come to have it. Annexation would invent some new objective element, like the command of God, as a way of reconciling the idea of what is impersonally best with the notion of a constraint on individual action. It is clear that neither elimination nor annexation would be consistent with the MLM. The MLM attempts to show why it is rational for us as individuals to take ACRs seriously, as representing truths about what we ought to do and the reasons we have to act, rather than as psychological facts to be explained. So the MLM does not follow the elimination alternative. Nor do we attempt to annex moral theory to something else like, for example, theological premises. So a different tack must be taken.

The relationship between collective and individual points of view would seem to be best characterized by another idea, that of subsumption. Both are subsumed under the simple idea of maximization. Thus the point of view of individual rationality is appropriate when the best is achievable directly through my action;

---

4 Nagel, 1979, pp. 210–11.
5 Thus Kagan, 1989, xii: "[I]n practical terms consequentialism may not differ in this area all that much from ordinary morality. Killing the innocent, e.g., will generally not have the best results overall, and so consequentialism and ordinary morality will typically be alike in forbidding it."

that of collective rationality is appropriate when the best is achievable through the general acceptance of a rule; that is, through group resolve and action in which I can participate.[6]

We must still explain, without resorting to reduction or elimination, what governs the adoption of one point of view rather than the other. It would not be quite right to say that we join with a group if and only if that action of joining produces the best results in the context of the actions of others in the group; that could easily be reductionist, for it would be consistent with reducing everything to a question of individual maximization. The answer that I propose relies on the commonsense idea of a rule's defensible rationale. The reason for having a generally accepted rule is to achieve good that would be unachievable if everyone were to act as so many separate maximizers. Yet we do best if we leave certain behavior untouched by rules. Now, suppose that there is a generally accepted rule forbidding everyone from walking across the lawn. Using the idea of a defensible rationale, we have some idea of how that rule is to be evaluated. It is usually quite clear what the rationale for such a rule is. There are certain paradigm cases of behavior, like that of walking across the lawn simply for one's own pleasure or convenience, that are the target of the rule. That kind of maximization is clearly prohibited, if anything is; for it is just the kind of behavior to which many people on many occasions are regularly tempted, and which they could, without obvious insincerity or fakery, justify to themselves and others. Now, the rationale enables us to distinguish among different kinds of maximizing behavior, not merely in terms of the degree of gains or losses at stake, but in terms of their kind. No reasonable person supposes that running across the grass in an emergency to save a life, or even to save someone from a nasty fall, is proscribed by the rule. This is the sort of individual maximizing that we want to take place. We would be quite happy if everyone in such a situation were to do just this sort of thing. It is not only that the good of saving another person is great; it is also that the other factors in the situation – its emergency character, the

6 Compare Parfit's (C9), 1984, sec. 26. From the fact that one has done the best act of those possible, it does not follow that one has done what one ought to do: One "ought to have asked whether he is a member of some group who could have acted in a way whose consequence would have been even better. If this is true, and he could have persuaded this group to act in this way, this is what he ought to have done."

difficulty of an agent's giving false justifications after the fact either to self or others – which make it special. We should consider these factors from the standpoint of their suitability for incorporation in a general, public and universalized rule. Whereas the main target of the rule was the typical person who tends to follow convenience and self-interest, emergency situations are sufficiently rare, perhaps also sufficiently hard to fake, that they are not included in the first place within the rationale of the rule.

The concept of the defensible rationale of a rule then serves to mediate between the bare notion of maximization and the choice of one point of view or the other; that is, that of individual, or of collective, rationality. Although it is true that the concept of a rationale is one that makes sense only from a collective point of view, being analogous to that of a legislator's point of view in framing and promulgating laws, the rationale also enables us to decide whether a special rule preempting the primary principle is appropriate.

Suppose that I am informed that it is wrong to walk across the grass, period. My informant, and lots of other people too, may think no further about it than that. Doing some further questioning, and thinking about the rule, I begin to realize what the rationale for the rule is. (I shall say more later about this kind of inquiry, an inquiry which is, I think, partly normative and partly descriptive.) Then I am in a better position to discriminate between situations calling for direct individual maximization and those calling for its disallowance. To summarize, our choice of a point of view is ultimately to be guided by the idea of maximization. The question is whether the best is achieved through individual maximization or through subscription to rules. Whether there is a rationale for having a rule, and if so what that rationale is, are then the central mediating questions. I address these questions further in Chapter 6 and in Section 4.9 of this chapter.

4.6. WHAT DO EXCLUSIONARY REASONS REALLY EXCLUDE?

The idea of an exclusionary reason may seem puzzling in its very conception. To some, the idea of excluding certain reasons from one's moral thinking seems to involve self-imposed blindness, ignorance, insensitivity, or even superstition; at the very least, it has seemed to bring with it an abdication of moral responsibility for making and acting on a full moral assessment of the situation. Because the tendency to misunderstand the role of rules, and the exclusionary reasons they provide in moral thinking, is so inveterate, I shall, out of an abundance of caution, attend more closely to the sources of unease.

To the skeptic, one who recognizes the force of exclusionary reasons reveals some or all of the following faults: (a) within some sphere at least, one refuses even to think "in moral terms about acts, but only about policies"; (b) one ponders people one meets "only from the viewpoint of the policies that apply to them," managing in the process to be more of a moral prig than a moral model; (c) even after balancing the wrong of breaking a rule against that of respecting it, and seeing that the action is morally unacceptable, one then makes the gross mistake of sweeping "this insight under the rug by saying that the individual act is not after all the logical subject of moral evaluation"; (d) one abdicates moral responsibility for one's acts, hiding behind the rule, claiming that it is not of one's making;[7] (e) one believes that, when a moral rule has once been justified, that simply blocks off any further inquiry into how it was justified, and whether its justification is strong or weak.[8] Let us consider these complaints more carefully.

(a) The moral agent need not refuse, on account of an exclusionary reason, to give space to any mere thought. (Though what one spends a lot of time thinking about may well reflect on one's character.) Of course, I may decide that I can gain better control of myself if I simply block out certain thoughts. Just as I may decide not even to have rich desserts anywhere in the kitchen, so that the thought of how nice they would taste will not even occur to me, I may decide not even to think of the better uses to which I could put my tax dollars if only I evaded my taxes. But respect for my

7 I draw this list of doubts primarily from Luban, 1988, whose stimulating book has made it largely unnecessary for me to construct a hypothetical skeptic. The quoted material is from pp. 120–5. Luban's point about abdication of moral responsibility was meant to apply mainly to the context of modern bureaucratic organizations. But if actually existing rules are taken to be morally binding, as the MLM takes them to be, the point would seem to have a natural application to the MLM as well.

8 "[O]nce the institution is justified, further inquiry into how it was justified is excluded. We must regard the justification as a given and ask only what it in turn justifies. The arguments pertaining to the justification of each link 'forget' those pertaining to previous links." Luban, 1988, p. 134.

duty to pay taxes requires only that that I reject certain reasons that would, were it not for the duty, be relevant. And that means that such a reason does not weigh in favor of the conclusion that I ought, all things considered, to evade my taxes. I can still think about these reasons all I want, even about how they might be relevant in another world in which I had no duty to pay my taxes.

(b) To view all one's actions, and their effects for other people, solely from the standpoint of abstract principles and policies, and without regard to the particular features of acts and persons, would indeed be a serious moral failing. Fortunately, we can take the exclusionary reasons of our moral rules seriously without falling into such vices. Indeed, we should notice that the opposite vice, which could as justly be attributed to denying exclusionary reasons their due, is as bad. When I am owed money, I don't want my debtor weighing all the features of my character, possessions, and likely uses for the money in determining whether he will pay me back or give the money to someone who will make better use of it. When people are calculating my salary increase, I don't want them to take account of my prior financial position, life-style, or details of family and religion. People who do these things are just as unattractive, in their own way, as the rigid rule-follower. Although the rigid rule-follower is cold, mechanical, and puts off too much responsibility on the rules, those who act always on the perceived merits of the individual case are arrogant, power-hungry, often as self-deceived as the rigid rule-follower, and leave the sticky fingerprints of their personal ideals everywhere.

But this only counters the vice of one extreme with that of the other. We need to know more about the place where virtue lies, and we need reassurances that respect for exclusionary reasons also lies at that place. The whole idea of "looking at things only from the viewpoint of policies" does not even make sense. For in order even to know whether there is a relevant policy or rule governing a proposed course of action and, if so, what it is, I need to have some idea of the particular features of this particular act: The rule says that we are all to save water by not consuming more than three gallons a day. In addition to the obviously relevant description of my action – that it involves consuming three hundred gallons of water – there may be the fact that it is necessary to saving the whole town from burning down. Far from refusing to consider this fact, I take it into account in determining that the rule could not rationally have been meant to apply to this kind of case. This inquiry is in turn not to be sharply distinguished from the fundamental question of whether the rule is justified in the first place. Even if I had been told time and again by authorities and ordinary citizens alike that one must never use more than three gallons of water even to prevent the town from burning to the ground, I could conclude that the rule, so taught, was simply not justified, assuming, of course, the absence of, say, demons or Martians who threaten to torture us all if we violate the rule. So, far from refusing to consider the particular features of acts, it is indeed hard to imagine how one could even know whether a justified policy applies to them (that is to say, what the policy is) without being constantly prepared to recognize and acknowledge the relevance of their special features.

The complaint about looking at things only from the viewpoint of policies is further flawed in that policies and rules – both on the MLM and on all but the most exaggeratedly rule-oriented moral conceptions – were never meant to govern all aspects of behavior. A social morality that did have special rules, over and above the primary principle, purporting to govern every piece of individual and social behavior would surely be a failure. Rules are appropriate in certain spheres, especially, though not exclusively, those involving behavior given to self-interested pursuit at the expense of others, and behavior for which social supervision is important because individual discretion leads easily to special pleading. But in many departments of life it is best simply to leave people to their own individual judgments of what is best. Thus the need to follow a justified rule does not even arise, because *no* rule would be justified.

(c) What if one has already carried out the balancing, and has recognized that the wrong done by breaking a rule is less than the wrong done from following it? Is it not then a gross mistake to reject this knowledge merely on the "logical" grounds that the act is not the proper subject of evaluation? Notice, however, that this way of formulating the problem very much stacks the deck in the objector's favor, but at the price of stating a tautology. Of course, when one has carried on a full comparison of the moral features of each act, and concluded, on this evidence, in favor of breaking the rule because it is the lesser of the wrongs, it appears that one has already taken account of whatever exclusionary force the rule had in the first place.[9] If this moral balancing does not take account of the exclusionary force of the rule, then the example is question-begging: For the defender of the exclusionary force of rules has claimed that violation of a justified rule is a wrong-making feature, and we now are to suppose that one can carry on a balancing of the moral features of an act without taking any account of exclusionary force. If this balancing has not yet taken account of the exclusionary reason, then it is not yet to be considered a valid piece of reasoning, not, at least, until those improperly weighed considerations are left out.

These points can be illustrated by considering our familiar example, the case in which I know that my failure to comply with a rule would maximize utility because the fuel or water that is saved would be of greater objective value to me than to the collective effort, which will succeed anyway. Now, the balancing here is between the overall good produced by compliance weighed against the overall good produced by my alternative use, the latter being the greater. If one were to say that failure to comply would nevertheless be morally wrong, that would amount to according some exclusionary reason its due. On the other hand, were the weighing of impersonal good to be the only thing that takes place in this moral balancing, that would amount to an act-utilitarian procedure, nothing more. So unless we assume the validity of an act-utilitarian procedure, which I obviously do not, we cannot attribute any kind of moral failing to one who, after seeing the results of the balancing, decides that it is right to follow the rule though doing so will not itself produce the most overall good.

(d) It might seem that to follow a generally accepted, justified rule, rather than to decide a case purely on its own merits, involves the plainest abdication of the moral responsibility to act on the basis of one's independent, autonomous judgment. Alternatively, it might seem that following a rule in those circumstances is just a shabby way of avoiding having to take responsibility for one's actions: "After all, the general acceptance of that rule is not my doing; I didn't institute my society's morality, and, had I done so,

9 Ibid., p. 122. After making this claim, Luban goes on to quote Bernard Williams, 1973, to the effect that it is irrational to follow a utilitarianly justified rule when doing so in that instance does not maximize utility. But Williams's formulation of the problem does not implicitly prejudge, as Luban's does, that one has already carried on a balancing of moral wrongs.

I would surely have made it better. But this is what I am stuck with, so I have no choice but to follow the rule." This would be the moral analogue of the often reviled "I was just doing my job" excuse.

These are indeed legitimate general worries. But, as a criticism of the idea that rules supply exclusionary reasons, they miss the mark. The complaint lacks force unless we *begin* with the premise that the agent has indeed done a wrong, and that he now seeks to escape moral responsibility for this wrong by shifting it to the group and its rules. In these circumstances, attempting to shift responsibility in this way would reveal a failure to reflect upon the moral dimensions of one's situation and actions: One ought, after all, to have seen that it was wrong. If this kind of excuse is frequently used by a lot of people, that may show a widespread deficiency in moral character and training: Too many people simply do not know how to interpret and evaluate a rule. Or, if the excuse is too frequently used in this kind of context, that may raise questions about the moral rules in this sphere that are generally accepted in the first place: They may be unjustified; that is, their existence may be worse than the utilitarian state of nature.

These quite legitimate general worries do not, however, demonstrate that rule-supplied exclusionary reasons have no force. Because they begin with the assumption that the moral agent who respects such reasons, in cases in which it makes a difference to the outcome, is doing a wrong, they cannot be used to establish this conclusion. So if the worries are aired in order to show the failure of the exclusionary-reasons approach, their recital simply begs the question. If, on the other hand, they are aired in order to show that following the rule in the teeth of contrary considerations is not always morally justified, or that people may sometimes be given to the vice of oversubservience to rules, these points can be freely admitted. At most, then, they would show that, in some particular context, moral training or moral consciousness, or both, are defective.

(e) From what has already been said, it will be easy enough to anticipate the broad outlines of our answer to the charge that taking rules seriously involves first determining whether the rule is justified up to some minimum threshold, and then following it unquestioningly, "forgetting" all but the bare fact that it is justified. It would be unfortunate indeed if this "forgotten justification" idea,

74

which is a caricature both of the concept of a moral rule and of an institutional role, were seriously taught. Even if someone were to attempt to respect such a rigid separation, it would be hard to apply the idea in practice – not, at least, without self-deception. For our conception of whether the rule is justified is guided by our conception of the acts that it justifies. Not even legal rules that are the product of outright statutory enactment, and which therefore have a privileged and authoritative formulation, come to us with the set of instances to which they are to apply neatly prelabeled and packaged. This is even less so in the application of moral rules, in which the agent is responsible for acting only under a defensible interpretation of a justified rule that is in turn to be understood in light of its rationale.

4.7. HAVE WE NOW DRIVEN A WEDGE BETWEEN THE BEST AND THE RIGHT?

Many, especially those most sympathetic to consequentialism, are impressed by what seems to be a close conceptual connection between the right and the best. If the underlying idea of consequentialism is that the rightness of actions is based squarely on bringing about good in the world, then it becomes hard to resist the further small step: that the rightness of actions is connected to bringing about the best, and not the merely good or the merely better. There is, after all, nothing particularly distinguished about doing good as such. Many of our actions involve net gains of utility, and the only plausible criterion for distinguishing them from one another would seem to be one which points in the direction of uniqueness. To most consequentialists, therefore, it has seemed obvious that the rational pursuit of the good must be the rational pursuit of the best.[10] Of course, the idea of the best without qualification may not even be a coherent idea, much less a usable one. But it does seem plausible to link the concept of the right to the idea of the best available. The idea, some might argue, of linking the rightness of action to accepted social rules severs this link in two ways: (a) Compliance even with the best rule may require action that has less than the best available consequences overall. (b) On the MLM, one

---

10 By no means all. See Slote, 1985a, for the idea of "satisficing" rather than maximizing.

is sometimes required to comply with social rules that are themselves not the best.

Stated in its simplest form, the answer to this objection is that the MLM does retain the connection between the right and the best. But it holds, at the same time, that the best cannot be directly achieved by the acts of individuals: instead, it must be indirectly pursued. This simple answer must now be followed by a much longer version. Because the most important have already been presented in this and the previous chapter, I shall not now repeat the arguments that directly bear on (a). Before considering the much more serious questions raised by (b), I should like to consider an objection, raised by Shelly Kagan, against the whole approach of linking the right to a set of rules. His concern is addressed to theories linking right action to optimific rules. Thus one who argues as he does would presumably have still deeper concerns about a theory that links right action to justified existing rules that might be less than optimific.

The main idea of this objection is that defenders of rule utilitarianism fail to motivate their use of the idea of rules; they fail to show the necessary link between rules and the morally right which their theories propose. Although it may be interesting and generally useful to know what moral code it would be optimific to promulgate, we have no guarantee that such a code would capture everything about acts that is morally relevant. As Kagan puts it:

[S]uch a possibility immediately raises the objection that there might be morally relevant considerations that would not be fully and precisely captured by the set of moral rules whose promulgation would be optimal. Yet such a possibility seems neglected by the two-level view, which simply assumes without justification that the moral status of an act is determined solely in terms of its conformity to the optimal set of rules.[11]

This point, Kagan thinks, undercuts rule-utilitarian ("two-level") attempts both to explain agent options to do less than the best, and agent restrictions on doing certain things even though they may maximize. As to options, even if it is true that the optimific moral code would lack a requirement to maximize, "the extremist [i.e., act consequentialist] will note that promoting the good may still be morally required nonetheless." And once we begin to believe that an optimific moral code "need not capture morality exhaus-

11 Kagan, 1989, p. 37.

76

tively nor completely accurately, we can see that the moderate has not yet given us an adequate defense of constraints."[12]

This criticism of rule utilitarianism rests on the idea that the rules the theory employs are designed to capture already existing moral distinctions, a project that, if attempted, could be done with greater or less accuracy, but one would certainly assume, never perfectly. If the purpose of rules is to serve as guides that help us to accumulate and preserve moral wisdom, and to avoid miscalculations, then it could hardly be otherwise. For on this conception, the moral data come first, and the rules are constructed based on this data. "Unless the moderate can give us reason to believe that the morally relevant considerations are presented with complete accuracy by the optimal set of social norms," Kagan writes, "he cannot show why the optimal rules should not be violated in the exceptional cases in which it would promote the best outcome to do so."[13] And above all, if the motivation behind the promulgation of an optimific set of social norms is to promote the good, then the claim that one must obey the rules even when it does not maximize good would seem to be unmotivated.

We can see by now the main ways in which this kind of criticism would be answered by the MLM. Kagan's argument strategy overlooks the possibility that we need, and would have reason to adopt, rules to provide moral distinctions rather than to summarize or "capture" moral distinctions that are already there. Further, the MLM does not propose that all moral judgments must somehow be referred to rules. So the moral status of acts is not solely determined by rules, not even by optimific rules. Sometimes no rule applies and the primary principle governs directly. In other cases, rules may conflict, and appeal must be made to the primary principle, combined with a conception of the rationale underlying each of the rules.

Most important of all, however, is the point that the project of using rules to establish, rather than reflect, moral distinctions, far from being unmotivated by the idea of doing good, is based squarely on it. As we have seen, it is based on the idea that some of the most important components of the good can only be achieved through mutual resolve to respect justified rules, and that the ben-

12 Ibid., p. 38.
13 Ibid., p. 39.

77

efits of this resolve cannot be cashed out in terms of the good consequences of acts. Thus adherence to a rule as a defining standard of the right is bound to appear unmotivated if one thinks of maximization solely as a matter of individual maximization of good through individual acts.

4.8. THE RULE-WORSHIP CHARGE

One of the most common charges against rule-utilitarian conceptions, especially those that give some priority to actually existing rules, is that they require us to worship rules for their own sake, and this does seem to be a blind worship indeed when we recognize how bad existing social rules may be. Of course, if those rules are not even minimally justified, they do not, on the MLM anyway, have any claim to preempting the primary principle. But even if we restrict our attention to minimally justified rules, they can indeed leave a lot to be desired.

Some rule worship charges are blunted when we allow (i) that consideration of the consequences is sometimes appropriate in deciding whether a particular case falls under a rule; and (ii) that social moral rules are to be understood against the background of their justifiable rationale. Thus Smart appeals to our intuitions about the putative irrationality of following rules with the following two examples.[14]

A promise to the dying: 'I have promised to a friend, dying on a desert island from which I am subsequently rescued, that I will see that his fortune (over which I have control) is given to a jockey club. However, when I am rescued I decide that it would be better to give the money to a hospital, which can do more good with it.'

Drought restrictions: 'Suppose that during hot weather there is an edict that no water must be used for watering gardens. I have a garden and I reason that most people are sure to obey the edict, and that as the amount of water that I use will be by itself negligible no harm will be done if I use the water secretly.'

Smart's argument, of course, is that it would not be wrong to give the money to a hospital, or to use the water secretly, provided my action would not have additional bad effects; for example, for my character, or for the behavior of others. Smart believes, incidentally,

14 Smart, "Extreme and Restricted Utilitarianism," in Bayles, 1968, pp. 109–11.

that the drought-restrictions example presents a weaker case for rule violation than that of the promise to the dying. I agree with this, but for reasons that are clearly different from any he gives.

First we should note that respect for an existing rule R, and the preemptive reasons it provides, does not entail, as some philosophers have thought,[15] that consequences are not in any way relevant to deciding what to do in particular cases. This is a common error. Smart's mistaken supposition about this recalls our earlier discussion. If R forbids using water for the garden, that prohibition is usually combined with a rationale, and some violations of R will be paradigmatic of the sort of thing R is meant to prohibit, while others will not. In the drought restrictions case, it is easy to see what kind of reasoning is the main target of the rule. It is that in which one reasons: "Everyone else is observing the restrictions, and I could do more good in the world by noncompliance. Of course, as a bonus, my doing more impersonal good will also be to my benefit, but that is incidental. What I ought to be concerned about is doing the most impersonal good." The rule's rationale excludes precisely this kind of reasoning whether or not it is otherwise correct, and whether or not one is absolutely certain that it is otherwise correct. However, if there were obviously no bonus of special benefit to the agent, and if the situation were genuinely rare, arising from circumstances beyond anyone's control, then, given this rationale for the rule, watering a garden to bring about the most impersonal good would not necessarily be wrong. As it is, the idea behind such a rule is that people are not to weigh considerations of impersonal good in the usual way where their own interests are involved. To permit such behavior would be to encourage opportunistic or self-deceived mistake, and in circumstances in which such mistake would be difficult to detect. In these circumstances, we would not be able as efficiently to exert collective influence on individual behavior, and mistrust might develop. Finally, discretion and power over outcomes would in practice be distributed unequally. For people are unequal in their abilities to notice opportunities and use them to their advantage. So if I notice an opportunity to benefit myself in the process of doing more

---

15 "The restricted utilitarian regards moral rules as more than rules of thumb for short-circuiting calculations of consequences. Generally, he argues, consequences are *not relevant at all* when we are deciding what to do in a particular case." [emphasis added] Smart, in Bayles, 1968, p. 107.

impersonal good in the world, relying on others' compliance with the rules, I must realize that my action is at the core of what is forbidden by the rule.

In Smart's example of making a promise to a dying person, the case which he believes would more obviously be an instance of rule worship, self-interest may not be an issue. If I see to it that the money goes to a hospital instead of the jockey club, I am not gaining anything for myself, except possibly an added measure of discretion that people do not ordinarily enjoy, being able both to make the promise and then, unconstrained by the promise, to do what I judge best with the money. This is one reason, I think, why we might be inclined to think that breaking this promise was not wrong.

But there is another, more compelling reason why breaking this kind of a promise might not be wrong: There may be no justified rule against breaking this kind of a promise. For this kind of promise raises all sorts of questions that promises in other contexts do not: Given that the friend is dying, can we assume that his expressed wish is what he would want on cool reflection? Can the promise made to a dying person, given the natural desire not to give hurt or cause upset, be treated as seriously as other kinds of promises? We already have the legal institutions of wills and trusts, so why did he not set up such an instrument when he could have? Even the law of trusts limits, for reasons of the public good, the ways in which one can determine the disposition of one's property after death;[16] so what could be the justification for having any moral rule prohibiting the breaking of promises like this one, given both the pressure and awkwardness of the situation, and the fact that carrying out the dying's wishes would put the money to an especially in-efficient use? I do not wish to deny here that there might be a good rationale for a rule requiring even the keeping of promises like this one, at least in some societies in some circumstances. When such circumstances exist, there would be good reasons for thinking that breaking the promise is wrong. But we can doubt this, and thus

---

16 I have in mind here the rule against perpetuities, which would, among other things, make unenforceable a trust designed to accumulate money indefinitely for the sole purpose of accumulation. The idea behind making such trusts unenforceable is that they are against the public good. Of course, the rule of perpetuities would not necessarily exclude a trust set up to endow the local jockey club.

we can share Smart's intuition, though not his reasons, that breaking this promise is not wrong after all.

It is time to consider the more serious version of the charge that the MLM drives a wedge between the best and the right. The idea that actually accepted, justified rules can be authoritative, even though less than optimific, may seem especially unmotivated. It would seem particularly vulnerable to the familiar rule worship charge so often directed against rule utilitarianism. Why should I ever consider myself bound by the less-than-ideal rules of a less-than-ideal code? Why not simply cut through all of this thinking and talk of what the existing rule requires and do that which produces the best overall results?

It would be implausible, as well as useless, to appeal to meanings here. We cannot maintain that judgments about the morally right really mean something like 'required by an existing justified code'. Many people, especially moral critics and moral philosophers, do not use the words 'is morally right' in this way. Even if they did, the fact would be of little use, for we could not settle substantive moral questions by appealing to meanings. We cannot, in short, make the moral recommendation that people follow an existing code simply on the ground that most or all people mean by 'is morally right' something like 'that which accords with an existing justified code'.

We can, however, return to the main idea that motivates our acceptance and use of rules in the first place. I suggest that when we reflect on this we can begin to see why even a nonideal rule can sometimes be binding on our thinking and action. In this way, we can see what it is about the general acceptance of a rule that gives it a certain priority over rules that would produce better results were they generally accepted. If a chief function of social moral rules is to provide the basis for mutual trust by placing understood limits on individual discretion, this function would obviously be undercut by returning much of that discretion to moral agents by allowing them always to appeal, in argument as well as in the privacy of conscience, to some ideal, even though nonexistent, rule. I may not be able to contribute to the good of mutual trust through my participation in the collective acceptance of ideal rule R_1, because others are not disposed to accept R_1; but I can still contribute to this same kind of good through my participation in the actual collective acceptance of R_2. Indeed, it is in precisely those circumstances in which rules are necessary to the collective promotion of good that to defy the existing justified rule in favor either of an ideal rule or of individual good-doing is most obviously immoral. Recall Keynes's comment, quoted on the epigraph page at the beginning of this book, that the claimed right to judge every individual case on its merits was "our most obvious and dangerous characteristic", making him and his group "in the strict sense of the term, immoralists." People who reserve this right for themselves are rightly understood to be immoralists, because they are unwilling or unable to see the point of having rules in the first place. And it does no good to object that such people do at least respect rules in theory, so long, that is, as the rules are the best that could conceivably exist (whatever that might mean); for it can almost always be plausibly claimed that the existing rules are not the best.

But let us return to an earlier example. The existing rule, let us suppose, forbids using more fuel than is necessary to heat one's residence to 50 degrees F. If I know that Smart's alternative rule – that each person throw dice and give himself or herself the appropriate probability, requiring 50 degrees on one outcome and 70 degrees on the other – would be ideal, I might follow that rule even though others do not, giving myself a chance to be among the lucky ones who would be allowed the 70-degree exception. Alternatively, I might use my recognition of the existing rule's shortcomings as justification for returning to individual maximization, allowing myself the 70 degrees because I know that, given the actions of others, more overall good will be done that way, via my own comfort, of course. But it is clear that, in either case, I would be missing the point of having a rule: I would be failing to recognize that a rule in this kind of situation is needed to set up a kind of Humean general concurrence, and that the concurrence itself, and the fact that it is rational for each to be true to it in action, is a major source of its value. Being true to the rule, of course, requires more than taking into account the disappointment, and diminished trust that might, or might not, be the consequence of my action. Thus my reasons for complying with the rule should not be confused with those of the act consequentialist who respects existing rules only in the sense that she or he is prepared to take into account the consequences of the particular action, especially those that result from its becoming known. My reasons apply even when my action will not become known. If I understand this, I must recognize that the general acceptance of a rule can give it a priority, both over a hypothetically better rule that is not concurred with, and over individual maximization.

These reflections can also help to account for the limits to the notion that the general acceptance of a rule gives it priority. Suppose that I not only know that Smart's alternative rule would be ideal if generally accepted, but that I am in a position to get others to adopt that rule. It is no longer a matter of my judging, and then acting, in secret to give myself access to a benefit; it is now a matter of making a public judgment which, given my position, will serve to bring the better rule into existence. The reasons for being bound and thinking myself bound by the inferior rule no longer obtain. Or, if they do obtain, it is only with much diminished force. For everyone could acknowledge the freedom, if not duty, of others to break away, at least in this kind of a case, from the existing rule. The good of having rules binding on all would not be undercut by this kind of freedom; quite to the contrary, it would be advanced. By judging and acting in public, I offer others the opportunity to use Smart's alternative rule. This confirms my willingness to adhere to rules that apply to all, and, in doing it, I do something that is rational from a collective point of view. Thus we can see in this the way in which the connection of the right to the best is not severed, but maintained.

4.9. THE CIRCUMSTANCES AND WEIGHT OF RULE PRIORITY

Having recognized the importance and priority of generally accepted rules to some areas of conduct, we must also recognize that large areas of our conduct and moral thinking are not suited to governance by rules. Or, if rules are appropriate in these areas, they are not the sort of rules that are understood to be applicable to everyone. Rather, they are rules that are understood to be largely a matter of individual choice and creation. A corollary of this is that, where universally applicable rules have no real point, it follows that there is also no real point in one's giving priority to any actually existing rule if one does happen to be generally accepted.

For one illustration of this, consider what W. D. Ross calls "the duties of self-improvement.''[17] On the MLM too the duties of self-improvement would be important; for one's own improvement is indeed a component of the good considered from an impersonal perspective. Most significant, however, it is a good that one is peculiarly well-positioned to bring about, and one, the promotion of which does not, by and large, conflict with self-interested motivation. But for this reason the duties of self-improvement are in most circumstances well accounted for by the primary principle alone. There is no need for any uniform, universally applicable rules of self-improvement. Indeed, such rules would in most cases be worse than otiose: they would be self-defeating.

But now suppose that there is some fairly wide agreement in my society as to how individuals are to fulfill their duties of self-improvement. Let us even suppose, for the sake of argument, that this wide agreement produces better results than if everyone were simply left to their own devices. If some alternative to this prevailing rule – one, say, that provides exceptions for certain categories of situation – would do even better, should I nevertheless accord priority to the prevailing rule? It would surely seem not. Because the usual point of having a rule – the need for a uniform and equal limitation of individual discretion – is missing, there is no need to think of the existing rule as having any special authority. Thus it has no priority except, perhaps, in the weak sense that it incorporates the wisdom of past experience. If there develop fairly uniform rules governing the duties of self-improvement, then, it seems most likely that they will turn out, on inspection, to be so many overlapping individual rules rather than rules binding on all. So these uniform rules may call for, say, getting as much education as one can as well as cultivating the arts. And I might for my part subscribe to these same rules. But I ought not to view everyone as strictly bound by them, though I might think that, so far as I know, they probably constitute wise strategies for just about everyone.

Much the same can no doubt be said about the duty of charity. It is one of the clearest kinds of case in which it will probably not be advantageous for behavior to be subject to public rules. In the case of charity, there is one benefit that will almost invariably be lost when charitable giving is made a matter of obligation: the

17 Ross, 1930, p. 21.

84

satisfaction of knowing that one has given, not because of pressure, but because of concern for the needy. This loss can be diminished somewhat if the duty of charity is made one of "imperfect obligation," that is, one in which the individual has considerable discretion in deciding on the type and objects of his or her charity. The argument against the use of collective rules would be strongest where (i) people are by and large sufficiently benevolent to be relied on to give sufficiently of their own accord; (ii) the objects of the giving tend over time to be, approximately, those who are indeed the neediest. When these conditions obtain, the usual arguments in favor of collective rules would ordinarily not apply to the case of charity. Given the existence of sufficient, properly directed benevolence, there is not the same kind of tendency toward deception, yielding to bad impulse, and adversely affecting the interests of others as there is in competition for scarce goods or in the taking of human life.

Those areas of behavior in which governance by rules has the most point, then, are also those areas in which an existing justified rule, though it falls short of the best, will have priority over an ideal rule. These are areas in which morality most appropriately takes on a legal aspect: The features of equal applicability of the rules, mutual restrictions on each individual's discretion to maximize, and uniformity of social moral judgment according to the rules all take on preeminent importance, as they do in the law. These areas do not constitute the whole of morality, to be sure; and many philosophers understandably think first of such things as personal moral ideals, life-styles, and individual standards of sexual behavior when they think of morality. Philosophers who do tend to think of these other areas of morality as paradigmatic will no doubt be inclined to miss the importance for moral thinking of rules and their actual acceptance in a social group. But neither do these areas constitute a minor segment of morality. Among the duties that seem best accounted for in terms of rules having the character of law are the various duties having to do with harming others or infringing on their personal domains; duties to keep promises; the duties that arise from cooperative schemes; the duties to respect property and individual privacy; and the duty to deal equitably and provide people with equal treatment.

We can now summarize the main features that mark those areas of behavior in which rules having the character of law are most likely to be appropriate:

(1) Where self-interest is feared because it is likely to produce undesirable results, as when:
    (a) individuals are likely to make mistakes in maximization;
    (b) individuals are likely to be tempted into maximization that also serves their own interests – cases in which everyone would like to avail themselves of the opportunity, but the enterprise would fail if they did (free-rider maximization);
    (c) individual action is difficult for the agent and/or for others to judge and supervise in the absence of uniform rules applicable to all.
(2) Where collective licensing of individual discretion to maximize is itself feared because of the terms of human interrelationship it expresses.

Those areas of behavior having several of these features are especially likely to need governance by generally accepted rules. Killing for the good that it will do would seem to be one of the foremost examples of such behavior. Thus a permission for individuals to kill for the overall good of it, given the self-interest and the strong passions that so often tempt people, encourages mistake. And the importance of this is in turn magnified by the fact that the mistake would be both irrevocable and so serious. Free-rider maximization is not precisely at issue in the case of killing for the good of it, except in this sense: Discretion is itself something upon which we place great importance, either as something we all want more of, or as something that we do not want to see unequally distributed. Discretionary power over life is therefore something which we would naturally want governed by fairly clear rules that are understood to be applicable to all, for without such rules, de facto discretion is likely to be very unequally distributed. And because of all of these factors, (1) (c) is relevant too, for the need for supervision of one's actions is especially great. Given the importance of the action, the temptations that lead to error, and the importance of general public confidence that de facto discretion is not unequally distributed, the dangers of deception and rationalization bulk especially large. Finally, for the reasons discussed in the previous chapter, (2) would seem especially applicable.

Doing one's part in a plan to save fuel reveals some of these same factors, though to a significantly lesser extent. Thus in some cases like this there is a point in having rules, but not so compelling a need. In a large group in which there are many contributors, the consequences of a few mistakes will not be great. As elsewhere, self-interest may motivate error, though any one person's stake in free-riding will not be large. Nor are strong passions likely to distort judgment. But in this kind of case (1) (c) still operates: Coordination is needed – not necessarily around a plan of action of general fuel-saving, for we may suppose that everyone knows this and is sufficiently inclined to save fuel that there will be no real problem – but around some shared conception of what constitutes having done enough. We all have an interest in knowing when we and others have too little (or enough), because we want to know when we and others are (or are not) open to the reproaches of conscience and the justified criticisms of other people.

In the cases in which one individual has charge of the distribution of burdens and benefits among a group, the duties of equitable treatment come to the fore. Here the importance of (1) (c) takes on a slightly different aspect. The value of judging in accordance with a rule rests on that of assuring impersonality: Decisions made in accordance with a publicly available rule carry their own confirmation that they are the decisions that could easily have been made by an unbiased, personally uninvolved judge. So the rule may function more to provide the basis for this kind of confidence than to guide others in their reproaches of the individual making the judgment.

5

Publicity, autonomy, and objective act consequentialism

Independence of thought is as necessary, even to light literature, the sciences and the arts, as air is to physical life. One might just as well make men work under a pneumatic pump, arguing that they are not compelled to breathe, but only to move their arms and legs, as keep the mind active on a given subject, while preventing it from exercising itself on those important objects which give it its energy because they remind it of its dignity.

The real cause of these vicissitudes in the history of peoples is that man's intelligence cannot remain stationary; if you do not stop it, it will advance; if you stop it, it will go backwards; if you cause it to lose confidence it will no longer exercise itself on any object without languor. One would almost say that, indignant at seeing itself excluded from its proper sphere, it wants to take revenge, by a noble suicide, for the humiliation inflicted on it.

Benjamin Constant[1]

5.1. INTRODUCTION

It is time to consider an alternative conception of the function of accepted moral rules, one that takes them, not as defining what is objectively right, but as providing individuals with useful or even necessary decision-making procedures. For the discussion of moral rules to this point has presupposed that they are public rules applying to all, that they are right-defining, and that they are therefore appropriately used as decision-making procedures. It is precisely this conception of moral rules that many philosophers will be inclined to call into question.

An objector might first agree with a number of the points this proposal includes: It is good that people do not always weigh the consequences of their particular actions, and it is also highly

---

1 Benjamin Constant, "Usurpation," in Fontana, 1988, pp. 122–4.

desirable that people observe rule-imposed requirements. Thus it is highly desirable that people, within limits, be faithful to the good moral institutions of their community or society, and that they regard their participation and their identity as a member as good reasons for action. But, the objector goes on, it does not follow that people really have those obligations; only that it is overwhelmingly best if they accept them as their obligations. The objector's strategy, then, is to explain away such obligations, admitting along the way how desirable it is for people to feel bound by them, and to be disposed to act as if such obligations objectively did exist.

For example, it would certainly lead to disastrous results if everyone were to reason as does Brandt's utilitarian Frenchman. But the act utilitarian may not be giving an account of how people ought to reason. He may be giving nothing more than an account of what is objectively right. So the act utilitarian might embrace the conclusion that, objectively speaking, it would be right for the Frenchman to disobey the rule even though, as a subjective decision-making procedure, his way of thinking, if widely followed, would lead to disastrous results.[2]

Defenders of the distinction between objective principles and subjective decision-making procedures insist that there is nothing unusual in it, and that it is common enough in other areas of knowledge to distinguish between what is true and what ought to be accepted. As Scheffler puts it:

He [the consequentialist] views the point of a theory of right action as being to provide a general account of what acts are right and what acts are wrong: no more and no less. And for him the distinction between the correctness or truth of any such theory, on the one hand, and the advisability of widespread acceptance of the theory, on the other hand, is a very important one.[3]

So viewed in this way, act consequentialism tells us only what actions really are (that is, objectively) right, and leaves open as a separate question what decision procedure ought to be employed if we are to do our best in performing objectively right actions. It tells us something like this: An action is objectively right if and

2 See Bales, 1971.
3 Scheffler, 1982, p. 50. See also Railton, 1984, on truth conditions and acceptance conditions.

only if it does in fact promote the most good of those available to the agent.

In this chapter, I shall focus mainly on two versions of this kind of proposal. Each argues for the possibility of adopting a host of devices, whether they be nonconsequentialist traits of character or rules that make no reference to consequences, for bringing about actions that are objectively right. Each proposal fails, I shall argue, both for reasons peculiar to it and for some of the same reasons that the other fails, namely, that they drive an unacceptable wedge between that which is objectively right and that which is an action-guiding reason.

5.2. OBJECTIVE TESTS OF RIGHTNESS VERSUS DECISION PROCEDURES

Proposed only as an objective test, act consequentialism avoids many of the objections that can be raised against it as a decision procedure. Thus it can easily be self-defeating, allowing us to yield to temptation and encouraging mistake, if we try always to act with an eye to the best consequences. More significant for the purposes here, act consequentialism as a decision procedure would not allow a place for exclusionary reasons like fairness to others, the keeping of promises, love for particular persons, loyalty to friends or to groups, or commitment to institutions. When actions required by loyalty and fairness do not do the most good of those available to the agent, the agent has overriding reasons not to perform them.

However, to hold that act consequentialism states only a criterion of rightness, and is not necessarily to be accepted as a decision procedure, is to leave open to empirical determination whether, and to what extent, people ought to be making up their minds about what to do by focusing on consequences or on something else, like fairness, loyalty, or commitment to rules. Thus, using Railton's term, the "sophisticated consequentialist" will be someone who "has a standing commitment to leading an objectively consequentialist life, but who need not set special stock in any particular form of decision making".[4] Like the sophisticated hedonist who realizes that the most effective way of getting pleasure

4 Railton, 1984, p. 153.

is often to seek things other than pleasure, the sophisticated consequentialist realizes that the most effective strategy for producing
the most good in the world is often to seek other things, taking
seriously such things, among others, as fairness to others, loyalty,
and loving commitment. Following this strategy, the sophisticated
consequentialist will no doubt make some errors, occasionally
doing that which is (objectively) wrong. But these action guides
may be more than worth the occasional errors they bring. They
may well constitute the best overall strategy for doing good available to the agent.

Further, these action guides need not have the mere status of
strategies or rules of thumb: They may be deeply internalized as
sturdy character traits. Indeed, we sense that there would be something morally deficient about one who acted as, say, a loyal and
loving husband because he views it as strategically the best long-
run way of producing good in the world. Being a loving and loyal
husband involves having special concern for one's wife as an individual person, and thus acting in certain ways out of love and
affection. Objective consequentialists can claim that the husband
who is a sophisticated objective consequentialist might very well
develop the needed dispositions, so that his concern for his wife is
direct and unmediated by impersonal considerations about doing
good in the world. His loving concern will be spontaneously directed to her and her needs: "[T]he objective act-consequentialist
can approve of dispositions, characters, or commitments to rules
that are sturdy in the sense mentioned . . . , that is, that do not
merely supplement a commitment to act for the best, but sometimes
override it, so that one knowingly does what is contrary to maximizing the good."[5]

5.3. THE TRAITS AND MOTIVATIONS
OF THE SOPHISTICATED CONSEQUENTIALIST

The objective act consequentialist's use of the idea of developed
traits — traits that focus one's attention and desires, and "lead" one
to do certain actions, often without thought of the consequences —
promises to soften the otherwise nagging and tyrannical demands
of act consequentialism when taken as a decision procedure. If

5 Ibid., p. 159.

certain traits are themselves optimific, and if those traits involve directing attention and desire to things other than producing good results, then, the argument goes, the consequentialist need not accept Sidgwick's often criticized claim that "a Utilitarian must hold that it is always wrong for a man knowingly to do anything other than what he believes to be most conducive to Universal Happiness."[6]

There are different kinds of approach to using the notions of motives and character traits within an overall consequentialist account. Motives and traits are desires or aversions that are directed to, and tend to result in, action. The term "motive" seems more appropriate for desires of a more short-term character, and for less general objects ("his motive was to embarrass her in front of her friends"). Now, we can distinguish instrumental accounts of motives and traits from right-defining accounts. On an instrumental account, a particular trait – say, the desire always to tell the truth – is to be ranked against other possible traits solely by reference to the good that having that trait leads to. By and large, the results by which a trait is to be evaluated are mainly the actions to which it leads. And for the objective act consequentialist, whether these are objectively desirable depends upon the good they bring about. On a right-defining account, there is no independent notion of the rightness of particular actions. The rightness of actions is defined in terms of optimific motives and traits. An example of a right-defining account is R. M. Adam's "conscience utilitarianism," which holds that "we have a *moral duty* to do an act, if and only if it would be demanded of us by the most useful kind of conscience we could have".[7] Right-defining accounts are more closely analogous to rule consequentialism than to act consequentialism, and so will not be my primary concern here.[8]

6 Sidgwick, 1966, p. 492. Robert Merrihew Adams refers this to the "totalitarian character of act utilitarianism" (1976, p. 478), and Railton says of Sidgwick that here he "is uncharacteristically confused" (1984, p. 160).
7 Adams, 1976, p. 479.
8 We can notice in passing, however, that right-defining accounts would seem to attract the same kind of objection made against many forms of rule utilitarianism. Just as the rule utilitarian must explain why it is not "rule worship" to adhere to an otherwise optimific rule even when compliance would not produce the most good, the conscience utilitarian must explain why it is not "conscience worship" to follow the dictates of the most useful conscience in particular cases in which doing so is clearly not optimific.

5.4. ACTING IN (OPTIMIFIC) CHARACTER:
SOME EXAMPLES

One view is a slightly more complex and mixed version of an instrumental account. It holds that (i) the objective act consequentialist has reason to develop and reinforce sturdy character traits if, of those possible for the agent, they will lead to the most good, and (ii) actions that are not objectively right may still have some merit or worth by virtue of the fact that they flow from character traits that are optimific. Railton's view seems to be of this type. I quote in full a central example of his, because it illustrates both (i) and (ii):

> Consider...Juan and Linda, whom we imagine to have a commuting marriage. They normally get together only every other week, but one week she seems a bit depressed and harried, and so he decides to take an extra trip in order to be with her. If he did not travel, he would save a fairly large sum that he could send to OXFAM to dig a well in a drought-stricken village. Even reckoning in Linda's uninterrupted malaise, Juan's guilt, and any ill effects on their relationship, it may be that for Juan to contribute the fare to OXFAM would produce better consequences overall than the unscheduled trip. Let us suppose that Juan knows this, and that he could stay home and write the check if he tried. Still, given Juan's character, he in fact will not try to perform this more beneficial act but will travel to see Linda instead. The objective act-consequentialist will say that Juan performed the wrong act on this occasion. Yet he may also say that if Juan had had a character that would have led him to perform the better act (or made him more inclined to do so), he would have had to have been less devoted to Linda.[9]

Juan's sturdy character traits "lead" him to do certain things on certain occasions that are not, strictly speaking, objectively right; indeed, he does them deliberately, *knowing* that they are not objectively right. Because no one can be expected to have a perfectly fine-grained set of dispositions or unlimited powers of discrimination, Juan's character traits may well be the best possible for him. The fact that Juan's character traits are optimific seems to lay the foundation for the further claim that they confer some sort of merit or worth on objectively wrong actions that are done in character: This action, while objectively wrong, is done from loving and loyal motives, and being loving and loyal are just the character traits (we suppose) that the objective consequentialist has reason to cultivate.

9 Railton, 1984, p. 159.

So the action itself would seem to have some merit, or even justification, on this score.[10]

Michael Slote has apparently taken the full step of concluding that actions springing from admirable character traits may be justified even though, objectively speaking, wrong:

So someone [a utilitarian] who regards these traits as good or right can say that if and when a person acts wrongly as a result of possessing one of them, there is none the less a moral justification for the tendency that leads to that action, and the particular action itself can then be said to be justified as an indispensable part of a morally desirable overall pattern.[11]

An example is the father who deliberately misleads police about his son's whereabouts, though he knows him to be guilty: "He may feel he mustn't let the police find his son, but must, instead, do everything in his power to help him get to a place of safety, even though he is also willing to admit that there can be no moral justification for what he is doing."[12] Evidently there is some kind of justification, in Slote's view, if we take the utilitarian position he refers to. For "the particular action itself can then be said to be justified as an indispensable part of a morally desirable overall pattern."

Contrary to these lines of thought, I suggest that the existence of an objective principle of the right imposes demands on moral agents, and that these demands cannot be escaped merely by acting in character. I shall argue for the following theses: (i) Doing an

10 Railton comes very near to claiming merit for such actions: "It might be thought counterintuitive to say, in the example given, that it is not right for Juan to travel to see Linda. But it must be kept in mind that for an act-consequentialist to say that an action is not right is not to say that it is without merit, only that it is not the very best act available to the agent. And an intuitive sense of the rightness of visiting Linda may be due less to an evaluation of the act itself than to a reaction to the sort of character a person would have to have in order to stay home and write a check to OXFAM under the circumstances." Railton, 1984, p. 160, n. 30. Railton also says that an objective act consequentialist can approve of dispositions, characters, or commitments to rules that are sturdy in that they "do not merely supplement a commitment to act for the best, but sometimes *override* it, so that one knowingly does what is contrary to maximizing the good" [emphasis mine] (p. 159). The "overriding" here means, presumably, a normative overriding, in which dispositions give *good reasons* for actions. Otherwise, such dispositions would have to be construed *in this case* as mere psychological obstacles to doing the objectively right.
11 Michael Slote, 1983, pp. 89–90. Since publication of this book, Slote has changed his view about this.
12 Ibid., p. 86.

94

action in (optimific) character confers no value on the action itself if the agent knows that that action is objectively wrong. (ii) Freely and knowingly to do a wrong, even if the action is itself in (optimific) character, is to act in a way that reflects badly on character. (iii) One who knows what is objectively right ought (morally) to do what is objectively right if it is sufficiently clear that it is right. The upshot is that the moral agent cannot escape responsibility for doing the objectively right thing unless that agent is nonculpably ignorant of what is right, either in the particular case, or in general.

5.5. JUSTIFIED VERSUS EXCUSED ACTIONS

We can conceptualize our evaluation of action and character in examples like Railton's and Slote's by using the legal distinction between an excuse and a justification. The legal distinction is fitting here, because we are reflecting on different stances that a person might have toward an objective standard of right action, in particular, whether ignorance of the standard itself or of its application in some situation reflects badly on the agent, and whether failure to comply because of generally desirable motives reflects well on the agent or the action. Now, claims that an action is justified generally challenge the claim that the action was really wrong in the first place. They tend to lend themselves to universalization, implicitly acknowledging a kind of public license to anyone to act similarly in similar circumstances; imply that the agent's situation provided objectively good reasons for him to act in the way he did; and constitute a basis for praising and respecting the agent. Thus it is wrong to burn down a building; but if the building must be destroyed in order to prevent a larger conflagration, burning it down is an action that is objectively justified, one which anyone in similar circumstances would have reason to perform. Claims that an action is excusable, on the other hand, presuppose that the action was wrong; do not constitute a public license that allows or encourages other people to behave similarly in similar situations; and, far from supposing that the agent had objectively good reasons for the action, tend to explain the action, making it understandable as something anyone might in fact do, though not for good reasons. On the contrary, an excuse tends to preclude an inference from the act to the actor's character.[13] For example, the driver who is forced

13 For a valuable summary of the main conceptual differences between an excuse

by unavoidable circumstances to make an instantaneous decision either to go over the cliff or kill two others in the road might then do the excusable thing, saving his own life at the expense of two others. But his response, while wholly understandable as a natural and very human thing to do, reflects no objectively valid, impersonal justification for the action. From an impersonal perspective, no valid goal is advanced by the killing of two persons in order to save one.

Our moral judgments about actions and the ways in which they reflect on character show much the same structure. Even when issues about praise or blame are not being raised, and we are concerned to reflect privately on the merits of our own actions or those of others, we are interested in knowing whether an action was objectively justified, or merely excusable, being the product of an understandable human impulse or frailty.

When we think of a wrong as excusable rather than justified, we are not required to assume that the motives which led the agent to do the wrong were themselves bad or disreputable. Thus there is nothing bad about instinctively trying to save one's life in an emergency, or in thinking of loved ones before thinking of impersonal good. As general patterns of motivation, these are harmless enough and may be part of the best possible motivation for ordinary human beings. But in particular instances, they can lead to objective wrongdoing, as when the agent's understandable concern for loved ones results in paying insufficient attention to what is objectively right, or when in a dilemmatic situation the agent's strong self-protective impulses dominate those of impersonal benevolence.

Now consider the two examples again. In Railton's example, Juan knows that what he is doing is not optimific, and that he could do otherwise if he tried. He knows also that staying home and writing a check to OXFAM would not change his character for the worse. Further, Juan is an objective act consequentialist, and thus holds the view that an act is morally right if and only if it in fact would promote the most good of the acts available. Assuming for the sake of argument that this is a correct account of the right, Juan is knowingly doing wrong. Does Juan have a justification for such an action? Clearly not. Having assumed that the action is not

and a justification, see Fletcher, 1978, pp. 759–62, 798–817. See also Brandt, 1985, pp. 165–98.

productive of the most good among available acts, and that objective act consequentialism is the criterion of rightness, it follows at once that Juan has no such justification.

But what about Juan's (excellent, we assume) character traits? They are traits that he had reason to develop and reinforce, because the pattern of actions springing from those traits is the best possible for him. But if Juan goes to see Linda instead of giving to OXFAM, his action is wrong. It has the same unattractive consequences as it would have had if done from some less admirable motives. Given this instrumental conception of what Juan's good traits are good for – the production of right actions and good consequences – we have here an action which is an unfortunate but inescapable consequence of having these otherwise excellent traits. But these traits only have value because of their consequences, including the right actions to which they lead; they do not in turn confer value, rightness, or justification on actions.

Can we say, then, that Juan's action is excusable? Given the description, it is hard to see how we could think of it this way. For the main avenues of excuse are closed off: First, Juan knows that the action is wrong. It is not as if, thinking of Linda so much of the time, he forgets to raise questions about whether his actions are objectively right. Nor is it that the act-consequentialist principle of objective rightness has itself somehow been withheld from him. Secondly, Juan could have done otherwise if he had tried. So it is not that his loyalty to, and affection for, Linda amounts to some kind of compulsion that he could not overcome. Indeed, unlike an excusable action, his free, deliberate, knowing wrongdoing does reflect badly on him. He could have done what he knew to be right, but he did not. Though he has many fine dispositions, this action of his shows insufficient motivation to do the right because it is right. He cannot use his otherwise fine character to shield himself from adverse judgment (whether blame, criticism, or a theoretical "charging against his character") for this action. We might, of course, use this occasion for thinking instead about what is good about Juan: his character. Though wrong, this action makes us think of the loving and loyal traits from which it emanated. But this serves only to change the subject, not to find something worthy or meritorious in the action itself.

Slote's example of the father who deliberately misleads police about his criminally guilty son's whereabouts fits the excuse model somewhat better. The father's devotion to his son may be in many respects like the almost unthinking, automatic self-protective re-action of the driver who avoids going over the cliff at the expense of innocent lives. The action is not the sort that allows us to infer that the agent is a bad person or has an insufficient desire to do the right thing. It is rather that the circumstances – the pressure, the need for instantaneous decision without reflection, as well as the naturalness of self-protective reactions in such situations – tend to explain why a good person with a strong motivation to do the right might nevertheless fail.

The upshot, therefore, is that one is morally responsible for what one knows to be objectively right, even if deeply entrenched and desirable motivations pull one in another direction. Thus the de-mands of objective act consequentialism are not softened by de-veloping such sturdy traits as those of loyalty, fairness, and love for family and friends; not, at least, in those cases where one knows that the objectively right action is different from what one's sturdy traits would lead one to do. (I leave open here the question whether moral considerations about doing the right thing always override, or are sometimes overridden by, nonmoral considerations and dispositions.)

5.6. PUBLICITY

So far, I have argued that knowingly doing wrong discredits the agent, and that one who knows what is objectively right ought to do the right when it is sufficiently clear that it is right. But this claim about the demands of objective act consequentialism depends on the assumption that the agent knows what is right. If Juan did not even know that it would be wrong to spend his money for an extra trip to visit Linda (and his lack of knowledge was not due to any fault of his), then his doing what he did would not have reflected badly on him. More important for our purposes, if Juan had had no idea whatsoever that act consequentialism was the correct cri-terion of the objectively right, this and all of his misguided wrong-doings would be excusable. We could still evaluate his character traits for their usefulness, but we would at least be rid of the knotty problem of Juan's responsibility for not doing the objectively right thing, in view of his not knowing it to be right.

Must principles of the objectively right be public and known?

Might it not even be possible for one to have act-consequentialist reasons for inducing oneself somehow to forget the criteria of objective rightness? Railton asks us to imagine "an all-knowing demon who controls the fate of the world and who visits unspeakable punishment upon man to the extent that he does not employ a Kantian morality." We would have reason to convert, and make provisions to erase consequentialism from human memory and prevent any resurgence of it.[14] Several philosophers have noticed that we recognize a distinction in other contexts between the truth conditions and the conditions for acceptance of a theory; so why not in ethics?[15] The evil demon example shows that there are imaginable cases in which consequentialists would have good reason to eliminate all belief in the truth of consequentialism. Short of this, there may well be consequentialist reasons for significant limits on publicity. And if publicity is sharply limited, it will no longer be true that moral agents may be held responsible for doing as objective act consequentialism requires. The proposal that knowledge of the objectively right be restricted or excluded, at least for most persons, must then be taken seriously.

Philosophical controversy about publicity conditions has often amounted to a dispute between those, on the one side, who hold that publicity is part of the concept of the moral or the right, and those, on the other side, who remain unconvinced by such claims about concepts or meanings and insist, like Railton and Scheffler, that in ethics as elsewhere we must mark an important difference between truth conditions and acceptance conditions for the claims of a theory.[16] In the following, I shall steer a course between these two lines of thought, arguing for the idea of the public character of principles of the right, but without direct appeal to concepts or meanings. I shall argue for publicity along broadly utilitarian lines, claiming that, as a matter of empirical fact, it is overwhelmingly likely, for conditions even roughly approximating those in which we live, that the evil caused by systematically withholding knowl-

14 Railton, 1984, p. 155.
15 In addition to Railton, there is Bales, 1971; and Scheffler, 1982. As Scheffler says of proponents of the view, "they do not regard the claim that a theory ought not to be widely disseminated as equivalent or tantamount to the claim that the theory is false." Schleffler, 1982, p. 50.
16 See Scheffler, 1982, pp. 46–7 for a brief survey of some of the main proponents of a publicity condition and their reasons.

edge of the right, from ourselves or others, outweighs the good it might do.

At the same time, it would be misleading to think of publicity as no more than an incidental feature belonging to some sets of principles in some conditions of society. The tendency to think of publicity as belonging to the very concept of morality itself has deep roots. The multiple connections between publicity and the very idea of a criterion for right action make it difficult to describe what things would be like in a world in which moral agents either had no knowledge of the objectively right, or in which some knew and others did not. Moreover, I shall argue that publicity plays several important roles in promoting the good, and that there is a broadly consequentialist argument in favor of the publicity condition. Most importantly, the value of actions themselves depends on the knowability of the right. Thus our attributions of worth to actions, as well as to character, depend in large part on the reasons for which actions are performed. Accordingly, if one does the dutiful thing because one knows it to be a duty, we ordinarily think of that action as having greater worth than the same external motions done for mistaken reasons or for no reasons at all. Or, to state a slightly weaker claim, right actions done for the mistaken reasons of a person deprived of the normal exercise of moral or intellectual powers have less value, other things being equal, than when done for the reasons belonging to an autonomous person who is exercising normal moral and intellectual powers. Providing for this good is so important, and so characteristic of the moral guidance of behavior, that there are reasons for thinking of it as an essential feature of that kind of governance of human behavior that we call "morality." To put it another way, in a world governed by the demon, there would seem to be no room for morality, not for humans, anyway.

5.7. PUBLICITY AND THE VALUE OF AUTONOMY

Consider for a moment the world that would result from the successful threats of Railton's demon. Having forgotten that consequentialism provides the true criterion of right action, moral agents would have complied with the demon's wishes by adopting Kantian morality, belief in which would have the status of belief in magic or taboo. The belief might be otherwise beneficial, but its benefits

100

would have been purchased at the cost of autonomy – loss of one's autonomy in moral reasoning and judgment, and loss of some of the value of one's actions.

Autonomy, in the broadest definition, is simply self-governance or self-direction. Moral autonomy involves having and using the capacity to sort through reasons for action, so that one's actions will be informed and rational to the extent possible, given normal human capacities. The demon example shows that in extraordinary conditions the exercise of autonomy might itself be too costly for it to be worthwhile. But, I suggest, the exercise of autonomy itself confers significant value on actions and, in ordinary conditions anyway, outweighs its costs. And yet our autonomy is diminished to the extent that publicity for, and hence our knowledge of, the right is diminished.

We can see this by considering some of the many ways in which we evaluate actions. Knowing the objective moral qualities of one's action confers on one more moral credit if the action is right, discredit if it is wrong. In either case, one exercises a characteristic power of rational beings with moral capacities. Further, the familiar Kantian point about the moral worth of actions, though Kantian, can be incorporated in a consequentialist conception of right action. To do the right thing because it is right has greater value than doing the same thing blindly or because of belief in magic or taboo.

One cannot regularly succeed in doing the right because it is right unless one has proper access to the right. Even if an action is, all things considered, wrong because its net result is worse than some alternative action, the fact that it was an autonomous act of one who possessed full information and exercised normal capacities, lends a value to it that it would not otherwise have. Thus it is easy to forget, when comparing a right act done out of ignorance to a wrong act done as the result of fully informed autonomous choice, that the margin by which the right act is better than the wrong one is reduced by the fact that it was not autonomous. In other cases, because of the good of autonomy, it is better, and hence right, that an autonomous and informed person do that which otherwise would be wrong, than that an ill-informed or deceived person produce the best external results. And, when considering the overall effects of many people living with limited information about the right, we must remember the overall value lost because so many actions are done in ignorance of the right. If there were nothing intrinsically bad in a state of affairs in which rational beings are cut off from access to principles of objectively right action, we could not give a satisfactory account of the difference between bringing about good results by turning humans into efficient automatons, and bringing about the, otherwise, same results through the exercise of normal human capacities, intellectual and moral.

The Kantian, of course, thinks of the knowability of the right as a prerequisite for actions to have moral worth. But for the consequentialist, unlike the Kantian, the moral worth of actions is part of the good that they bring about, and can even be part of what makes an action right, if indeed it is right.[17] As in nonconsequentialist conceptions of the importance of publicity, publicity constitutes part of the background framework within which moral deliberation and debate is to take place, and constitutes an essential part of autonomy. But unlike nonconsequentialist conceptions, publicity is taken to be a necessary means to the important good of autonomous action. This does not mean that we must always consciously aim at providing for our own autonomy in deciding how to act. For when we can exercise normal moral and intellectual capacities, when the principles of right action are publicly available, and when we then properly exercise our capacities, the good of autonomy has been provided for. We only sometimes need to bring considerations of the good of autonomy into our deliberations about the right thing to do.

The claim that publicity promotes the good of autonomy is of course limited by empirical considerations. As Railton's demon example shows, it may be possible to imagine extraordinary conditions in which autonomy, though a great value, becomes an unaffordable luxury. But there is no reason to think that actual conditions are anything close to being so bad. Publicity for the objectively right does not lead to such dire consequences, even though it arguably might lead to more frequent errors in calculating the consequences of actions.

17 G. E. Moore is an example of a utilitarian who holds, as part of his conception of goodness as belonging to organic wholes, that the value of an action itself, apart from its effects, must also be considered in determining whether it is right: "We must have all this causal knowledge, and further we must know accurately the degree of value both of the action itself and of all these effects. . . . " Moore, 1966, p. 149.

The way in which publicity promotes the good can also be seen when we reflect on the likely collective consequences of greatly diminished publicity. One problem is that of the instability of a nonpublic criterion of the right. If we have somehow succeeded in eliminating all knowledge of the criterion of objective right from the human race, there is the danger that someone, a philosopher perhaps, will rediscover its truth. Now, to understand the truth of the criterion is to understand that the criterion is inherently action guiding, at least in the following sense: Though the criterion might well be kept secret, and might itself recommend that it be shrouded in secrecy, *when* a person *A* knows that the criterion is correct, and *when* it is sufficiently clear to *A* that, according to that criterion, some action *X* is the right one, then *A* ought to perform *X*. If this much is not true, then it is indeed hard to understand what could be meant by calling this a criterion of objectively right action.[18] But this means that, if there is a conflict between *A*'s doing *X* and *A*'s doing what is required by the publicly received conception of the right, *A* ought to do *X*, which is objectively right. Another instability is then added by the fact that, if *A*'s doing *X* comes to general attention, *A* will either not be able to enter into the usual kind of free and open process of moral debate and justification, or *A* will need to "keep two sets of books," knowing that *X* is only justified on objectively valid principles, but constructing bad arguments for the conclusion that *X* is justified on the publicly received principles. If these bad arguments are accepted, then things might run smoothly for a time, and the instability kept at bay. But the badness of bad arguments tends over time to be discovered.

Another avenue might be open to someone in *A*'s position. So long as one knew the truth about what is objectively right, one

---

18 This is, I think, the element of truth in Williams's comment that "If that is right, and utilitarianism has to vanish from making any distinctive mark in the world, being left only with the total assessment from the transcendental standpoint – then I leave it for discussion whether that shows that utilitarianism is unacceptable, or merely that no one ought to accept it." Smart and Williams, 1973, p. 135.

would act on it, but without even proposing to give an acceptable justification to others. One might simply do what is objectively right, and be prepared to be regarded as an immoral person, a rebel, or one who stands above the morality of the masses. But that kind of approach cuts into the good of social union. For in thus setting oneself apart, the public sense that all are equals under the same rules is undercut. In these conditions, some labor under the publicly received though objectively false principles, while others publicly acknowledge themselves to be bound by principles they only privately know to be true, and which the others believe to be false. If they publicly demonstrate the truth of the principles, the secret is out; and if they keep the secret, they are likely to be regarded as arrogant, immoral, or contemptuous of others. And, if they succeed through some kind of discipline in returning themselves to an ignorant but sincere acceptance of the publicly received view, then they too have in the bargain lost their full autonomy.

Finally, we must remember the many other goods to which full moral autonomy and therefore publicity for the right are connected. In philosophical speculation we like to imagine the possibilities for selectively introduced ignorance and, thereby, selectively imposed limits on moral autonomy. But, as the passages from Benjamin Constant, quoted at the beginning of this chapter, suggest, the surgery is not so easily performed. How do you cut off knowledge of the objectively right in precisely those situations in which that knowledge may result in wrongdoing? How do you introduce just the right amount of prejudice and blindness in moral motivation without simultaneously cutting off the sources of creativity in science and the arts? Who is in a position to keep the separate sets of books – one for keeping track of people's beliefs about the right, the other for keeping a true tally of the facts about the right – without becoming the source of a cynicism that seeps ever outward? Unless it can be argued (and so far as I know it has not been) that false beliefs about the right tend, by a kind of spontaneous process, to stabilize in ways that produce the best results for action, we must assume that this would have to be carried out by the deliberate decisions of some human intelligence. And it would be assuming a great deal indeed to suppose that any human intelligence would have the capacity to carry this out.

It might now be objected that the desire to do one's duties is at most a small part of the full motivation of a morally good person. Yet I have argued, among other things, that freely and knowingly to do a wrong reflects badly on character, and that one who knows that X is objectively right ought morally to do X, at any rate if it is sufficiently clear that it is right. Combined with the claim about the importance of protecting the good of autonomy, these claims might seem to add up to a picture of moral agents as having to be constantly preoccupied, and even obsessed, with duty. It would seem that ordinary persons who were so preoccupied with duty would actually be morally unattractive persons. Thus to help a friend from a sense of duty seems to bring a cold impersonality to one's motivation that is out of place in a friendship. What seems to be lacking is the friend's sense of your importance as a particular person rather than as one who happens to occupy a certain type of position: The friend's concern for duty seems to take the place of, or override, a concern for you. Affections for particular persons would seem to fit badly with the impersonal and abstract point of view of objective duty. Thus too much duty-oriented motivation brings alienation.[19]

We must first distinguish two ways of dealing with these problems: One identifies the source of the problem in the concept of the right with which we began, namely, objective act consequentialism. The other attributes the problem to the very notion of acting from duty, holding that duty-oriented motivation can be too strong, and that it is sometimes good for us to act from other motives, like loyalty or affection for a particular person.

Indeed, a major source of the problem is the idea that act consequentialism is by itself the correct criterion for the objectively right. Though I reject act consequentialism, both as a decision procedure and as an objective criterion, and I believe that we would have little room for particular affections and loyalties if we did use it as a decision procedure, I wish to focus here on whether commitment to act consequentialism as an objective criterion only would also result in alienation. Because act consequentialism is

19 There is discussion of this in Stocker, 1976; and Baron, 1984.

prima facie such a demanding conception, to show that even it is consistent with genuine attachments and affections should be an encouraging prospect for conceptions of duty containing broad permissions sometimes to do less than the optimific. The exercise will help to make clear what traits and strategies the act consequentialist may adopt, consistent with being an autonomous moral agent.

Recall Sidgwick's comment that "a Utilitarian must hold that it is always wrong for a man knowingly to do anything other than what he believes to be most conducive to Universal Happiness." This comment is implausible if taken literally, so as to include belief on the preponderance of thin evidence. Thus I might believe, on the balance of my rather weak evidence, that giving five hundred dollars to some particular charity would do the most good. But if I have already adopted a reasonable strategy of caution because I have in the past been too inclined to temptation and mistake where charities are concerned, it would not necessarily be wrong for me not to do what I believe to be conducive to the most impersonal good. But if we amend Sidgwick's comment, substituting "knows with sufficient certainty" for "believes," then, assuming only an act-consequentialist conception of the right, Sidgwick is correct. If A knows with sufficient certainty that X is (morally) *the* right thing to do, then, assuming that A can do X, it is (morally) wrong for A not to do X. But this does not imply anything about how much A should be thinking about whether particular courses of action are right. Neither does it imply that we always know what is right; nor does it imply anything about how often we are reasonable in believing that our actions are right.

It may then be rational to develop personal strategies, as well as traits and dispositions, which have the result that one sometimes does not know with sufficient certainty that a particular right action is the right thing to do. For example, the development of sturdy character traits may include the disposition to pay attention to the needs of family and loved ones first. This might be a generally beneficial trait to have, though there will be occasions on which it causes one to overlook the possibility that one could do better with one's money by giving it to OXFAM. Not giving to OXFAM under the circumstances, though objectively wrong, would not reflect any character defect, nor would it be blameworthy. It would be an excusable and wholly understandable action, for no one can

106

be expected to be omniscient. Nor does this depend on any diminished publicity for the act consequentialist criterion of the right. A wholly reasonable person can know the general criterion of the right, but fail to know what is right in a particular situation. Similarly, it might be best to have a very strong disposition to be concerned about spouse and children first, possibly because of the great standing temptations there are to abandon them, and because of suffering that would ensue if such temptations ever dominated one's motivation. As a result, these very strong dispositions might be so strong as to make it impossible to do the objectively right thing in some situations, that is, might "lead" one to do what one knew to be the objectively wrong thing.

The traits one has developed, and the strategies adopted, for doing the right, may or may not be reasonable. They may or may not reflect a kind of moral negligence. If the potential occasions for doing egregious wrongs are many and unpredictable, then the reasonable person will devote a great deal of effort and attention to thinking about what is right, and avoiding wrongdoing. It is reasonable for us to develop intuitive guides, as we in fact often do, alerting us to situations likely to give rise to moral duty. Thus we know that to allow certain relationships with others to develop is potentially to give rise to duties; we know that when we are in the presence of people in our care, that we must be alert to their needs in special ways. Even when they are not especially in our care, the presence of others raises questions of duty: An act consequentialist would no doubt realize that being stranded on a desert island would give rise to far fewer duties of sacrifice than living among many people in need. The consequentialist will ideally give the amount of effort and attention to the identification of duties that is optimum in the circumstances: And the optimum will depend on whether the circumstances of duty are easily identified, being connected mostly to certain kinds of situations and not others, and whether the wrongs that one would be likely to do are egregious or minor.

5.10. TRAITS AND PUBLICITY: A SUMMARY

The alternative proposal we have so far considered – that the obligation imposed by social rules and practices be understood, not as part of what is objectively right (or the structure of objective reasons) but as the consequence of traits or beliefs (or both) that it

107

is useful for people to have – must be rejected. The alternative proposal proceeds by attempting to drive a wedge between what ordinary moral agents should be thinking and using as a decision procedure, and that which is a true, objective criterion of right action.

If traits are viewed only as instrumental in the production of right acts and other good consequences, then they provide no justification for doing what is objectively wrong. At most, what they do provide is either an explanation or an excuse, as when the trait was so strong as to dominate motivation so that it makes sense to think of the agent as being unable to do otherwise, or when the trait served to direct the agent's attention away from certain things, so that the agent did not realize that the act was objectively wrong.

If we understand act consequentialism to be the criterion of objectively right action, then that which is objectively right on the criterion ought to be done where it can be done, and where it is sufficiently clear that it is right. Thus suppose that someone has been able to establish the objective truth of the act-consequentialist formula, "X is right if and only if X is O [where O = optimizes]." If this formula is a correct theory about the objectively right, then it has a magnetism: If it means anything like what we ordinarily mean when we say that an action is morally right, to judge an action right is to recognize that it ought to be done, or, at least, that it is permissible to do it – that the moral person who recognizes that it is right will be moved toward it, and concerned to do it. Thus if I know the truth of the theory that the property of being O is what makes right actions right, and I also know with certainty that X is O, then I am correct in inferring that X is the action I ought to do, period. Even if X is designated as not right by some formula that I ought to (and do) accept, or by some decision-making procedure that I ought to (and do) follow, I still ought to do X. The only questions in such cases are whether to trust my judgment that X really is O, and whether I can bring myself to do X. Though one of my main reasons for accepting or following another formula may have been that it is in general more trustworthy, I must still acknowledge its failure in particular instances.

That a theory of the objectively right would have this kind of priority over other kinds of rules in matters of decision-making, is no doubt one important reason why many think of a theory of the right as inherently action-guiding. Thus the tie between action-guiding reasons and the right seems especially close: If we are supposed to recognize both that X is right and that X morally ought not to be done, then we have good reason to suspect that the concept of the objectively right being used here is special and technical, far from the more familiar concept of the morally right that we use in everyday life.

The instability of this distinction between action-guiding reasons and the objectively right emerges especially clearly if attempts are made to limit publicity about what is objectively right. For in thus depriving people of knowledge of the right, we inflict major utilitarian losses which would very likely cancel other gains. This is so because one important and typically overlooked good that derives from a public moral rule, knowable to the ordinary person of ordinary capacities, is that of participation in a process of self-governance, of adjusting one's own behavior to that which one knows to be the requirements of morality. Even when we deprive a person, through deception, perhaps, of the normally possible understanding of what makes some particular action of hers right, we deprive her of some of the good of fully autonomous action. When this deprivation is systematic, having to do with knowledge of what in general makes right actions right, the diminution of good that she can realize in her actions is much more greatly reduced. This exercise of the capacity to know what makes right acts right is part of the good of autonomy, and its opposite is a kind of alienation. The importance of this good, indeed, suggests that there is reason to think of it as more than an incidental good by which, along with other things, we measure the effectiveness of moral rules. Providing this good, it could reasonably be claimed, is so important and so characteristic of commonsense evaluation of character traits, motives, and actions that it is one of the essential defining functions of morality and moral standards, much as some minimal capacity to cut is part of what it is for something to be a knife.[20]

20 This idea appears at various points in the history of ethics. As a particularly good example, see St. Thomas Aquinas: "Now among all others, the rational creature is subject to divine providence in a more excellent way, in so far as it itself partakes of a share of providence, by being provident both for itself and for others." Aquinas, *Summa Theologica,* Q. 91, art. 2, in Pegis, 1945. Partaking of a share of providence in this more excellent way involves exercising the capacity to know what is right and to be guided by that knowledge. It is not merely a matter of behaving in an objectively right way.

Another line of thought seemingly available to the objective act consequentialist focuses primarily on the status of the rules that are to be used in everyday practical reasoning. Fred Berger has recently defended such a view as a plausible interpretation of the utilitarianism of J. S. Mill.[21] Whether or not it is a correct account of Mill, the view is interesting in itself, because it relies on something very like the distinction between act utilitarianism as an objective standard of the right, and act utilitarianism as a decision procedure.

The difference between the status of rules and the status of the act-consequentialist principle, Berger suggests, can be explained as we would the difference between the meaning of a term and a test for its application. Thus a familiar test for the presence of oxygen is the lighting of a match to see if it will burn, but no one supposes that the lighting and burning of a match is what it means to say that oxygen is present. Likewise, we can test whether a sentence is a tautology in the sentential calculus by constructing a truth table. But the construction or constructibility of a truth table is not what is meant by the statement that a sentence is a tautology.[22] Now, the same distinction can be used, in something like the following way, to explain the status of rules for the act consequentialist. What it means to call an act right is that it is the best available to the agent, or that its effects are predominantly good. But at the same time, it might be desirable to use well-accepted and familiar rules as a generally effective test of rightness. As a matter of strategy, the thought goes, following such rules as those requiring fairness, the keeping of promises, and telling the truth is likely to lead to doing the objectively right thing more often than is following the act-consequentialist formula. But it is nevertheless the act-consequentialist formula that provides us with the meaning of "right": Only it, and not the rule, is right-defining.

We should notice, in favor of this conception of rules, that it allows us to think of rules as providing, among other things, protected reasons for action. Thus it might be rational for me to make a strategy of adhering to the rule even though it appears that doing

21 Berger, 1984.
22 This explanation and the examples follow Berger's, pp. 69–70.

so will not produce the best consequences: I would be rational in excluding otherwise relevant considerations simply because I don't trust my judgment in such situations, because I so often make mistakes when I am swayed by evidence of that sort, making errors of calculation or yielding to temptation. Most importantly, the strategy conception of rules does not involve thinking of them as mere "summaries" of what has been found in the past to be useful, nor as "rules of thumb" in the sense that they are constantly open to scrutiny.[23] So a rule in the strategy sense might indeed be quite inflexible in its demands. In some areas of behavior, the dangers of mistake or temptation may be so great, and the consequences of error so bad, that a particularly stringent prohibition would be rational to observe. Stringent prohibitions like this are often incorporated in widely accepted moral rules precisely because experience has shown us the dangers.

The strategy conception of moral rules enables us also to allow for reassessment of well-accepted social rules and of our own policies, as circumstances dictate. Social rules may be outmoded, and the survival of a rule is no guarantee of its usefulness. When this is so, the reasons for accepting the rule evaporate, and the act-consequentialist principle may then be the appropriate direct test for rightness. Berger sums it up this way:

Rules which are part of a strategy may be as weak or as strong as circumstances dictate, and such an act-utilitarian need not give up a basically act-utilitarian criterion of right action by insisting on the relatively inflexible adoption of rules. Of course, should there be rare cases where one *can* be fairly certain of good consequences, or where the rules adopted conflict, the act-utilitarian must then sanction resorting to the Principle of Utility itself, judging the act directly by its consequences.[24]

So the usefulness of social rules varies, and the stance it is rational for us to take toward them should be flexible. Direct appeal to the principle is appropriate, though the occasions for it may be rare. It is also clear from these remarks that the strategy conception does not as such presuppose any limits placed on publicity, for a rational person can quite well recognize, in this as in other departments of life, what the real reasons are for observing a strategic constraint on action.

23 Ibid., p. 72.
24 Ibid., p. 73.

The strategy conception of rules constitutes an advance over the rule-of-thumb and summary conceptions. For it seems that, as a reflection of our commonsense intuitions about morality, we do view the seriousness of rule-imposed prohibitions as having something to do with the likelihood and seriousness of mistake, and that wisdom about these matters is in turn likely to have become incorporated in widely accepted moral rules. But at the same time, I shall argue, the strategy conception is inadequate, not because it conceives of moral rules as strategies, but because, for the most part, it attributes those strategies to the wrong entity; it mislocates them. It wrongly implies that the familiar moral rules which it seeks to explain, like the requirements to be fair, not to steal, lie, and cheat are person-relative strategies or policies – that the appropriate rule governing my lying, cheating, or stealing may be quite different from the appropriate rule governing your behavior in this sphere.

5.12. TWO KINDS OF STRATEGY: INDIVIDUAL AND COLLECTIVE

Much of morality, I have already suggested, consists of rules of collective, rather than individual, strategy. The difference becomes clear when we think first of some examples of strategies that are individual in the sense that they are strategies that it can be rational for a particular individual to adopt in the furtherance of a goal, say, happiness.

(a) For some people the wisest strategy is one of strictly refusing any offer of alcoholic drink, for they know that, so far as they are concerned, at any rate, they have little self-control after that first drink. For others, only some loose guidelines are needed: Don't yield to the temptation to drink alone; don't drink every night. Still others need not even think about policies for their own consumption of alcohol, for none are needed. They like it so little that there is never any danger of their using it excessively. There are perhaps even people for whom a policy of encouraging oneself to take an occasional drink would be a wise strategy.

(b) Investors vary greatly in the degree of their sophistication, knowledge, and skill. For some investors, it is a wise strategy to avoid anything more risky than investing in their own home, and in certificates of deposit in federally insured banks. At the other end of the spectrum, for the highly sophisticated investor with significant resources, it may be rational to use a wide range of financial instruments, including options and arbitrage strategies.

Individual strategies like these are clearly person-relative. The strategy that it is rational for an individual to adopt depends, among other things, on that individual's knowledge, skill, motivation, and psychological propensities; and on the amount of information he or she usually has. Although it might make sense to state some very general pieces of policy advice about such things as drinking alcohol and making investments, such advice would be inappropriate or pointless for some persons.

It is this person-relativity that makes it implausible to assimilate moral rules to individually rational separate strategies for optimizing. From the start, there is something intuitively odd in the idea that the appropriate moral rule for me to adopt about lying might be substantially different from the moral rule about lying that should govern your behavior. Yet this is precisely as it would be if moral rules were individual strategies for doing the most good. Suppose that you are the kind of person who is virtually incapable of telling a lie, and would probably not do so even if it were best. Suppose that I, by contrast, am the opposite, being naturally given to lying even when, as it is said, "the truth would do better." Without adopting and following some restrictive strategies, I will tell many more lies than would be deemed right by objective act utilitarianism, and you will tell too few, not even innocent "social" lies to avoid hurt feelings. The rational strategy for me would be something like a flat prohibition, and the rational policy for you would be something close to an encouragement with no prohibitions whatever.

To think of these two strategies as moral rules, the one holding for me and the other for you, is to embrace a relativism of a kind open to now familiar objections. For example, if A claims that lying is always wrong and B that it is never wrong, is it the case that they are not contradicting each other, each merely reporting the strategy that he, for his part, has found useful? If A claims that lying is always wrong, is A merely claiming that the best strategy for the average person, though not necessarily for everyone, is to resist lying on every occasion?

This second possibility would be to think of moral rules as individual strategies that are rational to adopt, at least for the average person of average knowledge, skills, and propensities. On this view, the moral rules that we are taught, and that we publicly discuss and defend are a kind of one-size-fits-all answer to the question, what decision procedure is best for me to adopt? But if moral rules were this kind of average answer to an individual's questions, it would be hard to understand why they should be taken very seriously. Thus if someone tells me that stealing is always wrong, I will be right in thinking of that as good advice in general and for the average person; but if I know that I am not an average person in the relevant respects, almost never even being tempted to steal for my own benefit, but only when I know that no one will find out and it can be used to help the poor, then I will know that the familiar prohibition just does not apply to me. It was made with the average person in mind, and I am not the average person. In this area of behavior, it might be rational for me to follow the policy of stealing, but only when no one will find out and when the proceeds will be used to help the poor.

It seems clear that we do not actually believe this about moral rules. We do not think of them as the most general sort of advice about policy, advice that must be accepted or rejected, and at any rate further tailored, to one's own peculiar situation, sophistication, and proclivities. When we claim that lying is wrong, we are claiming that lying is wrong for everyone, everyone, at least, within an understood moral community. We can, of course, argue about whether there are exceptions to the rule about lying. If we do, we are arguing about whether we as a community, perhaps of all moral persons, ought to recognize the existence of a different rule. We are arguing, neither about the personal strategies that certain individuals have found useful in promoting the good, nor about any strategy for the average person of average intelligence, skills, and proclivities. In short, particular moral judgments presuppose, and moral rules make a claim to, universality. To conceive of rules as individual strategies is to leave this universality unaccounted for.

The point here is not that individual strategies have no place in our practical thinking, or in the moral life generally. On the contrary, it is appropriate to develop policies and strategies to conserve energy, and to direct attention to the proper issues. Too much thinking about what is right can be counter-productive, and thinking about the right can be wasted time in situations where we are not likely to run afoul of duty anyway. The

114

important point is that moral judgments that state or presuppose rules ("Lying is wrong"; "One must never steal") presuppose a universality of application that is independent of such variations among persons as regards skill, intelligence, and psychological propensities.

Though we cannot really understand the universality of moral rules and judgments when we conceive of them as individual strategies for doing good, that does not require abandoning the strategy conception entirely. The notion of the universality of rules and judgments is easily combined with the idea that they are strategies by thinking of them as collective strategies. Law and legislation provide examples, but many moral rules can also be regarded as collective strategies.

(a) Suppose that we as a community, acting through the government and the legal system, make it a policy to reduce inflation. So we impose taxes to curb consumption. The taxes imposed by law are to be conceived as a collective strategy for reducing inflation. They are imposed, not by any individual, but by the collective (or someone or group acting for the collective) for the purpose of advancing a collective goal. Above all, the strategy they represent is not to be confused with a set of individual strategies that individuals might adopt as a means of reducing inflation. For first, it is not up to individuals, acting in the capacity of individuals, to adopt or reject or revise the strategy that has been adopted. This means, among other things, that the adopted strategy does not implicitly allow individual tailoring to individual cases; for example, depending on so many individuals' sincere and correct judgments about the rules they should follow to contribute the most effectively to the inflation-reduction effort. Second, it is therefore not up to individuals to comply or not to comply, depending on whether they sincerely or correctly judge that their noncompliance would better achieve the goal of reducing inflation. The point here is not that public rules can contain no exceptions or qualifications; it is that any such exceptions or qualifications are to be adopted by the collective and for reasons that are appropriate from a collective perspective. They are not to be adopted by the individual for reasons that are individually rational in pursuit of the goal, even if the goal is identical with that of the collective. In short, the public rules are universal in the sense that they apply to all.

(b) Suppose that, after some generations of relatively few problems with alcohol in our community, drinking and drunken behavior has come to be a serious problem. Not only have there been instances of behavior injurious to others as a result of drinking, but there has been an accumulated harm resulting from many people being drunk, often at the same time. These accumulated effects might well give thoughtful consequentialists good reason to claim that drinking and drunken behavior are morally wrong, that there is, or that we ought to adopt (for purposes here it does not matter which), a moral rule against drinking and drunken behavior. For the reasons already suggested, it does not make sense to think of this as a claim about the strategy or policy for doing good that it is individually rational for so many separate persons in our society to adopt. There are too many variations among individuals with respect to wisdom, degree of temptation to drink, and tendency to misbehave when drunk for this to be literally the case. Although there are people who would do best to follow an individual strategy of never again taking a drink, there are others for whom no strategy is needed at all, and who could just as well yield to any (as it would turn out, rare and harmless) impulse they might happen to have to drink. It does make sense, however, to think of this as a claim about the strategy or policy that it is rational to adopt from a collective point of view. Unlike the point of view of individual rationality, taking a collective point of view in the evaluation of strategy involves thinking of the strategy as applying to everyone so that some one person has discretion to disobey a rule only if it is public knowledge that everyone has the same discretion.

A collective strategy is therefore not the same as a set of well-coordinated individual strategies. In the example of imposing taxes to reduce consumption and hence inflation, we might all separately seek the reduction of inflation, and, somehow, however unlikely it is, succeed in coordinating our behavior toward that end. Or, walking down a crowded street, I, along with the others, seek passage without bumping into anyone. We may all succeed in our shared object, but without anyone ever taking a collective point of view, or adopting or urging any collective strategy. This point is worth emphasizing because it shows the connection between the need for coordination and the need for a collective strategy, but also the differences. A collective strategy is one way, often the best, for achieving coordination. Above all, the claim that moral rules are often better conceived as collective, rather than individual, strategies is not based entirely on the commonplace that coordination is necessary to realizing shared ends.

6

The existence of rules and practices

6.1. INTRODUCTION

One general feature that the MLM shares with "rule" or "restricted" utilitarian theories is the idea that what is morally right or obligatory, at least in many cases, is to be referred to social rules and practices. It is then the rules and practices, rather than the actions falling under them, that are to be evaluated for the good they produce. But here we encounter a fork in the road, each path corresponding to a very different conception of rule or practice as a test of rightness. We can take the right-defining rule either as (i) an actually accepted rule, or (ii) a justified, correct rule, where its correctness consists in its being best suited, among the alternatives, to promoting the good. Brandt's ideal-rule utilitarianism opts for the second course.[1] The MLM, on the other hand, represents existing rules as right-defining under certain conditions. As we have seen, the presumption favors existing rules because one of the main utilitarian functions of collective rules – that of promoting social union and trust via equal limits on individual discretion – would be largely defeated if the right were defined by the best rule, whether existing or not.

We must now examine more carefully than we have the concept of the existence of a rule. We shall consider two senses in which a rule or practice can be said to exist. I hope to show that the moral agent who bases moral judgments on an existing moral rule need not be in the position of merely counting opinions, and therefore does not relinquish individual judgment and autonomy in the interpretation of what a social moral code requires.

1 Brandt, 1963, p. 115.

One simple model of what it is for a social practice or rule to exist suggests itself.[2] It is one patterned after the idea of the general acceptance of a rule explained in Chapter 3. Where there is a social rule R requiring certain behavior, there is a pattern of behavior conforming to R, a pattern of individuals criticizing deviations from R, and the generally prevailing belief that deviating from R constitutes a good reason for such criticism.[3]

On the consensus model, a social practice exists in a group whenever there is a uniform, or nearly uniform, actual agreement about what constitutes a deviation and therefore a good reason for criticism. The consensus model reduces the question of whether a social practice exists to a question about whether virtually all people in the relevant group agree that such-and-such behavior is called for. The model focuses on what people's opinions are, as elicited by questions that do not allow deep reflection. Where there is no unanimity or near-unanimity on some proposition, the consensus model holds that the social practice does not extend to that question or, to put it differently, there is no practice with regard to that question. For example, if there is a practice requiring one to dress formally when meeting one's elder near relations, there may be universal agreement that one who goes to see his elderly grandmother should dress formally for the occasion. We would conclude that social practice requires one to dress formally when meeting his elderly grandmother. But there may be division of opinion about whether meeting one's slightly older third cousin requires more

2 The consensus model developed here, as well as the criticisms raised against it, owes much to Dworkin's discussion of conventionalism in law. Although Dworkin speaks of judges interpreting statutes or case law, we draw here the limited analogy of moral agents attempting to determine what a practice calls for. My notion of the difference between the consensus model and the DR-model parallels Dworkin's distinction between the explicit and implicit extensions of convention: The explicit extension of a convention is "the set of propositions which (almost) everyone said to be a party to the convention actually accepts as part of its extension." The implicit extension is that set which "follows from the best or soundest interpretation of the convention, whether or not these form part of the explicit extension." See R. Dworkin, 1986, pp. 114–150, especially pp. 123–4. See also Bell, 1983, pp. 9–21.

3 Here I follow Hart, 1961, pp. 54–5. This "criticism" can, of course, take many different forms and does not entail that a society containing social rules involves a lot of mutual blaming or criticism. It may involve primarily reminders and criticism directed by individuals at themselves.

formal attire than called for in meeting any stranger of roughly equal age and status. According to the consensus model, there is then no practice with respect to this behavior, though existing practice may eventually change to cover it.

We should first ask whether the consensus model provides us with a descriptively accurate account of what it is for a social practice to exist and to provide reasons for action. We can first notice that, as a descriptive account, the consensus model misrepresents our thinking in cases in which there is divided opinion, as there was in the imagined practice about attire. According to the consensus model, once we had concluded that opinion is divided about whether more than usual formality is required when meeting a third cousin of roughly one's own age, we would also conclude that, until changes occur in people's opinions, social practice is silent on the matter. In fact, though, we would explore the underlying reason for the practice in an effort to find out whether, properly construed, it already applies to this case. Thus suppose that the best understanding of the practice's point is that it develops and under-writes an attitude of respect towards one's elders. In that case, there would be a strong argument for thinking that the practice does not extend to meeting one who is not much older, and who had little role in one's upbringing. On the other hand, if the point of the practice has been to underline the distinction between family and nonfamily, and to reinforce respect, especially for family members, that would be a good argument for thinking that the practice does extend to meeting one who is only distantly related.

When we try to understand the point or reason behind a practice, we are engaged in an activity that involves both discovery and creation. When we conclude that the function of our practice is to reinforce respect for the elderly, we may be reaching a conclusion that no one has quite consciously and explicitly reached before. Certainly there is no explicit social agreement to that effect which on its face provides this answer. But what can count as this function is more than merely some effect or other, whether intended or not; for the practice might also have the result of helping the earnings of manufacturers of better clothing, and yet we would not single that out as the point of the practice. For something to be convinc-ingly called "the point" of a group's practice, it must have some effect that accords with the group's values and with what they, through their criticisms and reminders of one another, tend to show

120

as the point of the practice, however sketchy and dim their recognition of the point might be. Thus we could readily reject "helping the earnings of clothing manufacturers" as the point of the practice if nothing like that reason ever showed up in the reasoning people engaged in.

The descriptive and explanatory defects of the consensus model are that it represents social practices as more superficial than they are, taking them to be a matter of superficial actual agreement. Social practices have deeper layers that are partly revealed when we ask, of some specifically described behavior, *why* it constitutes a deviation. Reflection on the deeper-level reasons for thinking certain behavior to be wrong may reveal that so regarding it is a mistake. It may even be a widely shared mistake.

So the consensus model seems to provide an inadequate descriptive account of our actual practices. But we still need to ask, as a separate and normative question, what its advantages and disadvantages are in advancing the good. Will moral agents together tend more fully to realize the good when they adhere to practices as defined by the consensus model? Or is the good more fully realized when they adhere to practices in some other sense, or if they simply do what is best on a case-by-case basis?

One of the main advantages of the consensus model is the coordination it secures. The consensus model, tying the existence of a practice straightforwardly to actual agreement, reduces the occasions for controversy about what one is to do. Individuals can know what is expected of them, and can know with reasonable certainty what kinds of behavior will lead to criticism or feelings of guilt. Thus consider the different conventional arrangements there can be for apportioning responsibility for the welfare of children. One system would place it on the community collectively; another, on the father and mother; and still another, as in Brandt's description of the Hopi, on the "household" as defined by blood ties with the mother.[4] It seems clear that this is one kind of case where coordination is of great importance: It is important that one system be adhered to in the group, for some children may suffer if the mother's household abjures responsibility on one ground while the father abjures responsibility on another. Further, if each of several conflicting moral judgments can be supported by a plau-

4 See Brandt, 1963, pp. 136–7; and, generally, Brandt, 1954.

sible argument, assigning responsibility and blame becomes confusing and unfair.

But the consensus model's several disadvantages, as a system for promoting the good, are greater than its advantages. Its main disadvantages are that (1) consensus can contain important gaps, providing no answer for new cases that arise; (2) taking account of the point or justification of a practice, consensus on some particular issue can be mistaken; and (3) consensus-defined answers can be in conflict, either in requiring actions that work at cross purposes in advancing the good, or in the stronger sense of requiring actions that cannot jointly be performed.

The most fundamental problem for the consensus model is that there are often instances of behavior on which consensus is mistaken. That is to say, a deeper, reflective understanding of the practice and its point will show that it does not even advance the ends it is thought to advance; nor, perhaps, does it advance any valid ends, for that matter. There is no guarantee that following a consensus about the rightness or wrongness of some behavior has any bearing on advancing the good. Because of this, there are obvious disadvantages from a utilitarian point of view in accepting both the idea that existing social practices are binding on moral agents, and the consensus model of what it is for a practice to exist. If we regard a practice as defined by superficial consensus, then being bound by practice may mean that individuals are trapped: They must wait for a new consensus to develop. But waiting can involve a great and unnecessary disutility. It is especially unnecessary when the importance of maintaining coordination is not great, and the shift to a changed practice can be accomplished by so many individuals separately coming to recognize the superiority of the preferable practice, and acting on that recognition.

Finally, two different consensus-defined practices may exist simultaneously even though they conflict with one another. This may occur when role responsibilities are in a process of change. For example, suppose that an older, traditional moral code assigns women the burdens and benefits of the housewife, while assigning men the burdens and benefits of making a living, and of defending the country. Suppose that the consensus surrounding this traditional code shifts as a result of moral argument and political agitation. A new consensus develops in which women, as well as men, are understood to have the burdens and benefits of making a living and defending the country. Now, if part of the old consensus continues to exist, women still being held to their old duties as well as the new ones, the situation may be worse than it was before any change took place. The point is that moral rules and practices often work as packages, and not as so many independent parts. It is clearly a disadvantage of adhering to consensus-defined practices that one thereby subscribes to the inconsistencies and conflicts that consensus often brings with it.

6.3. THE DEEPER RATIONALE MODEL OF PRACTICES

On the deeper rationale (DR) model, social rules and practices are conceived more broadly, so as to include the rationale and ends they can be understood to serve. Given this broader conception, it becomes possible to think of consensus sometimes as mistaken, and sometimes as incomplete. What the social practice requires, therefore, is on this conception no mere matter of counting opinions, and serves to guide those opinions at least as much as it is constituted by them.

On the DR-model, the rationale underlying a rule or practice becomes the focus of efforts to determine what that rule or practice really requires. A rationale, if adequate, provides us with a link that connects the rule or practice to the good, though the link may only be an intermediate one. Thus suppose that, in a given society, people condemn as morally wrong any and all drinking of intoxicating liquors. When their basis for this condemnation is probed, they first cite the fact that drinking has historically been a very serious problem in their society; and they refer to well-known instances of brutality that occurred in connection with drinking. Prior to being asked, they may not even have reflected deeply on any rationale for the prohibition; instead, they have merely thought it wrong and associated it indiscriminately with various evil things. But we might then probe further: The cited rationale does not quite fit the flat prohibition. What they think prohibited is any and all drinking of intoxicants, and, as it stands, the cited rationale would only support a prohibition on heavy drinking. On further reflection, the rationale is refined: Our informants tell us that, for whatever reason, people in their society are incapable of moderation, and so a flat prohibition, rather than a limited permission, is called for.

This development of a rationale shows several things. One is

123

that, unlike the rationale that legislators usually have for enacting a statute, this moral prohibition against drinking is often supplied with a conscious, reflective rationale after it has come into existence. Second, the rationale provides an intermediate step to help complete the link between the rule and the good. In defense of this rule, informants don't say, uninstructively, that the prohibition is necessary in order to promote the good; instead, they say that drinking is wrong because it cannot be done in moderation, and the result too often is brutality. And brutality is an evil to be avoided. These considerations show how the prohibition is linked in this society, given its people and their circumstances, to the good. It can reasonably be construed, perhaps with other things, as the means they have chosen for dealing with this problem. Third, the rationale, once developed, must fit and support the prohibition in question. If it does not, and if no rationale can, then the prohibition will be correctly seen as mistaken.

Finally, when the revision or rejection of a prohibition occurs, it may amount, neither to pure discovery, nor to pure creation. In the example, it certainly had some of the flavor of discovery, in that it made sense to speak of a correct answer which was there to be recognized, and about which mistakes were possible. Thus if the only plausible rationale supports nothing more than a prohibition on drinking heavily, but does not support a flat prohibition on all drinking, our recognition of that fact constitutes a discovery of something that is independent of our will. On the other hand, the revision of a rule often contains a creative element, in that whether the rule is revised, and just how it is revised, is a matter in which judgment and interpretation play a role. It is implausible to deny either that the shape or even the existence of moral prohibitions sometimes depends on interpretation, judgment, and decision that might have been otherwise, if only because the ends to which they are the means do not by themselves always allow us to single out one set of prescriptions for behavior. Thus the severity of a social moral prohibition against drinking can vary greatly, depending on the outcome of judgment and interpretation. And while the facts about such things as the degree of harm that it causes, and the breadth and depth of the propensity to drink in that society, are matters which judgment and decision may not be able to alter, there is room for differences in judgment about how the harm of a

124

moral prohibition is to be weighed against the good it will produce. There is also the possibility that the good can be equally
well promoted using some other set of prescriptions, seeking to
alter through moral pressure some other aspect of behavior, a
change in which will indirectly reduce drinking, or make its
consequences less bad. Indeed, a sympathetic reading of the morality of a society very different from our own often proceeds in
this way: Although we recognize that they morally condemn (or
approve) some behavior that we morally approve (or condemn),
we may also recognize, after a deeper and more sympathetic inquiry, that, taken as a package, their practices constitute one
way, though different from our own, of reaching the same fundamental ends we recognize as universally valid. Certain parts of
their morality might be far less than optimific when transplanted
to our own cultural setting. Moreover, the background setting
of practices, against which some feature of a morality is to be
evaluated, is there partly because of the decisions and choices of
many people over time, and is a cultural artifact at least as much
as a discovery made by a culture.

Most importantly, there is even room for some degree of error
in these judgments. Some societies may impose a more stringent
moral prohibition on drinking than is actually warranted, even by
the kind of rationale they accept. But at the same time, it would
be implausible to claim that they do not, by and large, have the
moral obligations in this regard that they think they do, at least if
their moral views about drinking are backed by some respectable
rationale.

On the DR-model, then, what a group's social practice is, and
what it requires, depends partly on what members of the group
think it requires. But it also depends in part on what the underlying
rationale of the practice really supports, and on the success of that
rationale in connecting the practice to the promotion of the good,
whether members of the group actually see those implications or
not. What an underlying rationale really supports is partly a question of consistency between rationale and actual judgments and
reactions.

There are further issues of consistency which can form the basis for challenging current judgments, showing that they do not
really comport with a deeper understanding of a practice. One
of these is the issue of consistency in applying a moral require-

ment to different members of the group. Consider again the society that strongly condemns the drinking of alcohol. Suppose that this condemnation applies primarily to the young who are not yet beyond the teenage years: It is not thought wrong for adults to drink, unless they do it to great excess, but it is thought unacceptable for the young, and particularly so for girls. On the consensus model, we would stop there, identifying the social practice with widely shared opinions. On the DR-model, however, there may be serious grounds for questioning whether those opinions are not actually superficial and mistaken. One can imagine some people asking why it is considered so clearly wrong for them to drink, but not so for their elders. (Here I follow in general outline a televised discussion I recently saw of teenagers talking about moral problems. The example is not imaginary.) And one can further imagine some asking why moral opinion makes any distinction at all, with respect to teenage drinking, between male and female. These requests would call for an analysis of opinion and practice for internal consistency along several dimensions, an important one of which would be consistency of treatment of the various members of the group. In addition to some conception of a valid end which the moral prohibition promotes, acceptable answers would have to depend on further moral analysis. This moral analysis would reveal analogues of important elements of equal protection analysis in Constitutional law. Given that we condemn drinking because it results in hooliganism, what reason is there for thinking that teenagers are more prone to hooliganism than anyone else? And anyway, the question might go, how does that call for a more severe condemnation of drinking among teenage girls than among boys?

Now, suppose that the answer is first, that teenagers who drink are by and large more likely to be irresponsible and destructive than their drinking adult counterparts; and second, that teenage girls who drink are especially vulnerable to pregnancy, which gives their misbehavior important social and individual consequences that male misbehavior does not. From this sketch, we can anticipate how the argument will go from here, and how those attacking the prohibition are likely to answer. Of course, some of the factual claims may be false; for example, that drinking among teenagers leads to worse consequences than it does

126

among adults. But beyond that, even if the claims are true, there may be reasons to be especially suspicious of moral distinctions of certain kinds, for example, those based on sex. If one of the goals to which the society is committed (and, let us assume, is actually a valid end) is equality of burdens and benefits without regard to sex, then the offered justification of such a moral distinction will have to be especially strong. It will not be enough merely to give vague talk about girls being different; it will be necessary to show, both that the reasons for the condemnation are compelling, and that, in light of those reasons, the burdens of the prohibition fall on precisely the right people. An opponent of the distinctions might then argue that boys play as important role in bringing about pregnancy as girls, that in all probability the more severe condemnation of drinking among girls results from nothing more than a biased, male-dominated world view against which we should constantly be on guard.

Now to a summary of the main conclusions to which these illustrations lead. First, there are several ways in which a practice or set of practices can be checked for internal consistency: consistency between practice and its rationale, and between that rationale and some valid and legitimate ends. Second, it may be a separate legitimate end to tighten the demand of consistency for certain kinds of cases; for example, those in which an especially important interest of individuals is too likely to be given insufficient weight in the moral judgments of their fellows. Third, the terms of the moral debate are to some extent fixed, even if mostly at a deeper level, by moral views that happen to prevail and by moral judgments that have already been made. When we follow rules that are understood to be public and to apply to all, we think of the moral community as bound by the requirements of coherence and consistency among moral judgments, as well as among moral judgments over time, much as we think of individual persons as bound by the same requirements.[5]

5 R. Dworkin, 1986, p. 166; more generally, 1986, pp. 151–224. Dworkin bases this demand primarily on the idea that the community is personified in the dealings of its officials with its citizens; that is, that "the community has its own principles it can itself honor or dishonor, that it can act in good or bad faith, with integrity or hypocritically, just as people can." R. Dworkin, 1986, p. 168. The MLM too uses the notion of community personified, though it is the moral community that is personified in the making of ordinary moral judgments by ordinary moral agents. When we attempt to be consistent in our condemnations of some, and

Whether strict scrutiny of sex-based moral distinctions is called for may have been a matter about which reasonable persons in the imagined society could differ. But if it has been judged appropriate in the past, then the critics of this distinction have a moral argument for shifting and intensifying the burden of proof in this case. Citing past moral judgments and prevailing values, and pointing to the need for consistency with them, is a commonplace of moral reasoning. This becomes clear when we hear people accusing the group of internal inconsistencies in its moral views. "Ours is a hypocritical society," we sometimes hear people say, "because we condemn girls for behavior we find acceptable in boys." Notice here that the "we" does not refer to so many separate hypocritical individuals; for the hypocrisy belongs to the community over time, perhaps even over more than one generation.

A fourth and final point is that nothing in the example about moral prohibitions, moral distinctions, and equal treatment really suggests that anything other than a broadly consequentialist evaluation is involved when we ask the most fundamental questions about our practices. Although it is true that, when we respect the prohibition, we exclude considerations about advancing the good that the act utilitarian would not even be permitted to exclude, we evaluate the prohibition itself in terms of its rationale, and the rationale by determining whether the end to be promoted is indeed part of the good. Evaluating a practice to fit the best rationale is a matter of applying familiar means–ends rationality. And tightening the demands of means–ends rationality in the appropriate cases is done in the service of another goal, such as that of bringing about equality. And, as we have seen, though it is possible to think of equality as an intrinsic good, its value as an instrument to so many other goods, such as the management and productive redirection of envy, may be sufficient grounds for its incorporation in moral rules. Even the recognition of the rights of individuals can be included as a goal in that they are incorporated in the evaluation of states of affairs that are brought about by practices and rules.[6]

not other, behavior, and when we attempt to make judgments that fit other views and judgments that have already been reached, we personify our moral community.

6 This idea is borrowed and adapted from Sen, 1982a, who defines a "goal rights system" as "[a] moral system in which fulfilment and nonrealization of rights are

The claim that social rules and practices can impose moral constraints on individuals may seem to raise the specter of an unacceptable ethical relativism. Thus consider the moral prohibition
against killing the innocent. If it is wrong for X to kill the innocent,
does this constraint presuppose the existence of the appropriate
social practice in X's community? If so, that would generate some
very odd theoretical consequences. What if X is in no plausible
sense bound, as a member of any moral community, by a rule
prohibiting the killing of the innocent? It is very counterintuitive
to think of moral constraints, especially those of such central importance as this one is, to be dependent on the adventitious facts
of the agent's relationship to the appropriate society, and on the
nature of that society's social practices. It would seem, rather, to
depend on the nature and quality of the act itself.

On closer observation, this concern would seem to have less
warrant than might first appear to be the case. For only in the rarest
cases would people *not* have an obligation (in the sense of a preemptive reason) not to kill. When this obligation cannot be found in
the actually accepted rules of one's own particular community, it
can usually be found in the actually accepted rules of a larger, more
general community of human beings, for the protection of human
life from aggression is as nearly an indispensable and universal good
as any that can be imagined. It is one of those constraints, the
existence of which is necessary to any good society. The moral
prohibition against murder is one of the clearest examples of a
constraint protecting universal interests, since the temptation to kill
is recurrent and widespread. If human beings had the motivations
of angels, the possibility of a moral prohibition on killing, because
of its pointlessness, would belong to science fiction. Nor would
the prohibition have any point if humans were not vulnerable to
one another.[7] And if there is only potential, even if not actual,

included among the goals, incorporated in the evaluation of states of affairs, and
then applied to the choice of actions through consequential links. . . . " (p. 15) On
rights as goals, see also Nozick, 1974, pp. 28–30; and Scanlon, 1978.

7 This has been well stated by H. L. A. Hart in his discussion of "the minimum
content of natural law," most of which is directly relevant to my discussion here.
See Hart, 1961, p. 190.

general acceptance of a rule R forbidding killing, one may have reason publicly to judge and act in accordance with R in order to help bring about R's general acceptance. This reason would be especially strong in the case of rule forbidding killing, due to the great universal importance of the good involved. So in such a case, a kind of unilateral acceptance of R would likely be warranted.

Where there is not even any potential general acceptance of a rule forbidding killing, one's duties with respect to killing another human being would seem to be those generated by the primary principle of doing good and avoiding evil, rather than by any collective rule, hypothetical, potential, or actual. Of course, this primary principle would in most cases provide one with an all-things-considered judgment against the taking of human life, and in all cases would weigh killings negatively in the balance. Even in the worst case – a Hobbesian war of all against all – it would not be right to do what will exacerbate the conflict, and rational good-doing moral agents would often do best to follow individual strategies of restraining themselves against the temptations; for example, to kill some in order to save a larger number from being killed. For to take such discretion for oneself is in most situations likely to encourage others to take the same kind of discretion for themselves. Even if some were not likely to yield to temptation or error, many would be. And the prospects for establishing rules that publicly express more desirable terms of human relationship, with the benefits of trust and security that would bring, would be diminished.

6.5. CONSTRAINTS THAT ARE NECESSARY TO THE GOOD FOR SOME SOCIETIES, BUT NOT OTHERS

A clear example are those constraints needed to eliminate public accumulative harms.[8] There are some actions that are harmless, and sometimes even beneficial, when done by a few, but harmful when done by too many. Done by one or a few in circumstances where no one else is thereby inspired to do the same thing, walking across the grass is an example of an action that is harmless or even slightly beneficial. Individual negligible contributions to pollution are another example. It may not matter at all if a few people engage in

---

8 I borrow the term "public accumulative harm" from Feinberg, 1984, pp. 227–45.

some action, but if many do it, a threshold of positive harm may be reached. A type of action may become polluting, or it may become socially abrasive, precisely because there are so many people who are inclined to do it. Such social graces as gentility and formal politeness are necessary in a crowded society with unequal and potentially hostile social classes, but not necessary in a sparsely populated country with minimal class divisions. Other examples of moral constraints that would seem to be appropriate in some social conditions or societies but not in others would be the various constraints on consumption. At one time it may be highly important that people stress saving rather than consumption, and thus frugality may be elevated, not only to a moral virtue, but to a moral requirement. In another era, when saving is becoming excessive and depressing the economy, it may become necessary to reverse that teaching, and there may be good utilitarian reasons for thinking of frugality as a vice, and of consumption as an obligation. Of course, there are other, better known social devices for dealing with these problems: fiscal and monetary policy, for example. But their existence should not obscure the fact that changes in governmental policy often operate in tandem with changes in the moral teachings and judgments that people think appropriate.

These moral teachings and judgments have several functions that are analogous to those of enacted laws. To illustrate, let us begin by examining the form of the legal problem. Feinberg, in his discussion of the way in which the law deals with public accumulative harms, outlines what he calls the "common form" of the legislative problem.[9] In the following, I single out those features of Feinberg's account which are of direct relevance to the point here: (i) a threshold of harm reached through joint and successive contributions of numerous parties; (ii) each contribution is harmless in itself except that it moves the overall state of affairs closer to the threshold of harm; (iii) when the threshold is reached, the accumulation constitutes a public harm in that they "set back vital interests shared by almost everyone"; (iv) the activities producing these contributions are so beneficial in other ways that, prevented entirely, the resulting harm would be as great as the harm they now produce. Feinberg then goes on to suggest that legislation regulating or prohibiting the appropriate activities (if an adequate description of the

9 Ibid., 1984, pp. 229–30.

activity can be found) creates a standard of wrongfulness where none existed before. Thus there is nothing "inherently wrongful or right-violating in the activity of driving an automobile, generating electricity, or refining copper."[10] Feinberg's thesis is a plausible one. And, in some cases, especially where something like a "public accumulative harm" is involved, practices of moral judgment about wrongdoing also have the function of creating a standard of wrongful behavior. Such practices consist in a general agreement about the kind of actions that are to be judged wrong, an agreement which is supported by a deeper rationale. It is a kind of coordinated response which may be only one of several possible responses that would have solved the problem. Thus there is nothing inherently wrong about saving almost everything I earn. But if too much saving has recently inflicted great damage on the economy, and, to cope with this problem, a new teaching about the evils of frugality has begun to emerge, then I may be wrong in saving so much, even if my actions considered by themselves will have no material effects for the public problem, and even if my noncompliance would remain secret and have no damaging effects on public coordination to solve the problem. The creation of a moral standard of wrongfulness as a way of dealing with public accumulative harms is often masked by the existence of legislation of the kind Feinberg discusses. As Hume observed, when we construct our standard of moral wrongfulness, we seize on available analogies, sometimes using a legal standard already established somewhere.[11] But the establishment of general agreement need not be the result of legislation or governmental policy. It can arise gradually from moral debate and the consensus that crystallizes around it.

6.6. THE RULES OF MORALITY VERSUS THE RULES OF LAW

It is time to consider a set of related objections that might be directed against the MLM. These arise from what may seem to be its ex-

---

10 Ibid., 1984, p. 230.
11 As Hume put it, "In that case, the slightest *analogies* are laid hold of, in order to prevent that indifference and ambiguity, which would be the source of perpetual dissension." Hume, *Enquiry Concerning the Principles of Morals,* III, p. 2. See Aiken's *Hume's Moral and Political Philosophy,* 1972.

cessively legalistic character. I have argued that many moral rules function as public, right–defining standards which are necessary to collective supervision of the behavior of individuals; that part of the point of such rules is that they are to be applied equally to all; that is, that exceptions must be made a public part of the rules themselves; and that these functions are, among other things, important to reducing mistrust.

Thus it may appear that the MLM provides us with an excessively legalistic conception of morality. An initial objection would run like this: Granting that it is important that we have public rules understood to apply to all, don't we in fact rely on the law to provide us with these beneficial functions? And is this not satisfactory, from a utilitarian point of view? The law does provide us with rules governing property acquisition, rules prohibiting theft, murder, and rules defining what is permissible in various competitive situations, and the law's rules are universally applicable public rules enforceable by collective sanctions. So why is it even necessary to saddle people with additional rules?

These are important objections. I shall use two lines of approach in answering them, one showing that collective moral rules do not constitute anything like the imposition on individuals that the objection suggests; the other showing that such rules play an essential utilitarian role to which the rules of law are ill-suited.

Moral rules that are collective, public, and equally applicable to all are often needed as replacements for the primary principle. However, this does not entail that they are needed to govern every aspect of our behavior. Much of our behavior is properly left to the guidance of the principle of doing good and avoiding evil, supplemented sometimes by strategies that it is rational for individuals to adopt for their own particular cases. Thus the career choices people make can have major consequences, but it would in most conditions of society be disutilitarian to attempt to govern such choices by imposing rules for all, be they legal or moral rules. The same can be said of individuals' decisions to give to one charity rather than another.

Rules of obligation: Moral and legal

Ordinary moral thinking makes a distinction between that which is merely desirable and that which is an obligation, or duty. Some philosophers make a further distinction between obligation and duty themselves, holding, for example, that obligations are requirements that arise from special relationships and commitments while duties do not. For the most part, I shall not observe any clear distinction between obligation and duty. In order to fix ideas, however, we do need to have a concept of what it is for a social rule to impose an obligation, and of the differences between moral and legal obligation. We will then be in a better position to understand the advantages and disadvantages, from a utilitarian point of view, of moral rules of obligation.

Intuitively, to have an obligation is to be in some sense bound to do something, though it is not clear precisely what this sense would be. Some philosophers like J. S. Mill and H. L. A. Hart have attempted to locate the bindingness of obligation in the notion of the appropriateness of sanctions. Thus Mill held that duty, as distinguished from mere expediency, "is a thing which may be *exacted* from a person, as one exacts a debt." The sanction of punishment used for this exaction may be law, opinion, or the reproaches of conscience.[12] Hart's analysis of rules that impose obligations distinguishes them in the fact that the "general demand for conformity is insistent and the social pressure brought to bear upon those who deviate or threaten to deviate is great." Whether we would tend to classify a rule of obligation as one of law or of morality, he believes, depends in large part on the nature of the sanctions used to secure conformity.[13]

These ideas give a useful and illuminating starting point. But we must be careful about attributing too tight a connection between obligation and sanctions. Some relatively trivial moral obligations, like the obligation to return a favor or to keep an appointment, are clearly not backed by any great and insistent social pressure, as Hart's account would seem to suggest. Likewise, we must be careful not to embrace the false suggestion with which sanction accounts often leave us, namely that it is the presence or likelihood of the sanction that provides moral agents with their reasons for performing their obligations, reasons which, it might seem to be suggested, would otherwise not be sufficient.

Among the characteristic features of obligation is the idea that

12 Mill, *Utilitarianism,* ch. 5, in Piest, 1957, p. 60.
13 Hart, 1961, p. 84.

the performance of obligation is conceived to be a matter of legitimate interest and concern of others, whether they be members of some immediate group or community, or of humanity generally. This legitimate interest is typically manifested in an attitude that it is appropriate to exert pressure of some kind in order to secure performance of such obligations. Often, this pressure is not thought to be limited to those who have an immediate interest in the performance of the obligation, but is appropriately exerted by others who are conceived to be the legitimate defenders of society's interests in the obligation being performed. Sometimes the pressure takes the form of a moral teaching which, if successful, implants dispositions to feelings of guilt and remorse when one fails to perform one's obligation. A prevailing social rule of obligation, therefore, is connected with an attitude about the application of some form of pressure, whether in the form of sanctions applied by officials, informal opinion, or feelings of guilt and indignation. The mildest form of sanction, it would seem, comes in the form of the belief (or, if applied by others, the expression of opinion) that failure to perform the obligation is at least the business of others; failure to perform an obligation is thus not simply something that is in the abstract undesirable. The fact that sanctions are appropriate does not, of course, entail that any of them will be applied in a given case. A hardened scoundrel may well escape them all, including any feelings of guilt or self-reproach. Further, there may be good reasons for not applying sanctions in a given situation; for example, as when it is too costly to do so, or the wrongdoer is so sensitive that punishment or criticism may be harmful or counterproductive.

To summarize, we would probably not think of something as an obligation at all if we did not think that its performance was at the very least a matter of the legitimate concern of others. Typically, this concern is expressed or exercised in the form of concerted pressure on individuals to perform their obligations. No particular form of this pressure could reasonably be thought a conceptually necessary feature of obligation, though some form of the idea that performance is a matter of legitimate concern to others, and something that they have authority to insist upon, would seem to be necessary.

Another feature of obligation is that to have an obligation is to have a reason to act (or not to act) that is protected in the sense that it is both a reason for the action itself and a reason for excluding

135

certain things that would ordinarily be valid considerations against the action. To put it differently, we should not think of obligations as providing reasons of absolute, or even especially great, weight; for that view would make it difficult to understand how one could ever have rather trivial obligations, or could have obligations that sometimes conflict.[14] The concept of a protected reason is needed to capture the notion of an agent's having an obligation, something that is to be distinguished from the question, what it is for a social rule to purport to impose an obligation. Of course, the notion of someone's having an obligation is prior to the notion of a rule's purporting to impose an obligation, for it is by purporting to supply the rational individual with a protected reason for action that it is claimed that an obligation exists.

Tying the concept of obligation to the idea of the appropriateness of a sanction does not entail the quite different idea that the threat of a sanction is what provides a rational, autonomous moral agent with the protected reasons that having an obligation involves. Although the threat of a sanction obviously does supply reasons of a sort, those reasons would not qualify as moral reasons. I argued in Chapter 3 that the rational moral agent will have sufficient reason for respecting the requirements of generally accepted, justified moral rules. But the idea of an agent's fear of sanctions played no role in that argument. Rather, the reasons for respecting obligation-imposing rules spring from the primary principle, from the general duty to do good, combined with the fact that good-doing must often be a collective effort under rules.

With these distinctions in mind, we are in a better position to address the question of the differences between having rules that impose legal obligations, and rules that impose moral obligations. Following an earlier line of thought (Chapter 4, section 4.9), those areas of behavior that are most likely to be advantageously governed by public, collective moral rules would seem to be areas in which: (i) people are especially likely to be tempted by strong passions or personal interests, interests that come into conflict, not only with impersonal good, but with the interests of other individuals; (ii) it is important to have a single public criterion applying to all in order to make inquiries more efficient and to forestall rationalization; or

14 On the idea of obligation as connected to protected, or peremptory, reasons, see Raz, 1977, pp. 223–6.

136

(iii) where it is important to elevate judgments to the level of public discussion, pressure, and collective sanctions, the appropriateness of which can be efficiently decided in public moral debate. The possession of any of these features would provide a reason for the adoption of a collective rule. Behavior possessing all of them would be a paradigm case. Paradigm cases of behavior needing to be governed by such rules would thus be those involving the using and holding of things for one's own benefit (i.e., property), injury of other persons, and taking unfair advantage (defining, among other things, what is to count as unfair advantage). Widely occurring behavior that leads to accumulative harm but which does not directly conflict with the interests of other individuals, like alcohol or drug abuse done in private, would, if it called for the adoption of a collective rule at all, justify such a rule primarily because of (iii).

Advantages of moral rules of obligation

Even in those areas in which a collective moral rule is necessary, it does not follow that having and respecting such a rule will constitute an imposition or burden on individuals in anything like the same way that legal rules often do. Indeed, careful reflection on the differences between moral rules and legal rules will show, not only that moral rules do not impose the same kind of burdens, but that the interpretation and application of moral rules provides certain utilitarian advantages that a system of legal rules does not. In addition to providing effective direction of behavior in some areas where law fails, moral rules provide in a special way for the exercise of individual autonomy and a sense of participation in a scheme of self-governance.

Our reasons for using moral rather than legal rules begin with a familiar utilitarian observation. "We should be glad," Mill said, "to see just conduct enforced and injustice repressed, even in the minutest details, if we were not, with reason, afraid of trusting the magistrate with so unlimited an amount of power over individuals."[15] Distrust of the magistrate is justified in large part because

15 He goes on to say: "If we see that its enforcement by law would be inexpedient, we lament the impossibility, we consider the impunity given to injustice as an evil, and strive to make amends for it by bringing a strong expression of our own and the public disapprobation to bear upon the offender." *Mill Utilitarianism,* ch. 5, in Piest, 1957, pp. 59–60.

the power to apply legal sanctions is *centralized* in the hands of a relatively few officials. The dangers of mistake and abuse of power are therefore magnified. Though the decisions of even the highest court of final appeal may from a logical perspective be mistaken, the finality of its decisions is what matters to one caught up in the toils of the law. And the dangers of mistake and abuse of power are further magnified by the severity of physical sanctions that are commonly applied to enforce legal rules. Moreover, the law is ineffective in exercising control over many areas of life. Many aspects of interpersonal relations – for example, certain kinds of promises – are wisely left unenforced by the law, mainly because legal officials cannot reasonably be expected to know, or be able to find out, the details necessary to enforcement. But we as individuals, judging our own behavior and that of other persons, can exercise an influence that the law, with its centralized organs and often crude sanctions, could not. Thus we can and do hold people to promises which would be folly to make legally enforceable: We blame the uncle who fails to make good on a rash and gratuitous promise of a gift to his nephew; indeed, if the promise was a small enough one, we may pressure him to carry through with it anyway. But we would not think it wise for courts to get into the business of enforcing such promises. Conversely, when we decide whether to blame the uncle, we may not have the same reason to refrain as would a court of law. Our judgments and consequent blaming will scarcely have anything of the fearsome impersonality and coldness of legal judgments and sanctions. Here as elsewhere, our following one kind of a rule in law and another in morality is, or ought to be, driven by utilitarian considerations.

By now, these have become familiar points. But there is another point about the value of governing human conduct via moral, rather than legal, rules, a point that is equally important, though more often overlooked. Moral rules are applied and enforced, potentially anyway, by everyone who has normal moral capacities. Thus there is no finality in the making of moral judgments as there is in law; there is no person or persons whose moral judgment cannot be reviewed and, if need be, contradicted, with roughly equal effect, by another. No person is recognized as having any special competence to make moral judgments. Indeed, if some person were to be understood as having some such special competence, it would be doubtful whether we ought to regard that person as making moral judgments at all. And the benefits of this kind of equality of moral agency are clear. In exercising their functions in their role as moral agents, individuals must interpret, apply, and sometimes create rules, and in this they develop deeper moral understanding of the rationale that those rules do or ought to have. In this, they develop and exercise their capacities as autonomous moral agents. For in the exercise of their moral capacities, they are self-governing in a more direct way than they are in their control over the legal system, even assuming that that legal system belongs to a constitutional democracy. This last point provides a further reply to the objector who would claim that the MLM conceives of moral rules in a way that would make them burdensome and undesirable impositions of society on individuals. By participating in the process of moral reasoning and justification, individuals can come to understand, not only the general rationality of having such rules and then of respecting them, but the rationale and applicability of particular rules.

It might be thought that the MLM misrepresents moral thinking as having that rigidity and artificial precision that is more characteristic of the law than of moral thinking. The thought runs that, while these artificially imposed limits – this insensitivity to a broader range of possibilities – may be evident in the law, with its use of public rules guiding the application of sanctions, moral thinking can contain no arbitrary distinctions like the "year and a day" rule, which says that an assailant can be charged with homicide if the victim of the assault dies within a year and a day of the assault.[16] In the law, there are practical reasons for cutting off controversy, thus making the reaching of an authoritative and final decision a necessity. This is so because, to use Feinberg's words, "judgments of legal responsibility are strongly influenced by ulterior practical purposes,"[17] while "judgments of moral responsibility can often be safely avoided, for nothing practical need hinge on them."[18] So,

---

16 The example, as well as the claimed distinction between law and morality, is drawn from Feinberg, "Problematic Responsibility in Law and Morals" and "On Being 'Morally Speaking a Murderer,'" both in 1970, pp. 25–54, esp. pp. 26–9.
17 Ibid., 1970, p. 26.
18 Ibid., 1970, p. 30.

on this line of thought, the determination of legal responsibility, unlike moral responsibility, is a matter of decision, and not simply discovery.

It is true that there are some such differences between legal and moral thinking. But it is, I think, a common mistake to overemphasize them, taking moral distinctions to be more a matter of discovery, and less one of creation and legislation, than they really are. Moral thinking does sometimes contain some rather arbitrary distinctions that would seem to amount to the drawing of a line primarily because some line or other is needed. Thus it might be thought improper for a recently widowed woman to engage in any kind of association with another man until a year has passed from her husband's death. And a prohibition like this might well amount to a moral rule rather than any mere rule of etiquette. Such a rule might or might not have a utilitarian justification. We would need to know much more about the particular context in order to know whether it did. But it is surely doubtful that we could exclude in advance the possibility of a utilitarianly justified morality having a rule that makes such an arbitrary distinction.

Moreover, judgments of moral responsibility are in many contexts guided by practical considerations, though very different sorts of practical considerations. As in the case of legal judgments, we sometimes simply refrain from making a judgment that would otherwise be justified. We may simply consider the matter closed because blame, reminders, or "charging against one's record as a man," to use Feinberg's phrase, would be pointless or counterproductive. Just as lawyers can talk about an instance of theoretical legal liability which will in fact never be judged in a court of law, moral agents can theorize about that which is really wrong, whether or not anyone will ever find out, and whether or not anyone would in fact blame anyone or charge anything against anyone's moral record. It can likewise make sense to ask, of one who has been acquitted of murder, whether the judge and jury made a mistake, even though any mistake may not be capable of official correction. And moral judgment, like its legal counterpart, can sometimes be deliberately forgetful. Given what is at least a strong de facto connection between the moral norms we use and our behavior in judging, praising, and blaming, it would be surprising indeed if our moral distinctions did not reflect the practical difficulties we typically experience in making adequately informed moral judgments.

140

Just as a utilitarian moral theory will need to take into account the practical problems of teaching, remembering, and applying moral rules in one's own case, so too will it need to take account of how readily a rule can be used as a basis for action guidance, as well as blaming or praising.

Though the differences between legal and moral judgments are easy to overemphasize, they do exist, and they are important. Earlier in this chapter, I argued that moral reasoning with public, collective rules need not be conceived as a mechanical operation – that, say, of simply counting opinions as if taking a poll. In this respect, moral and legal reasoning are alike. But there are several important differences between the functions of such moral rules and their legal counterparts.

(i) *Special adjudicative competence.* One is that legal rules must lend themselves to application by formal, centralized organs of adjudication, the decisions of which are either not open to appeal, or appealable only to officials who have special competence to make authoritative decisions. Thus it is part of our understanding of legal rules that the official interpretations of them are not open to question in many of the ways that the interpretations of moral rules are.

(ii) *Special legislative competence.* A second difference is that legal rules are in large part explicitly created by organs (legislatures) understood to have the special authority to create rules. Because morality as we understand it does not include the idea that some people have special authority to legislate its rules, we do not think of any person's formulation of a rule as authoritative merely because it is that person's formulation. So here again, we can expect a difference between our ways of thinking about moral and legal rules. We think of the existence of legal rules, at least those whose source is a legislative act, as beyond question in ways that moral rules are not.

(iii) *Predominant use of external sanctions.* Finally, there is the obvious difference that the law guides our conduct more extensively through the explicit application of external sanctions than does morality. So to a much greater extent when dealing with legal demands than when dealing with moral, our concern is what some other persons are likely to do to us or with us if we act in certain ways. And what those persons decide to do must be decided in a public forum, according to public procedures, taking into account only that evidence that has been gathered consistently with proper procedures. So we can expect that the predominant focus of legal rules will be behavior that is, in principle anyway, ascertainable by formal public procedures. The focus of moral rules being less on the external, and more on the internal, their point is as much to guide the individual in the privacy of conscience as to guide people in judging, praising, and blaming others.

7

Practical reasoning

The central features of the MLM having been explained, it is now necessary to get a clearer idea of how the MLM would structure one's moral reasoning. We need to know how our reasons for action can come under the influence of existing collective norms, most of which are less than utilitarianly perfect. No doubt everything that deserves to be called "the morality" of one's society or group implicitly makes the claim to legitimate authority over one; for if a large proportion of society hold that one is morally bound to follow accepted moral rules, they are in their way claiming a kind of authority for those rules. But the fact that legitimate authority is claimed for a moral code does not, of course, entail that it actually has legitimate authority over anyone.

No plausible moral theory could expect the moral agent, who must decide what is morally right or wrong, to ignore the facts about the prevailing morality of his or her culture, and of other people generally. What people are thinking, doing, and expecting of one another and of me is a fact that bears in at least many indirect ways on my own moral conclusions. It is a fact that may give me genuine moral reasons bearing on my own decisions and actions. What differentiates theories from one another are their different views about the way in which these facts are relevant. Though I fear that my account of how people ought to reason – especially when, like everyone I have ever known, they find themselves having grown up and living within a culture and morality that is largely ready-made – may seem overly complex to some readers, my answer is that moral reasoning *is* very complex, even at the level of adequate theory. This is particularly so if we represent what moral reasoning is and ought to be like when we deal with moral conflicts, and if we attempt, as we sometimes must, to uncover the deeper rationale for some element of a moral code. If elegant simplicity

143

were a mark of truth and validity, the act-consequentialist formula
– that the right action = that which produces the most good overall
– would be philosophically unassailable.

Beginning with the primary principle that one is to do good, one
recognizes that there are certain goods that can only be achieved
through collective action, and that a moral code containing public,
right-defining rules, in certain spheres of behavior anyway, is necessary to their attainment. We recognize that the most common
situation is that in which we and most people do live in communities in which there is some such moral code, though sometimes
consensus only exists at a deep level. We recognize also that the
mere fact that a code exists is no guarantee that it has any legitimate authority, or that it ought to be accepted. Yet we ordinarily
do not question the code of our own community, and we normally
accept most of its elements. Whether it is rational to give such
a presumption of acceptability to a prevailing moral code depends on a variety of factors, all of which focus ultimately on our
reasons for believing or not believing that that code's general acceptance constitutes an improvement over the utilitarian state of
nature.

For example, suppose I have on balance the most reason to believe
that the existing moral code arises from the influence, the false
example, teaching, and power of a minority whose interests alone
are really served by it. I would have basis for the presumption that
none of the code really did constitute an improvement over the
utilitarian state of nature, and I would have reason for denying that
the code had any authority over anyone. But a reasonable presumption is only that and nothing more. I might on closer analysis
discover that, whatever the history of the code, it, or at least some
of its most important elements, actually is justified in this sense,
that is, of constituting an improvement over the utilitarian state of
nature. The presumption would then be reversed. It is easy to
imagine how rational reflection about an existing moral code might
move in the opposite direction. A Burkean conservative's presumption in favor of an existing code might be reasonable even
though the reasonableness of that stance could disappear on the
availability of additional evidence.

144

We must pay closer attention to what this presumption in favor of, or against, an existing code would be about. A plausible test for the minimal acceptability of a code or rule, I suggested, is whether its general acceptance produces greater overall good than that which would be produced if members of the society whose code or rule it is were, in that sphere of behavior, to govern their actions by the use of the primary principle. When I apply this test in practice, I will first need to remember that the idea of people governing their actions by the use of the primary principle is a matter of their accepting, using, and sometimes teaching the primary principle. This idea is therefore not the same as effective, actual compliance. This is as it should be, given our conception of a moral code as a public, generally knowable instrument for the guidance and evaluation of actions. When we ask what it would be like if people were to govern their behavior by use of the primary principle only, this notion of self-governance does not then entail that they will always succeed in complying with that principle, even when its requirements are unambiguous and clear. For it is a notorious fact that people are not always impersonally benevolent, but are often selfish, impulsive, resentful, opportunistic, and self-deceiving. A moral code is partly an instrument for correcting the collective consequences of such defects in motivation.

Recognizing this, we are in a better position to determine what is relevant to the question whether some rule or code is minimally acceptable. Immediately relevant are some empirical questions about the kinds of defects of motivation that exist in a particular society. In a society of genuinely benevolent, reflective people who have an especially developed capacity to control their behavior by the deliverances of benevolent reason, no doubt the need for collective moral rules would be less than in a society of selfish, power hungry, and competitive people. Although these latter might also have significant benevolent impulses, and even acknowledge that the basis of moral action is the primary principle, they would still have greater need of collective right-defining strategies backed by the collective authority of society. These variations in the kind and degree of defects of motivation imply appropriate variations in the justifiability of specific moral rules, and even of whole moral codes. Evaluating these rules and codes, I will need to examine their social

145

context: If a particular society contains an especially strict code about the special deference that men are to show to women, is there perhaps a rationale for this in the fact that, in the absence of such a code, men would treat women with roughness and brutality? Does it give everyone, especially women, a beneficial sense of security to know that such rough and brutal behavior, which, in the abstract at least, might be condemned most of the time anyway by the primary principle of doing good, is also collectively condemned by the use of generally accepted moral rules? Though condemned anyway by the primary principle, that condemnation does not have the same force in practice, for the principle is of necessity highly general and vague, and does not provide people with immediately useful descriptions of behavior that is to regarded as wrong.

Chief among the factors that would serve to justify a collective rule, then, would seem to be whether the behavior in question is under the influences of self-interest and strong temptation, especially where the interests of other persons will be deeply affected by mistakes, where self-deception would likely result, and where a coordinated plan of action using a public conception of the right needs to be followed. Where such factors are present, the likelihood of mutual mistrust may be increased if individuals are left to their own strategies in pursuing the good.

We can notice here an incidental benefit that accrues when people attempt to analyze moral codes in this way. Though I might, because of my own acculturation, have difficulty in understanding why other people could have such an odd moral code in which women are accorded such an extraordinary degree of deference whereas men are not, I am likely to have more understanding and sympathy once I have probed deeply into the underlying rationale for their code. I will have some intellectual basis for resisting a kind of moral imperialism that is directed against other cultures. At the same time, I will not be forced back to a moral relativism that holds that every moral code is as objectively good and as much a source of legitimate moral authority as any other.

7.4. WHEN DOES AN EXISTING CODE HAVE LEGITIMATE AUTHORITY OVER ME?

When one surveys and evaluates the rules of this or that moral code, one may be warranted in concluding that some code is indeed

146

justified, even that it is the best available; but that much by itself does not necessitate the conclusion that one is morally obligated to comply with the requirements of that code: Though I may acknowledge the great good that adherence to some code produces, that fact is not sufficient to show that that code embodies any moral authority over me. There must exist a more intimate connection between that code and me. This particularity problem is reduced to manageable proportions by a number of considerations, most of which spring from the limits that are inherent in one's duty under the primary principle. These limits include the following: Because there are certain good results that I am simply in no position to bring about, helping to bring them about cannot be my duty. And, because goods are of various kinds, only some of which represent central and fundamental interests of all human beings, their importance varies, and the first priority (if not the only requirement) under the primary principle is to contribute to the advancement of the most fundamental of goods.

Physical proximity

However much good it would otherwise do, I cannot comply with fuel-saving requirements in another country if I am not there. That, it seems, is the first and most common reason why I am untouched by so many of the regulations, programs, and schemes that exist on this planet and whose most plausible justification is that they bring about some benefit or other. This list of contributions to the good that I cannot make goes on and on: I can do nothing to reduce consumption of alcohol in the Soviet Union; to reduce consumption of luxuries in Argentina; or to lend a hand to a poor soul trapped in a well in Texas. If any of these problems involve the recognition of duties as part of their solution, those duties do not extend to me. If there is no other reason for this, the reason of simple physical distance suffices.

Psychological and social proximity

Sometimes I cannot join in proud solidarity with an oppressed group, because I am not one of them, and they do not see me as one of them. If theirs is a program of action designed in part to be symbolic and expressive of their history of oppression and suffer-

147

ing, my own history may disqualify me from participation. My attempt at participation may not be accepted at all, and might correctly be viewed as an obstacle, rather than as a contribution, to the advancement of their goal. To take another example, I cannot comply with the requirements within a religious sect to give up the things of this world, not, at least, if the function of the requirements is to give expression to that sect's collective self-subordination to the God of their belief. Not sharing their belief, my outward actions would not have the needed effect.

Sometimes the distance that makes for my inability to participate is simply a matter of my own psychological makeup, due in part to my own cultural background. Even if nothing else would disqualify me from taking some role in another culture, my own lack of the needed dispositions and skill for that role would. I would always look like a clumsy, third-rate actor in a play, a play in which it would be especially important for the actor to be effortlessly at one with the role. My clumsy attempts would therefore do little to reinforce a sense of cultural identity, pride, or unity.

Considerations such as these help explain, I think, why, on the MLM, one would lack certain obligations under the moral code of another group, even though one may physically be in their presence, and yet in some cases, one's physical location would make a crucial difference. Thus if I am in a foreign land, and there is a sudden bread shortage, I would have a genuine moral obligation to comply with the rules announced for curbing consumption. I am there, I am capable of making this contribution, and collective compliance with public rules is a matter of protecting a central and fundamental interest, that of insuring enough food. But even if they need additional priests for the practice of their religion, and the practice of that religion were otherwise justified (which would in fact probably not be the case), they would probably not even think of accepting me in the role, and if they did, they would be making a mistake. So I would not be doing wrong in rejecting this possible claim on me. And this conclusion is, I think, consistent with commonsense intuitions about the matter.

The availability of better alternatives for doing good

Even if I find myself in the extraordinary situation of being able to perform my share of good-doing in the world by acknowledging the obligations imposed by some group's moral code, that will in all likelihood not be the only such possibility open to me. For example: Though I find myself living in my own culture with its own code, I might be quite capable of adjusting to another culture, doing good by complying with the code accepted there. There are numerous reasons for affording the presumption of valid authority (over me at least) to my own culture: I am adjusted to my own culture's expectations and demands, and it therefore comes easiest to me. Even if I could make a marginally greater contribution to the good after (international or intranational) migration, the costs of a transition, once the effects on friends, family, and me are reckoned in, would probably outweigh the overall benefits. So the idea of doing the most good again affords a basis for narrowing down the range of moral codes and rules that might otherwise be thought to have some legitimate claim on me. It also opens the way for an additional factor that further narrows the range, that of one's own choice. Faced with several alternatives that are otherwise equally meritorious from a good–doing standpoint, I recognize, or once recognized, that I must choose. I can join a religious order, join the military to fight in a just war, or obtain citizenship in another country in which I could make a life-long contribution. But I cannot do all three. There may, of course, be marginal differences among these alternatives in the amount of good that I could do. But these differences may be narrow enough to make disagreement about them reasonable. Thus I make (or once made) a choice which continues to be reasonable, and that choice serves further to narrow the source of my obligations under a code to that of the code belonging to the enterprise I have chosen.

Whether the good resulting from acceptance of the code is discretionary or essential

I may be able to promote the beneficial ends of the local topiary garden club, but doing so is at most one of the many optional ways for me to promote good in the world. The mere fact that the club does good things – conducting tours of local topiary gardens, developing an interest in the history of topiary gardening, and doing something to add to beauty in the world – is not enough to obligate me to do my part in that organization. One reason for this is that the duty to do good would seem to leave much to individual discretion. In particular, it leaves open for my decision many questions about what ends to promote. As between doing my part to promote the cause of historic preservation, topiary gardening, chess, philosophy, or seventeenth-century keyboard music, the general duty to do good would seem to be silent; unless, of course, one of these things is connected to other goods, or other more fundamental goods, as would be the case if, for example, successful preservation of historic buildings were necessary to the tourist industry in my small country, and that in turn were essential to economic survival. In short, if the rules, practices, and ideals of the topiary garden club are to have legitimate claim on my aims and efforts, there needs to be a much tighter connection between them and me. The most typical way in which this connection is supplied is through my explicit consent, agreement, or promise, perhaps an act of "joining up."

Whether one has consented, agreed, or promised

If I have taken an active decision to join an organization, accepting its code of conduct, then, assuming that acceptance of the rules of the organization does good rather than evil, I have an obligation to comply. I have joined an organization with the understanding that the point of its rules is to restrict the actions of its members. Of course, we do not usually accept moral codes in this way, and cases in which the demands of a moral code are linked to a particular person in this way are rare. What comes closest to this in everyday experience would seem to be an individual's acceptance of a professional code of ethics. Thus in everyday life, I have an obligation not to lie, but, arguably, no obligation to tell the whole truth when asked. But this ethical standard might be raised for me if I have taken an oath, on entering a military academy, that I will tell the whole truth, and not quibble in any way.

To summarize: A justified moral code attains legitimate authority over me by virtue of the fact that my compliance with its requirements would fulfill my general duty, under the primary principle, to do good. But the occasions for fulfilling my duty in such a way are limited by physical, as well as psychological and social, distance; by the availability of presumptively better alternatives; or by the discretionary character of the ends the code promotes. Thus I typically do not do wrong if I refuse to acknowledge the authority of

150

some particular code, even if it is justified.[1] But for these same reasons, a justified moral code of my own society, in which I am living, and which represents the best or only opportunity I have to contribute to essential ends, presumptively does have legitimate moral authority over me.

7.5. NONIDEAL SOCIAL NORMS

Once I have satisfactorily answered the questions about minimum acceptability of a code and its legitimate authority over me in particular, I face further questions. Perhaps the most common case is that in which an existing rule or code passes these tests, but falls significantly short of being ideal. It is no doubt greatly preferable that we should have some fairly specific moral rules governing the use individuals can make of physical force against other human beings; but the accepted rules may be less than the best. And it may also be the case that my society is better off because of a recognized moral prohibition on the drinking of alcohol or on the use of drugs. But it may also be the case that the prevailing prohibition is not optimal, either because it is overly restrictive, or insufficiently so, or places the restrictions imprecisely, on the wrong behavior.

What normative force does an accepted rule have for me if I realize that it falls in the range above minimal acceptability but somewhere short of ideal? First, a brief recapitulation of an earlier argument. Initially, one must recognize that the whole idea of complying with public, collective strategies for doing good is inconsistent with the idea that individuals may separately act on strategies that *would* be ideal, *were* they publicly acknowledged and generally followed. If individuals were to follow their own judgments as to the rules that are ideal in this sense, their attempts would often be

---

1 We can notice at once that the argument provided in the text largely avoids what Simmons, 1979, pp. 30–5, calls the "particularity problem"; that is, that of particularizing a general duty to do good, uphold just institutions, or whatever to the institutions of my country or group. Simmons rejects physical proximity as a particularizing factor on grounds that "If we allowed such a move, it would follow that when I go to live for a month with my friends in the domain of just government *B*, all of my political obligations would transfer automatically to government *B*, regardless of whether I have any other significant relations with that government" (p. 33). But the answer to this is that physical proximity does bring some obligations with it. The transfer of obligations need not be entire.

self-defeating. This is so because individuals are likely to make too many mistakes when they attempt to act by their own judgments about what rule would be ideal. Further, even if we assume that no mistakes are made, it is implausible to suppose that there will always, or even very often, be some one rule that is *uniquely* ideal: Two or more incompatible rules may be tied for first place. So if the reasons for having a public collective strategy have mainly to do with reducing both mistakes of judgment and mutual mistrust about the exercise of discretion, and with making everyone's actions accountable by a single standard readily available to all, the injunction that everyone should adhere to ideal rules will fail.

But if the claim is that I am bound by a less than ideal social norm, that claim would seem open to the following kind of objection. Suppose that I know that some alternative rule is better than the de facto rule. Ordinarily, it would seem, we simply begin to act in accordance with rules we recognize as better, and when enough people do so, the rule changes. That, at least, allows us not to be trapped by the rules of a deficient moral code. But if our duties are defined by an existing imperfect code, the objection goes, we would be doing wrong – rejecting the authority of that code – if we were simply to begin acting in accordance with the new code.

This objection assumes, however, that the only, or even the most typical, way of bringing about change in an existing code is immediately to begin acting in accordance with the better code. But we are often in a position to comply with the existing code even while publicly criticizing it, seeking general acceptance of the better code through argument and persuasion. To return to the example of fuel-saving in wartime, recall Smart's suggestion that a rule better than a flat prohibition on house temperatures above 50 degrees might be one using a mixed strategy: Each person is to throw dice, then is to allow himself a higher temperature if and only if a certain number of successive sixes turns up. If accepted, that rule might indeed produce better results than the simple prohibition. And that fact would no doubt give me good reason for publicly calling attention to the better rule. It would not justify my simply going ahead and acting upon it without further ado. And the reason for this seems clear. If I were simply to act, privately and without giving any accounting of myself, on that rule which I sincerely and even correctly judged to be ideal, that would defeat the purpose of a collective strategy which is supposed to be binding on all. This is a compelling reason even if no one else will find out, for such a rule presupposes that rational and autonomous moral agents, recognizing the value of such a rule from a collective point of view, will thereby recognize that it provides them with a reason for action, a reason that is independent of considerations about causing a scandal or setting a bad example.

That there is such an independent reason is often masked by the existence of other reasons for complying with a deficient rule. For example, in virtually every society there are accepted rules of role responsibility determining, among other things, which family members and relatives have the duty of caring for children. It is clear that there are many possibilities for placing these duties, ranging from equal parental responsibility to primarily maternal or paternal familial responsibility. Now, if the existing justified though imperfect rule places the burden primarily on the mother and the mother's family, and another, and better, rule would place it on the father and the father's family, a mother would usually have an additional reason for caring for her child as the rule requires, rather than abandoning her child to chance. For the child would almost certainly suffer, possibly even starve. Yet this kind of reason, important as it is, should not be allowed to conceal the sort of reason that concerns us here. Even if, by abandoning one's child on a doorstep somewhere, or placing her directly in the hands of some benevolent others, one could know the results to be happy ones – the child is adopted and well cared for by loving people – the fact that doing so would violate an accepted and justified rule of obligation would imply that one had done a wrong.

Fortunately, we usually have more than the bleak pair of alternatives of either doing something that is outright wrong or passively accepting an inferior code. What we can and actually do in various situations can be understood if we reflect on the point, or rationale, for having a public, right-defining moral code in the first place. In addition to the familiar role of moral rules as action guides for individuals, there are the additional functions of promoting mutual trust and, partly to serve the end of mutual trust, facilitating collective supervision. So one possibility for one faced with such a dilemma was mentioned above: One might act in compliance with the existing rule while publicly urging acceptance of the better rule. Not only does one then do no wrong, and respect the point of having generally accepted rules that apply equally to all, but one thereby does more good by contributing to the improvement of the de facto moral code. This course would seem to be most justified where little is lost by my compliance with the prevailing rule, and where the very point of having such a rule in the first place is to exclude reasoning of this kind. The restrictions on wartime fuel use would be an example. If I comply with the existing imperfect rule, all that will be lost is the possibility of some additional heat for my home, and the purpose of having rules for fuel usage is precisely to exclude considerations about optimizing that would coincide with self-interest. Thus if I know that Smart's dice-throwing rule would indeed be better, if generally accepted, than the existing rule, that certainly does not justify my using it. For little good is lost to the world if I don't use it, and if I do use it, I could thereby slightly increase, though not decrease, my own expectations. Here the reasons for optimizing are too weak to override the exclusionary reasons provided by the rationale for the rule; that is, we don't want people thinking about ways in which they might individually optimize where such optimizing would so neatly serve their own interests, and where the resulting net good would be marginal.

Another possibility for dealing with the dilemma would go a step further: Take a public stand in favor of the better rule while acting on it and failing to comply, if need be, with the existing rule. In the example of fuel-saving, this would be the most justified procedure where there is potential general acceptance of the better rule, and where one's publicly defended action is especially likely to bring about the general acceptance of that better rule. The argument for this course gets stronger as the amount that would be gained by acceptance of the improved rule increases. Here one might ask: Isn't it still the case that, in violating the existing rule, one is doing a wrong? The answer here would seem to be that, given the whole rationale for having such a rule in the first place, it would not. For the rationale behind the rule is to secure the saving of fuel and to limit individual discretion in a publicly supervisable way so that mistrust will be reduced. But then to violate such a rule publicly, and in order to get acceptance of the better rule where one's action will have this result, is not really to violate this rule taken in light of its rationale. One's violation of the old rule is publicly admitted and there for all to see, and there for others to follow with collectively beneficial effect. The argument that there is no real wrongdoing would be especially complete if one's violation did not advance one's own interests.

These observations bring us to a more general problem that may seem to be serious for any conception of right-defining rules that are at the same time conceived not to be absolutely binding in all conceivable circumstances. Whether a social norm is ideal or not, noncompliance with its requirements may be justified. Though such a norm may create valid protected reasons for action, and protected reasons exclude certain sorts of normally relevant contrary reasons, protected reasons do not exclude every kind of contrary reason; nor do they necessarily exclude all contrary reasons of the same kind, no matter how great their weight.

This claim has seemed to some critics to be especially unclear, even unintelligible. For to hold that one is sometimes justified in not complying with a social norm might seem hard to square with the idea that rules provide protected reasons for action. As one critic has put it, the difficulty arises from the unclarity of the relation between primary principle (here the principle that one is to do good) and secondary rules:

In theory mixed restricted utilitarianism does represent a different theory from extreme utilitarianism. In practice it is difficult to determine whether the two have been assimilated. Unless we are told how to weight the practice against the consequences and how much weight to attribute to the practice qua practice, it is difficult to know how the mixed version works out in detail and whether its exponent has or has not fallen back into the outmoded extreme utilitarian calculus.[2]

This complaint seems prima facie applicable here. We need to have a clearer idea of the exclusionary effect that acceptable rules have.

The critic has an especially strong objection if we think of reasons for and against a particular action as measurable and directly comparable. For example, if we used a Benthamite utilitarian calculus, conceiving of every reason in favor of an action and every reason against an action in terms of expected utility, then, even if we had no difficulty explaining how some of these reasons could exclude

2 McCloskey, "An Examination of Restricted Utilitarianism," p. 139, in Bayles, 1968, p. 117.

others, it would still be hard to understand why they should exclude to some particular degree, but neither more nor less. And if reasons exclude in this way, the thought might run, perhaps they don't really exclude at all, but simply have weight sufficient to outweigh other reasons.

But if we examine familiar instances of practical reasoning, we can see how to make sense of the relationship between the primary principle about doing good and the secondary rules adopted as means to advancing the good. As we saw in our initial examination of what exclusionary reasons exclude (in Chapter 4), exclusionary reasons typically exclude certain kinds of reasons but not others. For example, if I make a promise to do a small errand for you, my promise serves especially to exclude some contrary reasons. It clearly excludes considerations about my being inconvenienced: That is precisely the sort of consideration that we both understand to be ruled out by the promise. But it does not exclude considerations about risk to my life, or the saving of someone else's life. Again, it is wrong to cheat on an exam, and we can understand very clearly the rationale for this rule. It excludes, above all, considerations about advantages for one's own career. But if cheating (in the sense of a student's going to an examination and getting answers to questions using unauthorized methods and materials) were necessary to conduct a major study on how students cheat in today's classrooms, it would be much less clear just how, or even whether, the rule against cheating would apply. In short, the typical practical question that will arise about the relationship between primary principle and secondary rule has to do with the rationale for the secondary rule: What sorts of considerations is it supposed to exclude, and to what valid end? This question is not the same as asking, how much weight a particular exclusionary reason has. Thinking of it in this latter way, we are thus invited to attach some particular weight to the exclusion. And, presumably, this particular weight will be arbitrary. But if we think of rules, in morality as in law, as having or not having a good rationale, and, given the rationale, as excluding some kinds of contrary considerations but not others, the problem for practical reasoning becomes much more tractable. In principle, this kind of relationship between rule and background rationale is no more difficult or mysterious than it is in the law, where grappling with the relationship is common, difficult, though hardly impossible.

156

It is sometimes thought to be a defect of rule utilitarianism that it would make it difficult to understand the person of conscience, the person who attempts to rise above common morality. Brandt puts the point this way:

> One might argue that the existence of an accepted moral rule is not sufficient to make particular actions wrong or obligatory but is a necessary condition. To say this, however, is to say that men have no obligation to rise above the commonplace morals of their times. Whereas in fact we do not think it right for men to be cruel to animals or to slaves in a society which condones this.[3]

As the discussion so far should make clear, there are many ways in which the MLM allows us, not only to understand what the person of conscience is, but even to understand individuals as having an obligation, arising from the deeper principles to which they in conscience ought to be committed, to "rise above" commonplace morals.

First, there is a point about the judgment and understanding of the autonomous moral agent. Though under some conditions the existence of a social rule excludes certain reasons for action, the moral agent is not deprived of knowledge of the right, nor, in general, of the means or ability to judge what is good and what is right. It is no part of the proposal that moral agents would be better off if they usually had false beliefs about the right or the good. Thus to claim that one sometimes has exclusionary reasons is not to suppose that any facts must be excluded from one's consciousness, any more than embracing the logical truth that P entails not-not-P is to suppose that one's believing P must be to exclude not-P from one's consciousness. Living in a society of commonplace morals, the person of conscience, therefore, need not be in a position of mindless assent to the existing order, but can, with enough information, reach the conclusion that the moral code of her society is indeed commonplace, and ought to be changed.

A second way in which the person of conscience may "rise above" commonplace morals is built into the idea that a moral code or rule must be minimally acceptable in order to preempt the pri-

3 Brandt, 1963, p. 118.

mary principle. Let us consider more carefully the two examples Brandt provides: the condoning of cruelty to animals or to slaves. What it means to say that my society condones cruelty to animals or slaves is presumably that cruelty to animals or slaves is tolerated and not thought wrong. Or it may mean something stronger than this, that such cruelty is a generally accepted rule of obligation, and that one is criticized if one does not, in appropriate conditions anyway, do cruel things to animals or slaves. To take the latter case first, if cruelty is regarded as an obligation in my society, the first question I shall have to ask is how such a rule could be utilitarianly justified. And it seems overwhelmingly likely that the answer would be that it is not. Could the general acceptance of such a rule constitute an improvement over the state of affairs in which there is no rule specifically about cruelty, but that, already armed with the theory of the good, people are instructed merely to adhere to the primary principle as best they can? The most familiar and obvious utilitarian arguments against cruelty – about suffering, coarsening of those who are required to perpetrate it – would still hold, though perhaps with even greater force than usual. For when we imagine a generally accepted rule of obligation, we are imagining a situation in which there is, through the acceptance of that rule, a kind of collective expression of the terms of human (or human and animal) relationship, and the public knowledge of this may well cause insecurity, fear, or even contempt for one's own society.

Now, let us consider the other possibility: that cruelty to animals or slaves is condoned only in the sense that it is fully allowed, though not a matter of obligation. The crucial difference here is that there is arguably no generally accepted rule about cruelty to animals or slaves. Instead, there is permissive silence. How should I determine what is the morally right thing to do? One thing is clear. From the fact that my society thus condones cruelty, I may not straightaway infer that it is ever morally permissible for any person to do cruel things. For even if I am indeed not bound by any social rule of obligation, I am still bound directly by the primary principle. Anyone in such a position must then ask whether, after reckoning in the effects on others and on one's own dispositions and character, doing something cruel to an animal or a slave really will do more good than evil. And if one decides that it does do more good than evil, one needs to realize that one is especially likely

158

to make mistakes, and yielding to a temptation to cruelty will very likely be objectively mistaken.

A third way in which a person of conscience might rise above commonplace morals would make use of the idea that the existence of a social rule is, as I argued in the preceding chapter, no mere matter of counting opinions, but involves a sound interpretation of the rule in light of its most plausible rationale linking it to the good. So, for example, suppose that the widespread opinion is that cruelty to human beings is wrong, but that cruelty to slaves is not. Exploring the rationale for the wrongness of cruelty to human beings, the person of conscience recognizes that there is no way consistent with that rationale to deny that it is also wrong to be cruel to slaves. In recognizing this and pointing it out, the person of conscience does indeed rise above commonplace morals. (For one thing that an objector like Brandt might mean by "commonplace morals" is something like "commonplace moral opinion.") Indeed, one's duty under the primary principle requires that one point out the loose or inconsistent connections between superficial, popular moral opinions and the deeper rationale of social rules. For this constitutes one of the most important ways in which the moral agent can bring about good in the world.

A fourth way in which one can rise above commonplace morals is also consistent with one's obligations under justified social rules. There is clearly a place for the moral leader who attempts to persuade others, by example or argument, to accept a rule, either in a sphere of behavior where none existed, or where the existing rule ought to be rejected. Finding myself in a society in which cruelty to animals is both routine and tolerated, it would of course be good if I don't also participate in the cruelty; it might do even more good if I devote myself to persuading others to regard such cruelty as a wrong – not just a bad strategy for each of so many separate individuals, but as wrong for anyone to do, *period*. When I publicly argue this position, I will express myself by saying that "cruelty to slaves and animals is wrong." But both the aim and function of my judgment will be to establish a new rule rather than to use an existing one.[4]

Finally, there is a sense in which one might "rise above" com-

---

4 The idea of standard-using and standard-setting uses gets its inspiration from Stevensonian emotivism's handling of judgments about goodness. For the distinction itself, see Urmson, 1968, ch. 5.

monplace morality by doing morally wrong things from motives that are, in their general and fundamental orientation, morally good motives. The person who fails to comply with valid moral rules that are genuinely applicable may do wrong without justification. However, this conclusion does not entail that that person is wicked, or insufficiently concerned about doing good. On the contrary, such a person may have good-doing motives to an especially high degree. Perhaps we should admire such people, at least if there aren't too many of them. We can admire them for their motives, and we may rightly believe that the world is a better place for having some such people. Social moral codes are sometimes improved by the morally wrong actions of highly benevolent people. Indeed, codes are sometimes improved by the morally wrong actions of wicked people.

7.7. CONFLICTS AMONG RULES

What ought one to do when faced with two rules that impose conflicting duties, apparently requiring one both to do X and not to do X? The most plausible immediate suggestion is that conflicts are to be resolved by going back to the primary principle. But critics have pointed out that this is an ambiguous piece of advice, and the solutions it offers have seemed implausible to some. McCloskey is again a good source for the criticism:

Even the restricted utilitarian has to face the conflicts of duties so commonly supposed to be fatal to the Kantian theory. There are either of two possible courses open to him. One is to argue that we should judge between the conflicting duties in particular situations on the grounds of the value of the consequences of the respective *actions*. But this either amounts to the extreme utilitarian position, or at least exposes it to extension along the lines of making the consequences always relevant, as after all they really are. Alternatively, the restricted utilitarian could choose between the prac tices on the basis of the value of the practices. This . . . leads to the absurdity of always preferring one practice to another.[5]

Fortunately there are alternatives beyond the two McCloskey imagines. The first of McCloskey's criticisms, if otherwise sound, would show only that there are some cases, possibly fairly numerous, in which appeal to rules would yield no usable conclusion. But that does not amount to the extreme utilitarian position; it merely would

5 McCloskey, in Bayles, 1968, pp. 126–7.

show that right and wrong cannot always be settled by reference to rules. And this conclusion surely seems correct. I have argued that moral rules are not always necessary, and that it is sometimes best, from a collective point of view, to leave individual moral agents morally permitted to choose their own courses of action, guided either directly by the principle of doing good, or indirectly by it, as when individuals develop their own dispositions, traits, and strategies for doing good.

As to the second criticism, it would be a mechanical procedure indeed that required individuals always, in case of conflict between existing rules, to opt for that which has the greatest overall value. That procedure would have the virtue of simplicity, but little else would recommend it. Instead, the first step of a more defensible procedure for dealing with conflicts would be to gain a deeper understanding of the two apparently conflicting rules. For the conflict may be apparent only. Once we probe more deeply into the reasons we have for making a moral requirement of, say, truth-telling or promise-keeping, we may discover that one of the rules does not really apply after all. Or we may discover that, although both rules do apply, the rules or their rationales include ways of ranking violations of rules so that there is a way of grading wrongs according to something like their degree of seriousness.

Consider some of the ways in which lies and promise-breakings might then be graded. First suppose that the rationale for requiring truth-telling and promise-keeping focuses primarily on the importance of making it possible for people to rely on one another, allowing people to have well-founded expectations upon which they can reasonably rely in their pursuits. The rules, we may suppose, make all lies and promise-breakings wrong; but, when forced to grade their seriousness for purposes of resolving a conflict, it would be reasonable for us to consider the seriousness of their consequences for the disappointment of reasonable expectations. Thus to lie to the local gossip in order to protect a confidence that you have promised to keep, the revealing of which would pointlessly damage a person's reputation, would be a less serious wrong than to break the promise. The reasonable expectations of local gossips about the reliability of their information need not be protected with the same depth of concern that we have for other reasonable expectations. It is important to notice that this procedure is not equivalent to an act-consequentialist procedure, for it applies only to grading wrongs in situations of conflict, and it uses for the grading a fairly specific rationale standing behind the rules. It thus presupposes, as an act-consequentialist procedure would not, that the action being graded is wrong because it violates a rule. And it is clearly different from a procedure which calls for a gross assessment of one rule – truth-telling, say – as having greater value than another. For it might even be the case that the rule of truth-telling secures more good in the world than that of promise-keeping. Even if that were true, it would be simply irrelevant to the grading of this lie as compared to this promise-breaking.

Another, very closely related way to deal with conflicts among rules is to choose that action which, though a wrong given the rules as they are presently accepted, would not be wrong if the rules were revised in the most desirable way feasible. Applied to the example of lying to the local gossip in order to protect a confidence, it is reasonable to suppose that an exception to the rule about lying – one covering some general category of situations like this one – would be a more desirable rule to have. Because in cases of genuine conflict among actually accepted rules one will do a wrong either way, it would be desirable to do that which would not be wrong on the most desirable revision feasible. When people deal with conflicts in this way, their actions tend over time to bring about beneficial changes in prevailing morality. But again, the procedure would not amount to an act-consequentialist one; for it invites one to solve conflicts by thinking of revisions in rules which it would be desirable to have accepted. One who thinks, and publicly reasons and acts, in this way thus takes right-defining rules seriously in a way that the act consequentialist could not.

Some cases of conflict of rules are not genuine conflicts at all, but are only apparent conflicts between two judgments having the two different functions explained earlier: between judgments whose function it is to use an existing rule and those whose function it is to help establish a new rule. This possibility can arise when one person, judging that X is wrong, means approximately that, as things stand, X is (the kind of action that is) wrong, whereas another person, judging that X is not wrong, means that we ought not to regard X as wrong, that we ought not to include it within our conception of wrongs. For example, suppose that, on our well-established practices about truth-telling, even "white" lies and "social" lies are taken to be wrong, and that rather than telling such

162

a lie, it is better to evade answering a question, which, it is understood, should not be asked anyway. Suppose that I make the reasonable judgment that things would be better if we had a different
practice – one on which it was well understood that white lies and
social lies are morally permissible, and, if "lie" includes the idea of
wrongness, are therefore not lies at all. I might be justified in
claiming that knowingly telling a falsehood in such circumstances
is not really wrong. But you, making another kind of judgment,
one focusing on the practice as it stands, might be equally justified
in judging that it is wrong.

To summarize the main points about dealing with conflicting
rules: There is no simple algorithm, no mechanical procedure, for
deciding what to do when rules appear to conflict. As an initial
step, one looks behind the rules for the best interpretation of their
rationale or rationales. After such an examination, it may turn out
that the conflict is one in appearance only. And even if the conflict
is genuine, and it is both the case that doing X and not doing X
would be wrong, an examination of the utilitarian rationales for
having these separate rules may enable one to grade the wrongs,
so that one can at least do the lesser of the two wrongs. Doing the
lesser of the wrongs will presumably be the same as doing that
which would not be wrong on the most desirable rule-revision
feasible. If there actually are moral dilemmas that resist all of these
methods, then one must dispense with further consideration of the
rules themselves, and simply retreat to the direct use of the primary
principle. Even if there are such cases that can only be decided using
the primary principle, that fact by no means implies that the whole
set of procedures somehow amounts to act consequentialism.

7.8. CONFLICTS OWING TO MULTIPLE CONNECTIONS
TO GROUPS

We may belong to more than one group. Because there are so many
groups in the world, it would seem that the potential for conflict
of obligations is enormous. Given that there is rarely just some one
group to which we are connected, but often many, how is one to
avoid or solve the inevitable conflicts?

We should first take note of the several factors that tend to reduce
the incidence and likelihood of such conflicts, for they are in fact
not as persistent and pervasive a problem as might appear. First, a

point made above about conflicts in general applies here: that which appears to be a conflict of duties may only appear to be, and a deeper examination of the rationale for a rule may reveal that there actually is no conflict. Secondly, there is a related point about the rationale and applicability of rules. The possibility of conflicts is to a large extent anticipated and then avoided in the development and acceptance of moral rules, as it often is in the case of legal rules. For example, it is often part of the teaching, the accepted rule, within religious faiths that certain things are properly the authority of the nation's government whereas others properly fall within the province of religious authority. And though my membership in a bridge club may be understood to commit me to certain rules – for example, that I am to play host to the club at least once a month – it is no part of the understood obligations of bridge-club membership that they are to take priority over my obligations to protect and care for my family. In case of conflict the decision is ready-made: Familial obligations come first.

But, although genuine conflicts may be less frequent than is often supposed, when they do occur they must be resolved by appeal to something beyond the conflicting rules themselves. Before going all the way back to the primary principle to resolve a conflict, other methods need to be exhausted first. The most important of these uses the distinction between the promotion of central human interests or goods, and the promotion of secondary, or discretionary goods. Thus a plausible account as to why the obligations of bridge-club membership take second place to familial obligations is that one's bridge-club activities promote discretionary goods whereas one's discharge of familial duties presumably promotes the more essential goods. Notice again that to rank one set of obligations above the other in this way is not the same as an act-consequentialist procedure. Nor is the procedure of doing that action which would not be wrong on the most desirable feasible revision of the rules. For again we are supposing that the conflict between one's bridge-club obligation and one's familial obligation is genuine, that the one cannot be discharged without violating the other. So one is doing a wrong either way, because either way a rule is being violated, and the remaining question concerns which wrong is the more serious, or which action would turn out not to be wrong under properly revised rules. On an act-consequentialist account, there would be no genuine conflict because only one action would

164

be right, unless the two actions would produce equal overall good, in which case neither would be wrong.[6]

7.9. THE NONEXISTENCE OF SOCIAL NORMS

One familiar difficulty for at least some forms of rule utilitarianism arises in connection with those situations in which people judge themselves or others to have moral obligations even when there is no generally accepted rule that corresponds to the judgment. Indeed, situations in which no social rule exists may be fairly common, given the fact that technological developments create new possibilities that had not been taken seriously; for example, surrogate motherhood and organ transplantation. It seems clear, not only that people do make moral judgments of obligation in the absence of generally accepted rules to validate those judgments, but that they often have good reasons for such judgments. They can have good reason to conclude, for example, that some such judgments are mistaken whereas others are justified. How can we account for this?

Here again it would be tempting simply to go directly to the fallback position offered by the primary principle. We might say simply that, where behavior is not governed by any generally accepted rule, one must do that which produces the most good of any available alternative. But this would be too simple. From a descriptive point of view, it does not approximate the way in which moral reasoning is actually conducted. From a normative point of view, it would be undesirable for moral reasoning to be conducted in this way. Our actual moral reasoning, as Hume noted, seizes upon the slightest analogies, particularly those provided by rules in some neighboring area of behavior, and so even our judgments in the absence of existing social rules tend to be guided indirectly by rules, if only those from adjacent areas. Moreover, it is desirable that moral reasoning should proceed in this way; for in doing so

6 I do not consider here more complex forms of act utilitarianism on which genuine moral dilemmas might indeed be possible; for example, an act utilitarianism that requires for the rightness of an action both that it produce consequences at least as good as any alternative available to the agent, and that the action be on balance good. On this possibility, see Slote, 1985b. (Even on such an act utilitarianism as this, the example of bridge-club versus familial obligations would not turn out to be a conflict of one wrong against another, for to discharge either obligation would be on balance good, not bad.)

we both reflect on the underlying reasons for existing rules, and we take seriously the enterprise of governing appropriate areas of our conduct by collective rules that apply to all. In many cases, therefore, the moral agent need not face the false dilemma of either applying an existing rule or of following the act-consequentialist procedure of doing the most good. What appears to be a gap in existing rules may, on a deeper inspection of the rationale for those rules, be no gap at all. And even when existing rules are indeed silent about some behavior, that does not preclude the possibility that one ought to think, judge, and act as if there were a rule so that, by precept and example, one can bring a new or revised rule into being. In still other cases,. no collective rule of behavior would be justified.

Initially, we can make a rough distinction between two types of situation, analogous to the legal procedures of interpretation and legislation. In one kind of situation, an existing rule, properly understood and interpreted, actually does apply to the new case. A moral prohibition against killing, like a law against murder, presumably applies no less to killings that use recently invented techniques than to killings done in the old, familiar ways. Though disagreement even about something as plain as this is conceivable, the long-accepted rule would clearly apply. On the other hand, if some technology were invented enabling us easily to bring the dead back to life, with their memories, and mental and physical characteristics remaining the same, it would be doubtful that the old prohibition against killing would apply, or would apply with anything like the force that we understand it to have. If killing by some special method were to permit this sort of returning to life, then the prohibition would not so obviously apply to killing by this method. Whether, in the end, the existing rule does apply or not, the interpretion of a rule in light of its rationale is one way in which we can have good reasons for making rule-based judgments about moral obligation even when dealing with new situations that are seemingly not governed by existing rules.

Analogical reasoning from other sources can provide the basis for judgments even in those areas where there is no generally accepted rule of moral obligation. For example, if there is already a morally defensible legal rule that draws property rights boundaries in some new area like that of rights over computer software, and some such rule is also needed for the making of moral judgments,

166

it may well make sense for moral judgments to track legal judgments. The existing legal rule can then serve as the model for our moral judgments. In this kind of case, one may again have excellent reasons for making a rule-based moral judgment even where there is no general moral opinion about the matter. The moral judgment that one kind of use of software is, in effect, theft of another's property, whereas another kind of use is not, employs an existing legal rule as a device for coordinating moral opinion, creating a moral rule of much the same content.

In some cases, though a generally accepted collective moral rule may be highly desirable, it may not exist. Further, there may be no existing rules which apply even when correctly interpreted in light of their rationale, and there may be no acceptable legal-rule or other analogies to be seized upon. For example, consider a moral question about which there may well be no existing moral rule: Whether it is wrong to keep a hopelessly defective infant alive in order to use its various organs for transplantation. We may fear that leaving this sort of matter up to the discretion of those in a position of power – such as medical personnel and family – is a dangerous thing. For various reasons of the kinds discussed earlier, it might be the case that a rule limiting the discretion of all in this sphere is a desirable thing. In these circumstances, one might be well justified in making a kind of legislative, rule-establishing judgment to the effect that keeping a hopelessly defective infant alive for the purpose of using its organs is wrong. I will no doubt have reason to do what I can to get other people to accept this judgment of mine, for if it becomes generally accepted, I will have played a beneficial part in a process of moral legislation. But even if it plays no such causal role, the judgment may be justified. It could not, of course, be justified by the fact that there is a generally accepted rule against this behavior, for there is not; instead, it is justified by the fact that such a rule ought to be accepted. If I and others are quite conscious of the fact that no such rule is already accepted, and perhaps that the matter is a controversial one, then the language used in my judgment will no doubt reflect that fact. Instead of saying, flatly, "It is wrong . . . " my language might reflect the obvious fact of controversy and uncertainty. I might then say, "We should not accept the idea that a hopelessly defective infant . . . " or "We ought to consider it wrong to . . . ."

8

Moral analogues of interpretation and legislation

8.1. HOW DOES MORAL LEGISLATION OCCUR?

This chapter is devoted to further exploration of the processes by which people do (and ought to) reason and act using moral rules. We shall examine some hypothetical examples of moral reasoning and debate, both in contexts in which judgment has an adjudicative character, and those in which it is more like the legislative. First, we need to understand how moral debate can take on a kind of collective character, aiming at a collective conclusion which is understood to apply to everyone, rather than merely being a process by which so many separate individual moral opinions tend to overlap. Secondly, we need to understand how collective moral agreement can be reached in large groups, such as nations. Although people in very small groups may often be able to reach a consensus, in a large and pluralistic nation there are obstacles that make this more difficult. Thus, it might seem unrealistic to suppose that a moral rule can come to be generally accepted, by any kind of process of public deliberation anyway, in a large group.

The very topic of this chapter warrants a special caveat. To think of social moral rules as the outcome of utilitarian reflection, assessment, and deliberate legislative actions may seem to presuppose a commitment to what Hayek has called "rationalist constructivism": the view that

all institutions which benefit humanity have in the past and ought in the future to be invented in clear awareness of the desirable effects that they produce; that they are to be approved and respected only to the extent that we can show that the particular effects they will produce in any given situation are preferable to the effects another arrangement would produce; that we have it in our power so to shape our institutions that of all possible sets of results that which we prefer to all others will be realized; and that our reason should never resort to automatic or mechanical devices when conscious consideration of all factors would make preferable an outcome different from that of the spontaneous process.[1]

No doubt Hayek is right in his claim that much moral philosophy in the utilitarian tradition has made just such mistaken assumptions. But we, at least, can opt for a consequentialist moral theory that does not suppose that our powers to reason about and adopt moral rules are so great. We may allow for the possibility that, in many departments of human interaction, the best available result will likely be that which will be arrived at through spontaneous mutual adjustments that individuals make to one another, and reflected in the moral judgments emerging from this process. Just as it may sometimes lead us much more reliably to the better result if we allow production and prices to be set by the interplay of free market forces, so too we might be best advised to allow moral rules to develop through long-term incremental processes of interaction on the part of many individuals. We might be systematically deceiving ourselves if we suppose that we can do better than that through some single person's or group's conscious deliberation and planning. Thus in speaking of "adopting" or "replacing" moral rules, we need to keep our limitations in mind. We also need to bear in mind the limits of rational understanding when evaluating an existing moral rule or code. For that which has developed out of a spontaneous process of mutual adjustment among the aims and information of many people may have functions and benefits which are difficult or impossible to grasp from some single perspective with minimal information. Most importantly, to recognize the limits of our capacities to understand, and then to adopt or change, moral codes is not to opt for a mindless conservatism, or to reject rationality or rational criticism; it is itself the rational thing for a consequentialist to do.

8.2. A PROBLEM ABOUT THE UNIVERSALITY AND SCOPE OF MORAL RULES

A preliminary question must first be addressed if we are to understand how moral rules can be created or changed. Nearly all philosophers agree that moral judgments are universalizable, that if an action X is wrong, then any relevantly similar action Y is wrong.

---

1 Hayek, 1967, p. 85. See also Hayek, 1978, ch. 1.

Expressed using the idea of moral rules, moral rules are to apply to all. However, if we are to think of moral rules, to evaluate them, formulate them, argue for them, as applying to all, it is obvious that we need to know more about the scope of this "all." There are different ways in which this universality might be understood. We can distinguish two general lines of approach. One is to think of moral rules as holding for, say, all human beings, whatever their society or historical period. On this conception, the important differences between the obligations attaching to different roles, circumstances, and cultures are provided for within rules that themselves have intersocietal validity. Another line of approach is to introduce a degree of relativity to society, thinking of at least some moral rules as valid for, and applying to, a particular society only.

There are problems connected with each of these lines of approach. As others have noted,[2] if rules are thought not to have intersocietal validity, then we must embrace a degree of relativism, to the extent, at least, that we admit that the same type of action that is right in one society is wrong in another. And this may seem odd. Further, if the validity of rules is linked to a particular society – the society of the agent, say – we have the task of explaining just what "the society" of the agent is. On the other hand, if we think of moral rules as only those that have intersocietal validity, we encounter the equally difficult problem of explaining what they are without conceiving them to be absurdly complex. (It is very likely that this demand for universality, combined with the demand for simplicity, has been for many philosophers one of the leading attractions of act consequentialism.) This enormous complexity would also make such rules ill-suited for everything connected to action guidance; for example, understandability and teachability.

Another important consideration weighs in favor of restricting the scope of the validity of at least some moral rules to particular societies. Given the fact that collective rules must be understood by members of a group to apply equally to all its members, and that distinctions made by a rule will be public and at least knowable to all, it will usually be worse if everyone thinks of themselves as bound by a single rule that makes too many distinctions among

2 My discussion of this here and in the previous paragraph owes much to Brandt, in Bayles, 1968, esp. sect. 7. More generally, see Wong, 1984.

individuals than if members of separate groups think of themselves as bound by two separate rules. When we think of rules as public and applicable to all, there can be a crucial difference between (1) group $(A + B)$ collectively addressing a single requirement to its members, though explicitly making an exception for members of B, and (2) group A collectively addressing a single rule to members of A only, with group B collectively addressing either no rule or a permission to members of B only. The crucial difference is that in case (2), the solidarity, mutual respect, and sense of equality that prevails in each of the two groups can be preserved; but in case (1), the use of a single rule making a public exception for a whole set of individuals is likely to be perceived as making an invidious and arbitrary distinction. Thus (1) would, in some cases anyway, be inconsistent with solidarity, mutual respect, and a sense of equality. That the rule's source was the combined $(A + B)$ naturally raises the question, why should that entity treat its members A differently from its members B? The demand for consistency and nonarbitrariness applies to *its* rules. Such is not the case if there are two rules emanating from two unrelated sources. For there would then be no single entity, to which attributions of inconsistency or arbitrariness would make sense. This is an additional way in which, when rules are conceived as public, collective strategies addressed by a collective entity to its individual members equally, rules that are materially equivalent in the logician's sense may not be equally desirable.

Indeed, there seems to be no a priori reason why a moral-legislative judgment must apply, or be intended to apply, to all human beings. In claiming "X is wrong," I do presuppose universality, at least for an understood group; but that group need not always be the largest group imaginable. It may apply to a much narrower group. I might judge, for example, that drinking alcohol is wrong, understanding thereby that it is wrong for *us,* in our group, tribe, or nation, to drink alcohol. If the drinking of alcohol has been the cause of serious social problems in my community, that might well give me reason for judging that it is wrong. But I need not be so presumptuous as to suppose that a moral permission to drink would have the same bad results in your community, the members having always been able to drink in moderation.

On balance, the most promising line of approach for our purposes is that which conceives of at least some moral rules as having a

171

restricted scope of application. Given the premise that moral rules and principles are to be publicly available guides to action, rules of restricted scope will often have significant utilitarian advantages over rules that are understood to be valid for, say, all beings with moral capacities. Moreover, the primary principle is still understood to have unrestricted scope. Should conflicts between rules of restricted scope arise, moral agents can still make appeal to an unrestrictedly universal principle as a method for filling gaps and resolving disputes.

This leaves us with the problem of determining the range of application of particular moral rules. In practice there are a number of factors that enable us to make sense of this. Indeed, the natural boundaries of the group to which the rule ought to be addressed are often clear. Given such factors as physical and social proximity to other people – living among them and being accepted by them as one of them – one can recognize oneself as a participant in an enterprise of mutual self-governance through moral rules. Recognizing that excessive drinking of alcohol is a problem in community X, that X is my community because of my presence there, my recognition by others as one of them, and because of the expectation that others have of me, I know that the rule forbidding all drinking of alcohol except on special ceremonial occasions applies to me, and that it applies to me by virtue of my membership in the community. Making the claim that drinking except on ceremonial occasions is wrong, I might reasonably want myself to be understood as claiming that it is wrong for this community, thereby making no further claim about larger communities, or all moral beings. It is, after all, these people, living in their circumstances, who have this social problem to be addressed. I am one of them in the sense that I am regarded as having equal status, both as a participant in moral legislation and as one subject to the rules of the community. I am therefore in a position to advocate a solution as one of them, rather than as an outsider attempting to impose a solution.

One of the main questions about the legislation of moral rules is how they can be brought into existence by a process of collective deliberation, particularly when the group is large and heterogeneous, and it would be appropriate for the rule to have a wide scope. It may help to consider some examples. The examples that follow were chosen mostly because they lie close at hand. Many other examples, some of which would no doubt have worked better for illustrative purposes, could have been chosen.

8.3. AN EXAMPLE: SOFTWARE PROPERTY RIGHTS AND THE ROLE OF THE LAW

In morality as in law, we frequently must provide answers to questions that are either new, or newly troubling. Thus we all know that it is wrong to go onto a farmer's land and take the potatoes that he has planted, irrigated, and cultivated; but when someone has created a new piece of computer software, we may be faced with an entirely new question: It may be wrong to make direct copies of the program, but is it wrong to copy its look and feel; that is, the way it presents material on the screen? Is it wrong to copy the commands that it recognizes?[3]

Now, it might seem that the only question about wrongness that would interest anyone here is the legal question. Of course we are interested in knowing whether copying software will lead to liability in a court of law. But how can this be a moral question? As a legal question, the thought runs, it will be decided authoritatively in a legal forum. As a moral question, it is idle. No doubt it is true that the bulk of whatever attention this question gets will be focused on its likely legal resolution. But this should not obscure the moral analogues to the legal questions. I need to know whether I am doing a moral wrong in copying someone else's software for my use, perhaps even for my business use. If the question has not yet been resolved in the courts, I still need to reflect on what is morally right; that is, on the kinds of rules and practices we ought to adopt, and the moral teaching and example that need to guide behavior. Even if the question has been resolved in the courts, and the resulting legal rule is a reasonable one, reasons may remain for thinking of certain things as morally wrong even though they are legally permitted.

---

3 Esther Dyson, "New Product or Knockoff?" in *Forbes Magazine* (June 15, 1987), p. 272. Dyson's perception of the need for laws to settle these questions is that "new situations require new ethics. Problems arise when ethical issues aren't clear – or rather, when there are several clear answers, depending on who you are. That's when laws come in, not to resolve ethical questions but to make everyone play by the same rules."

Now, one procedure for arriving at answers to questions like these would be to engage in moral analysis and debate. Out of such a debate would emerge additional rules defining the boundaries of property rights such as these. But the disadvantages of such a procedure are obvious. The debate would need at least to be a national debate, given the importance of nationally recognized property rights boundaries, and such a debate would be nearly impossible to conduct with any hope of satisfactory resolution. If property "rules of the game" are indeed necessary, we would no doubt rely on the legislative action of the United States Congress to settle, not just the legal disputes that are likely to appear before the courts of the land, but some of the moral issues as well. Our reliance on the law to develop a legal rule would be especially appropriate if the need to have some rule or other was at least as important as having a good rule. If a legal rule is then created, and it is a plausible (though not necessarily ideal) solution to the problem, it will tend to be regarded as the moral solution to the problem as well: If the law prohibits even using the same screen formatting that another successfully marketed software uses, those who think about such issues at all will tend to accept the notion that to do such copying without the creator's consent is indeed morally wrong. If the law explicitly permits this, then such copying will tend to be regarded as morally permissible.

My claim here is partly a sociological and psychological claim, but partly a claim about the kinds of facts that provide good reasons for moral conclusions. As a matter of sociological fact, we do rely on the legislative and judicial actions of legal organs for definitive solutions, not just to legal questions, but to their moral analogues. This is no doubt one reason why people often pay such close attention to legal decisions in areas in which they are highly unlikely to be touched by legal disputes. Some (potentially) moral questions are simply too complex and technical to be settled using the everyday methods of opinion, persuasion, and debate. In other cases, our need to reach some wide, useable national consensus would simply be impossible to satisfy in a heterogeneous society that has no national priesthood or institutionalized religion. Lawrence Friedman has advanced the thesis that it is precisely in a large and heterogeneous society like our own in which people tend to rely on the law as a way of resolving difficult moral issues:

174

As other authorities weaken, the role of law becomes stronger, as an impartial, impersonal arbiter of disputes. Law is a way out of the dilemmas of politics and controversy. Even if this idea of law above and beyond all politics is a myth, it is still a valuable way to appeal to people's inner voices, to motives higher than their crude self-interest. All this may explain the trend so many have noticed: the trend to adjudicate all sorts of social and economic questions. In court, these questions get answers; and both sides usually respect what the courts decide.[4]

This crystallization of collective moral opinion might be brought about through decisions of the courts, or through actions of the legislature. In either case, a moral debate about how we, as a nation, are henceforth to regard certain behavior – from a moral, as well as from a legal, point of view – can be settled. On the assumption that the resulting legal rule provides a morally justified model for a moral rule, the resulting moral rule is presumptively justified too. In this way, the validity of the resulting generally accepted moral rule is not a function of the mere fact that it is patterned after a law; rather, it is valid if and only if it is morally justified.

The use of the law as a model for moral reasoning does not require that the law on the relevant subject be widely known. If the questions of software property rights get a definitive legal resolution, it is unlikely that many people other than specialists will even know about it. In what sense then does a generally accepted moral rule result from the legal resolution? For it would seem that a generally accepted moral rule could hardly be modeled after an obscure, little-known legal rule. But this difficulty is not as significant as it may appear. In practice there are not many people who face immediate ethical dilemmas about the copying of software features. When one does need to reflect on those questions, it is reasonable to turn to the existing law for help. If there is already a legal rule defining software property rights, and if a moral analogue of this legal rule would be morally justified, then one will be reasonable in accepting the analogous moral rule. This is reasonable because, among other things, it is reasonable to suppose that other moral agents will come to the same conclusion: If there is need for moral agents to coordinate their judgments and actions around some justified rule, and the law already provides a model for such a rule, then moral agents will presumably model their

4 Friedman, 1984, p. 275.

moral thinking on the legal rule. Its existence provides the most salient and natural focus of coordination, and it will be reasonable for everyone to believe that it does.

8.4. THE PRIVACY OF CANDIDATES RUNNING FOR PUBLIC OFFICE

If the issue about the rights of software makers over their product ever gets definitively settled, it is likely to be settled first in the legal system. There is not likely to be any spontaneous national debate about the subject. In the case of at least some of the boundaries of privacy rights, however, the moral debate has already taken place to a large extent outside of any legal forum, and it would be easy to imagine some fairly clear-cut consensus emerging without reliance on any action of a legislature or other legal organ.

We have some generally prevailing understandings about the circumstances under which individual privacy must be respected. For example, we do not think it appropriate to ask highly personal questions either about, or of, one who is interviewing for a job. In recent years, the view has become accepted that it is improper to inquire into a job applicant's, especially a woman job applicant's, marital status. And it would be considered an invasion of a job applicant's privacy to station investigators outside of his or her home at all hours in order to obtain information about that person's various relationships with other people.

Yet, in the spring of 1987, precisely that kind of scrutiny was conducted by the national press of an individual's private life, albeit the private life of a very public individual, Senator Gary Hart. After repeated rumors in the press about adultery, and after Mr. Hart issued a dare to reporters to catch him in a compromising situation, newspaper reporters had camped out across the street from Mr. Hart's home on Capitol Hill, watching the house to observe who entered and left, and at what times. The subsequent reports in the media eventually led, by a series of events familiar enough to obviate recounting here, to Mr. Hart's withdrawal of his candidacy for the Presidency of the United States. There ensued a major public debate on whether the newspaper reporters had violated Mr. Hart's moral right to privacy. First, there was the question of whether such information is even relevant to one's candidacy for office, however high the office. Many held that it was not, and that there

176

is many a democracy in the world that flourishes without any such understanding that the press or public are free to intrude on a candidate's private life. However, most commentators seemed eventually to concede that such information was relevant to the public's assessment of a candidate's character, but that, relevant or not, getting the information in that way was a violation of the candidate's right to privacy.

On one side of this debate there were those, including some distinguished journalists, who argued that watching, and reporting on, the comings and goings from somebody's house is simply wrong; that the right of privacy belongs in equal measure to everyone, whether candidates for high office or not, and that newspaper reporters must show that they adhere to the same standards of ethical behavior to which everyone else is held. Apart from claiming that Mr. Hart had in fact dared reporters to watch his every move, those on the other side of the debate claimed that we should not think of candidates for public office, especially the Presidency, as having the same right to privacy that is enjoyed by the ordinary citizen. Given the importance of the office, and the public's legitimate, fundamentally important interest in knowing even rather intimate details of a potential president's life-style, such behavior as that of the *Miami Herald* reporters should not be considered wrong.

Much of this moral debate was framed in legislative terms, as if the main question were one of how we ought henceforth to regard such intrusive behavior on the part of the press. Questions of interpreting and applying our existing moral understandings to this particular instance of behavior tended therefore to be treated as less important than questions about what general rules we ought to accept from now on. No doubt one of the reasons for this moral-legislative focus was that conventional understandings were simply unclear about the boundaries of the right of privacy in this area. Both judgments – that the particular instance of behavior was wrong, and that it was not wrong – were uncertain precisely because of the lack of clear consensus about such a case. A second reason was the perception on the part of many that, whatever the rules might be as they stand, they ought henceforth to allow for a greater degree of intrusiveness into the personal lives of candidates for high office than of ordinary people. A panel discussion of the ethical issues, conducted by Morley Safer of CBS's "Sixty Minutes," fo-

177

cused in just this legislative way on the rules that ought to be accepted. According to the published account of the discussion, Safer told a Stanford audience of two thousand alumni and guests that Democrats owe "a debt of gratitude" to the *Miami Herald* for their actions. Other panelists said they were "inordinately proud" of the *Herald* for its actions. The report went on:

All three panelists defended the press' role in the Hart story, noting that the so-called 'right to privacy' is a relatively new judicial concept that does not necessarily extend to public figures.

'The responsible press has never peeped into the keyholes of private people, and rarely into the keyholes of public figures. But when a man runs for president, the zone of his privacy becomes very small,' Watson [Washington Bureau Chief for ABC News] noted, 'People whose personal lives can't stand scrutiny should get out.'[5]

Of special interest is the reference here to the right to privacy as a "relatively new" concept that "does not necessarily extend to public figures." Whereas this is an indirect reference to the law, it is not mainly about the law, but about morality. If such matters had been debated and settled either in the legislatures or the courts, that, presumably, would be a different matter. For then we would no doubt use the law as our model for moral judgment. But things are unsettled as they stand, and a rule is called for. It is clear that the three panelists believe that certain limits on the right to privacy should apply to candidates for high office. If their view is influential and persuasive, and if it comes to be shared by enough others, the matter will become settled. The very public case of Senator Hart versus *The Miami Herald* newspaper will come to constitute something like a precedent to which future reporters can point in defending the claim that they are not only not violating any rights, but merely doing their duty, performing a vital function in a democracy. And if it is in fact better that the right to privacy is circumscribed in this way, and if the resulting generally accepted rule is justified, they may be right.

It is necessary to pause to consider an objection. It would seem that the actual process by which moral norms of any kind get changed is one in which individuals act separately; that is, we see that an existing moral norm is unacceptable, and we just start acting in the way that we think right. We do not wait for some community

5 The *Stanford Observer*, May, 1987, p. 24.

consensus to develop. But if there is a norm in place, then to act for the best would seem to constitute a violation of the authority of the existing norms of the community. Consequently, the dilemma for those who accept the authority of the existing norm in such a situation is either to reject the existing norm, or to wait for the needed new consensus to develop. As a descriptive claim, the objection proceeds, this seems false; for we do not wait for consensus. As a normative claim, the method would be impractical for large groups because of the sheer difficulties in coordinating moral opinion around a new norm.

The privacy example provides a useful illustration and test case. For the behavior of the reporters may constitute just the kind of actions that, although wrong given the de facto standards in force at the time, come to be regarded as permissible under the new rules. (Another possibility which I presently ignore is that the rightness or wrongness of this kind of invasion of privacy is still unsettled and indeterminate; that it is important that there be some generally accepted rule about this, though it is not clear which would be best.) Now, suppose that that is what the reporters did: their action was an invasion of privacy, and wrong according to then-prevailing standards, though permissible by the standards that come to be accepted in the wake of the rule's violation. There are several questions. First, a descriptive question: In such a case, do individuals simply act on their own best judgment of what the best rule would require or of which action would produce the best results in the circumstances? The person concerned about doing the right thing, it would seem, will consult the generally accepted rules about such behavior. If it is well understood that a certain type of behavior lies well over the accepted borderline and in the area of invasion of privacy, that fact ought to be taken seriously, even though, on a different and better drawing of the boundaries, the behavior would not count as a violation of privacy. This accepted borderline will be viewed, not as a generally useful guide to the sorts of actions that are right on act-utilitarian grounds, but as a standard of right behavior that excludes some of the normally relevant considerations about promoting overall good. Above all, in considering what is actually accepted or has potential acceptance, one is not simply acting alone. One does not simply follow the course of individual rationality, attempting to act in a way that has the best consequences.

179

Secondly, if the prevailing rule is then violated, does that not constitute a wrongdoing that defies the authority of the prevailing rule? It may indeed. It may be both a wrongdoing and something about which we can, in retrospect, be glad that it happened. Perhaps it was wrong for that violation of privacy to have taken place. We need understood boundaries of privacy, and those were the understood boundaries at that time. The reporters did wrong in not respecting the boundaries, but, as a consequence, some beneficial changes have been brought about. Now, one reason why it might be difficult to think of such an action as wrong is that it did produce more overall good. Because the action did produce a beneficial revision in accepted boundaries, it would seem to be the kind of action that is right and to be encouraged, not the opposite. Moreover, if the action is wrong, that would seem to imply that the most typical route to bringing about improvements in prevailing morality is one that involves wrongdoing. Presumably we want to encourage people to bring about beneficial changes, but if we do so, we would be encouraging wrongdoing. If we do not, we must settle for the status quo.

Fortunately, this is a false dilemma. We need not worry about being stuck with the status quo morality. Not everyone will in fact be so respectful of existing rules that there will be no violations. There will always be rule violations that can then help to bring about the benefits of an improved morality. Indeed, it might be collectively rational for people in a group to agree upon, and then teach and otherwise reinforce, a standard or right behavior, knowing that (i) that standard might turn out to be imperfect and open to improvement, and (ii) that the standard should not itself include exceptions for violations aimed at its improvement. Again, the reason for (ii) might be that to authorize and encourage such behavior would be self-defeating, and that, anyway, there will be quite enough violations and disrespect for the rule to perform the function of allowing for change. But even this grants too much, for it overstates the case for bringing about changes in the de facto morality through deliberate violations of that morality. There are many other ways in which an accepted rule can be challenged without acts of defiance. For what the rule requires is that people act (or not act) in certain ways. If it is well recognized that to spy on a person – any person – at their home is a wrong because a violation of their privacy, then it is the spying that is wrong by the accepted

180

standard, not the public questioning and challenging of the accepted standard. It just happens to be the case that many of the best publicized moral debates have arisen because of putative violations of accepted standards. But there is no necessity in this. Accepted standards can be, and are, debated in the absence of violations, and moral opinion can change as a result. Perhaps this sort of public moral deliberation ought to occur much more often than it does. Perhaps we ought not to have waited until the case of Senator Hart versus *The Miami Herald* to reflect on what public opinion ought to be on the question of spying on candidates for high office, and whether the public has a sufficiently important and legitimate interest in knowing about private lives in such cases as to carve an exception in the currently understood right of privacy.

Finally, if one is in such a position, ought one to violate this code, doing wrong in order to bring about an improved moral code? The very formulation of the question may seem to give it an air of paradox. For one ought not to do wrong, but it is also the case that one ought to do good by bringing about improvements in the moral code, and this violation of the code may be the only way an improved code will result. We should first notice how unlikely situations like this will be. Thus in many cases the rule, understood in light of its justifying rationale, will clearly prohibit ordinary intrusions on the ordinary person's privacy, but will be at least unclear if not silent about the case of the candidate for high office, the public's need to know, and the dare that the candidate issued to reporters. But even if spying on a presidential candidate really is a violation of his generally understood right to privacy, it still does not follow that those who violate that right ought to have done as they did, nor that we ought to encourage them to do as they did. In retrospect we might be correct in judging (i) that, given the situation before the fact, the action ought not to have been done; (ii) that the action was and remains wrong; but (iii) that it all turned out well in the end; and so (iv) those who did it ought not to be blamed, or at least, not blamed severely, for what they did. In short, with respect to some wrongs, we can in retrospect be glad they occurred. This helps to dispel the air of paradox. It may seem odd that wrongdoing can sometimes be a benefit to society and its moral code, but it is true.

Nor does the judgment that the action was or would be wrong entail that its agent is in any way an immoral person. An immoral person, we may suppose, is one whose concern for, and disposition to do, the right is defective. One who knowingly does wrong, or is insufficiently concerned about whether his actions might be wrong, is an immoral person, especially if these deficiencies are part of a general pattern actually manifested in action. But a particular instance of knowing wrongdoing does not add up to immorality; indeed, if the sincere purpose behind it is to bring about improvements in prevailing moral thinking, it may be evidence of an especially deep concern for morality and the right. Just as the immoral person can often be one who usually does the morally right thing, a highly moral person can, and no doubt will, sometimes knowingly do wrong. This is not to say that the knowing wrongdoing itself adds anything good to one's character, or that by itself it reflects positively on one. It is rather that, given the larger context – that the action arises out of a deep concern to do good by improving moral opinion, the action tends to confirm, rather than disconfirm, what we knew already: that the agent is a highly moral person sincerely concerned, perhaps even too concerned, to do good.

8.5. SNOWY EGRETS AND THEIR FEATHERS

We are rightly concerned about the continued flourishing of animal species, even though we typically do not show the same degree of concern about any particular animal, the major exception, of course, being family pets. For a variety of reasons, the continued flourishing of a species is at least useful to us in many ways, providing aesthetic enjoyment, ecological balance, and possible benefits to medical research, among other things. The continued flourishing of a species may also be an intrinsically good thing. So when our human behavior threatens a species, we have reason for directing and restricting our behavior.

Snowy egrets, an exceptionally beautiful bird, were near extinction about a century ago. They were being killed in great numbers for their feathers, which were in demand for the dresses, fans, and hats of fashion-conscious women. But public opinion turned against the killings, mostly because of the efforts of leaders of public opinion. One writer, Henry C. Mercer, described painful scenes of the killings, and of "ethereal parents, whose instinct brought them hovering back to the trees where their young cried from the

182

nests, and their mates in wedding plumes lay bleeding." These descriptions powerfully affected the climate of moral opinion:

As more and more reports like these were published, reaction set in. Women wearing feathers were jeered at on the streets as those in wild furs sometimes are today. Queen Victoria decreed that military officers should no longer wear egret feathers in their hats. Fledgling Audubon societies worked for legislation that would outlaw plume hunting. They hired their own wardens to enforce new laws, men who risked their lives for the lives of birds.[6]

This shift of moral opinion about the killing of snowy egrets, I suggest, is most plausibly construed as having the effect of a piece of moral legislation; that is, as a case in which the general acceptance of a new rule itself alters the normative position of members of the society in question, making an action wrong that, without the general acceptance of the rule, either would be permissible or would have an unclear and ill-defined normative status. It is, I suggest, the moral analogue of legislation that serves to deal with an accumulative harm (Chapter 6, Section 6.5) by setting a standard of wrongfulness where either no standard or only a vaguely applicable standard existed before.

Before arguing for this construal, however, I should like to consider two other possible construals. On each of these, the shift in public opinion would be understood only as a recognition of wrongness, a "waking up" to the fact that what people had been doing was already wrong independently of the acceptance of any rule. One possibility is that it is virtually never consistent with the primary principle to kill such creatures merely for human ornamentation, that the value of an individual egret's life is almost always greater than the value of satisfying the desires of the fashion conscious. This possibility is to be taken seriously if the snowy egret population has already been considerably reduced, if not endangered. But it is much less plausible if that has not yet happened. Indeed, if our concern is the flourishing of the species, the moderate thinning out of a heavy population of egrets might actually do positive good. Then there is a second possibility: that for some number X between 0 and 100, it is the case that after X percent have been killed by humans, the action of killing an egret for its

6 "Reprieve for the Showy Snowy Egret," *Smithsonian Magazine* 19, no. 8 (November 1988): 104, 106–07.

feathers becomes morally wrong. Thus X represents the theoretical threshold above which the killing of egrets becomes a bad utilitarian bargain, even though X may be a number that no one can discern with any precision.

Now, if the killing has clearly gone beyond the threshold, one can safely, though not with absolute certainty, presume that any individual killing will do more harm than good. In that case, a "recognition" construal would be fairly plausible. Yet even at that we would not have anything like a categorical prohibition, but only an especially strong indication that, in the absence of specific information to the contrary, any particular instance of killing one of the birds is likely to be wrong. But if the amount of killing has only gone within the neighborhood of the threshold, the presumption becomes much less certain. So if at this time writers like Henry Mercer, leaders like Queen Victoria, and groups like the Audubon Society manage through their influence to bring about a strong consensus against such killings, so that there develops a generally accepted rule that such killings are wrong, period; that in applying the rule people are not to balance in the usual way considerations about doing good and harm, but are to exclude some of those considerations; and that this rule is understood to apply to all rather than merely to serve as the best, most advisable strategy for the average person, then the most natural construal of this is as a social rule that preempts the primary principle. And that is to say that it not only claims to preempt the primary principle, but does preempt it. Part of the reason for this, we must here again recall, is that the having of some such rule in the circumstances is itself a utilitarian benefit over and above the behavior it secures. It serves to clarify and further define the right in an area of behavior where such clarification is needed. In addition, it may be collectively rational to adopt such a public rule even well before the X percent point has been reached. Thus if it is clear that the tendency to kill these creatures is so strong as eventually to bring about the destruction of the species; at least in the absence of moral counterpressure, the general acceptance of a prohibiting rule may be collectively desirable. That this is so shows that the rule cannot be regarded merely as a good indication, or summary, of the fact that acts of killing egrets have now reached the point of becoming (most of the time) wrong on other (e.g., act-utilitarian) grounds. For that

184

point has not yet been reached, though it will be if moral pressure is not exerted well in advance.

It might be objected here that this analysis supposes individual persons, like Queen Victoria or Henry Mercer, somehow to have special legislative authority to place ordinary people under moral obligations, as if, say, Queen Victoria, in addition to her authority to place her military officers under an obligation not to wear egret feathers, also has the authority to create a moral rule placing the ordinary citizen of the world under an obligation not to kill egrets. And this would surely be an odd conclusion to reach. But the objection would rest on a misunderstanding. Queen Victoria, because of her great influence and salient position, can play a causal role in bringing about a change in moral opinion. Perhaps she can even act to coordinate moral opinion around a quite specific rule. But none of this implies that she has authority to create valid moral rules, or that she is understood to have the normative power, through her decrees, to limit anyone's moral liberty, imposing on them a duty not to kill egrets (i.e., a duty that they would not have but for the decree). Nor does it imply that she is a moral authority in the different sense that her moral judgments are especially likely to be correct. Her power consists rather in the ability to bring about the general acceptance of a moral rule, the justification and legitimate authority of which then rests on independent grounds. The idea of moral legislation therefore presupposes neither that any person has special moral insight or judgment, nor that any person has the authority to create moral duties. Neither, for that matter, does it presuppose the negation of either of these ideas.

Correctly understood, the intended and justified scope of the resulting rule prohibiting the killing of the egrets would seem to be all of humanity. This broad scope would be justified if, as was no doubt the case, the problem to which the rule was addressed was itself of world-wide scope. By this I mean something like the following. We can suppose that, given the price for their feathers and the wide-spread operation of the profit motive, the killing of snowy egrets would be a problem anywhere they could be found. Moreover, we might be justified in supposing that the killing of snowy egrets anywhere endangers the species as much as it does anywhere else, and that the use to which the birds are put constitutes a bad utilitarian bargain anywhere. Therefore, as members of the

185

world community, we all bear some responsibility for the solution of this problem, if only to acknowledge the authority of this justified rule.

But it is easy to imagine a different set of facts. Suppose that there is an isolated tribe of people who have long had the practice of killing a few snowy egrets so that they may use their feathers for ceremonial and ornamental purposes. Because they never sought to market the feathers, they were never even tempted to kill more than a few of the birds from time to time, and the result is that their actions never threatened the species. It might then be quite reasonable to exclude these people from the scope of the rule. The rule would not even be addressed to them in the first place, and their occasional killing of one of the birds would not be wrong. For the circumstances justifying the rule include the fact that, in the rest of the world anyway, there is an undesirable tendency to be counteracted, and the natural sphere of that undesirable tendency does not include the isolated tribe. In this way, it is not simply the number of acts of killing that we are attempting to affect by use of a rule; it is also the thinking and the tendencies of a group, the natural boundaries and membership of which are determined partly by culture and geographic location.

Indeed, we can imagine what the reply might well be if we were to present to the tribe the judgment that their killing of egrets was also wrong. They could reasonably reply that their actions never came close to endangering the species; that, if the species is endangered today, the responsibility for it rests chiefly with people of other cultures, even though those other people ultimately use the feathers for the same purpose of personal ornament. The reasonableness of this reply would depend upon such factors as the degree of social interaction between the tribe (T) and the rest of the world (W) – in particular, whether any sense of a social unity between the two cultures had developed. If such a sense of social unity has developed, then members of ($T + W$) will come to think of themselves as appropriately governed by the same standards of conduct, and thus as sharing responsibility for the directions and tendencies of their group ($T + W$) and its collective behavior. It might then still be possible, though perhaps less likely, to make a justified exception for members of T, but in the same single rule that applies to all. Because such a procedure presupposes a single moral community, and the idea of some one source of the moral rules that

186

are addressed to all, the procedure makes greater demands for a showing that the exception is nonarbitrary. If on the other hand the sense of social unity has not developed, as we have supposed, it will be reasonable of members of T to think of their behavior as constituting a separate sphere. Indeed, if they discuss what they ought or ought not to do, it need not be with any sense other than that they are literally determining what they ought or ought not to do.

9

Other utilitarian conceptions: Some comparisons

9.1. RAWLS'S "TWO CONCEPTS OF RULES"

The conception of moral rules on which I have relied – viewing them as public, applicable to all, and right-defining – owes much to Rawls's important discussion of the subject. Accordingly, it is necessary to examine the position Rawls took in that article, both in order to state the points of agreement, but also, and more importantly, to explain the differences. For some of the most significant points that Rawls made there as a way of strengthening the case for rule utilitarianism have unfortunately been obscured by ambiguities and gaps in his argument.

Rules as "logically prior" to particular cases

On Rawls's view, what he calls "the rules of practices" are *logically prior* to particular cases in the sense that "there cannot be a particular case of an action falling under a rule of a practice unless there is the practice."[1] He explains this by saying that a particular action would not be described in a particular way unless the practice existed as a background. The main illustrative example is that of a game in which an action – for example, that of stealing a base or striking out – could only be meaningfully described as such against the background of a set of rules. Thus "[i]f one wants to do an action which a certain practice specifies then there is no way to do it except to follow the rules which define it."[2] Assuming that one is engaged in the practice in question, it just does not make sense to raise the question whether the practice applies to one's own case.

---

1 Rawls, 1955, p. 25 (subsequent references are to reprinting in Bayles, 1968, p. 88).
2 Ibid., 1968, p. 89.

For if the form of action contemplated is one defined by the practice, then it does apply.

Taken just as it stands, it is difficult to give this idea a very wide application to moral questions. For it is simply not true, of many morally prohibited actions anyway, that they can only be meaningfully described against the background of an existing practice. For example, an action can meaningfully be described as murder or as the telling of a lie, and thus as wrong, in the absence of any general practice one way or the other.[3] But the notion of rules as logically prior to their instances can, I think, be put in another way. As we have seen, we can think of the point of some rules as that of setting a public standard of rightness in some sphere of behavior. It need not be thought to follow from this that, without such rules, it would make no sense to attribute rightness or wrongness to actions. Here there is a useful parallel in the law. Legislated rules have the function of setting a standard of legal rightness. For disparate areas of human behavior, ranging from criminal law to contracts and torts, legislated rules serve to supplement or replace other standards of rightness already available to legal thinking. Thus legislated rules setting forth the duties of care of, say, real estate developers or manufacturers of cosmetics serve to define those duties. But it certainly does not follow that, in the absence of such legislation, we or the courts could not meaningfully talk about the duties of real estate developers or manufacturers. Nor would courts be bereft of any standards by which they could reach meaningful judgments in these areas. The existence of legislation defining these duties, however, can constitute a great utilitarian advantage, one that could not be secured if we did not have the concept of a rule which is legislated in order to be an important component of the standard of right.

Shorn of what appears to be its false suggestion – that only a few actions could be meaningfully or correctly described as wrong in the absence of an existing practice – the valuable core of Rawls's practice conception is, then, that of a legislated rule, the very function of which is to define the right rather than merely to provide a general summary of what has been found, or is likely, to be right on some independent criterion. However, several important ques-

3 This point is made by McCloskey, in Bayles, 1968, p. 131: "[M]urder and abstinence from murder are activities *logically prior* to a general practice and have a reality independent of a general practice in a way that promise-keeping does not."

tions remain open. Some of these arise from the legislator's top-down perspective, and others from the perspective of the ordinary person who must live under the rules. The main question belonging to the former category has to do with the utilitarian point of having such rules. Rawls gives only a few remarks about their utilitarian point, and more must be said to make a compelling case for rules whose function it is to serve as a right-defining public standard applying equally to all. In the latter category is the troublesome question of how it can be rational to comply with the rule of a practice when doing so would not maximize the very good that it is the point of the practice to advance.

The utilitarian point of having practices

Rawls recognizes that to have a practice, with its associated rules, can confer important utilitarian advantages. In the case of promising, the utilitarian advantages of abdicating "one's title to act in accordance with utilitarian and prudential considerations" are that the future is tied down and plans are coordinated in advance.[4] Now, there can be no doubt that tying down the future and achieving coordination are important utilitarian advantages of rules. But reasons of coordination would seem by themselves to be quite insufficient to justify a rule that is supposed to serve as a public, right-defining standard, and this insufficiency makes the case for such rules appear weak.

Such reasons would seem to justify nothing more than rules that serve as general sign posts or public guides as to the proper course that individuals are to take. For example, it is important that we coordinate our behavior when we are together trying to lift a heavy object, or when we are attempting to pass each other without mishap when traveling in opposite directions on a mountain road. And there are various useful devices for achieving coordination in such cases, like counting to three, or posting signs on the road. But if, in a particular case, we should happen to achieve coordination in some other way, even a coordination that is the opposite of the one called for by the implementing devices upon which we rely, then all has gone well. Indeed, we have each done the right thing. Thus suppose that the road signs indicate that each is to drive

4 Rawls, 1968, p. 76.

on the right. You see me coming around the corner, driving on my left. (This may even have been the result of a reasonable attempt on my part to coordinate with you.) So you, in defiance of the coordinating sign post, drive on your left, too. As a result, we coordinate, and no harm is done. Though we both acted in contravention of the coordinating device, each of us acted rightly. We can even imagine getting into a discussion of the case after the fact. If we did, the crucial question would be whether each reasonably did his part in arriving at coordination. That would be the standard of right action if the road sign is conceived as having a purely coordinative function. So the coordination of action – tying down the future, as Rawls puts it – would seem by itself to provide insufficient rationale for having a rule, the function of which is to define the right; that is, to be, in his terminology, "logically prior" to its instances.

However, if we take into account some further though equally important functions of moral rules, we can see what the utilitarian point of right-defining rules might be. The first clue can be found in Rawls's own choice of words in describing what happens when we reason about promise-keeping. The point of the practice, he holds, is to "abdicate one's *title*" to act in accordance with certain kinds of reasons, and thus to deny the promisor "as a *defense,* any general appeal to the utilitarian principle in accordance with which the practice itself may be justified [emphases mine]." This legal terminology attracts our attention to an important fact about moral principles and rules: Their function is not only to guide our own actions toward individually and collectively good results; it is to serve as a public standard to which we can look in evaluating, justifying, praising, and blaming both our own and others' actions. This function is particularly clear in Rawls's own example of the institution of promising. The institution of promising enables me to know that certain acts of mine, made in the appropriate context, will place me under certain obligations. Having made a promise to you, for example, not only will I know what I morally ought to do, and that certain justifications for action that would have been valid without the promise are valid no longer, but you will know this too. You will be able to make a public issue of it, if only on a small scale, if I do not do as I have promised. You know that you will be able to do so because of the existence of the right-defining standards provided by the institution of promising. Unlike the purely coordinative rules designed to bring about the good state of affairs in which actions are coordinated, these right-defining rules will authoritatively cut off certain lines of defense and justification that would otherwise be available to me. In short, if do we regard the value of right-defining rules as coordination, that valuable co-ordination would at the least have to include the coordination of reason and argument about actions. Quite literally, then, right-defining rules serve as partial authoritative definitions of right action, and as such they perform the role that definitions do elsewhere, enabling us to understand one another and to follow the same paths of reason, argument, and justification.

But the value of right-defining rules still comprises more than coordination, even when this is taken to include the coordination of reasoning and justification. Thus the use of rules that are public and known to apply equally to all advances the good of social union. Their existence provides an additional but important assurance that the demands that morality makes are in practice the same for all persons, and that any exceptions must become part of the rules, knowable to all, and hence justifiable by public standards of justification.

The logical distinction between justifying a practice and justifying a particular action falling under it: The distinction of offices

On Rawls's view, if one is engaged in a practice, it does not make sense to question whether the practice applies to one's own actions. But it can make sense to question the practice itself and ask whether it ought to be changed. To think that particular cases can always be decided on general utilitarian grounds is to make a logical mistake, "misconceiving the logical status of the rules of practices."[5] The rules of practices, unlike the summary conception of rules, provide for a distinction between *offices* and the various forms of argument appropriate to each. "If one seeks to question these rules," he says, "then one's office undergoes a fundamental change: one then assumes the office of one empowered to change and criticize the rules, or the office of a reformer, and so on."[6]

At several points, Rawls strongly encourages the thought that

5 Ibid., pp. 79–80.
6 Ibid., p. 92.

the point he is making is a logical point only, and that it is by itself consistent with virtually any political attitude, conservative or radical. The point, he says, "is simply that where a form of action is specified by a practice there is no justification possible of the particular action of a particular person save by reference to the practice." And no inference is to be drawn as to whether one ought to accept the practices of one's society.[7]

Given these characterizations, two possible objections loom. If something like this conception of moral reasoning is to be made plausible, they must be answered. Otherwise, the distinction between offices, and the distinction on which it rests – that between justifying a practice and justifying a particular action falling under it – are in danger of collapse. One objection, developed by an act consequentialist, would run along the following, by now familiar lines. Even if we suppose that the rules themselves are the best, such that general adherence to them produces the most good of any available set of rules, it does not follow that compliance with them in each case will produce the most good. If in some particular case I know that I can maximize the good by noncompliance with optimific rules, then what reason is there for compliance? Here it will not do simply to cite for me the logical distinction between practice-rules and summary-rules, and to insist that if I really did understand the logical difference between the two, I would know that I can logically only apply the utilitarian principle to the practice-rules rather to particular instances falling under them. What I still need to know is why, given that I am to do good, my doing of good requires acceptance of this particular rule as a practice-rule rather than a summary rule. The point about the "logical distinction" between the two kinds of rules and the differentiation of offices, I take it, does show that *if* I have compelling, good-doing reasons for opting into a practice in the first place, then it is rational for me to comply with its requirements, even if, in some particular instance, I could maximize the good by noncompliance. For I recognize that that sort of "abdication of title" is the whole point of the practice in the first place.

A second objection goes a bit deeper, threatening to destabilize and collapse the distinction between the office of acting under a practice and that of criticizing it. Thus David Lyons argues that,

7 Ibid., p. 97.

even if we do grasp the point of rules on a practice conception, it will always be possible to gain permission to maximize under a de facto practice. For if in some cases better results could be obtained from noncompliance, this

> entails that for every such case there is a class of exceptions that might be allowed by the rules. If such exceptions were allowed by the rules the results would be better on the whole. That is to say, better results would come from observing an alternative set of rules that allowed exceptions in such cases.[8]

To put it somewhat differently, one might say that if criticism of the rules involves a fundamental change of one's office, then so be it: The distinction is only a logical one anyway, and there are no evident barriers to putting on a different hat, switching from judge applying the rules to legislator framing the rules. However one cares to describe the shift to direct application of utilitarian considerations, if Lyons is right there will always be a way to frame an exception in terms of a generalized rule. Then that rule, rather than the de facto practice, is to be taken as defining the right in particular instances.

As Lyons himself would acknowledge, his argument applies when the rules being considered are evaluated solely in terms of their "conformity utility," the utility that would result if behavior were generally to conform to their requirements. It does not apply when the rules are evaluated for their "acceptance utility" as public standards by which people are taught, and their actions guided, judged, praised, and blamed. For it seems clear that the attempt to formulate an exception in a rule that is then to constitute a public standard of the right will sometimes fail because the proposed rule would result in diminished acceptance utility. So the fact that Rawls's rules of practices are to be understood as public rules diminishes the force of Lyons's argument.

But there is a related challenge that goes deeper yet. If one can freely act on one's own, "switching offices" by "legislating" a new and better rule that allows for the needed exception, then the distinction between justifying a practice and justifying a particular instance under a practice will again be threatened with collapse. This is so even if we acknowledge that any such newly "legislated" rule must be evaluated for its utility as a possible public rule, and

8 Lyons, 1965, p. 185.

194

not only for its conformity utility. The point can be illustrated by pursuing Rawls's game analogy. In baseball, if a batter were to ask whether he could have four strikes because he thinks it would be best on the whole for him to have four rather than three, this, Rawls observes, would be most kindly taken as a joke. But it would also be taken most kindly as a joke if the batter were to propose taking four strikes then and there because of his correct assessment that such a rule would be demonstrably better than the present rule. If individuals are virtually always free, on their own and for themselves, to make an allowed exception of their otherwise noncompliant behavior, the only condition being that a formulable rule allowing for the exception be a better public rule than the de facto rule, then Rawls's distinction between offices and the forms of argument appropriate to each would have little substance in practice.

This threat to the stability of Rawls's conception arises from our difficulties in making use of a fundamental fact about the differentiation of offices in more familiar contexts. We can understand what it is to keep separate the roles of judges and legislators in our legal system because that system comprises an actually existing set of rules and practices, around which concrete expectations have been built. We know that there is a time and place for legislation, and a specific group of people elected to consider and enact that legislation. We also know that there are other times and places and procedures for applying already enacted legislation to particular cases. And in baseball, the batter knows that, having already decided to play the game and finding himself at bat, his is not the time and place for obtaining changes in the rules. But moral agents, on the other hand, have no separate, designated legislature, and they know that virtually every occasion for making a moral judgment is potentially an occasion for making some critical assessment of social moral rules. Yet they know that a necessary component of any acceptable moral reason for respecting those rules is that those rules be capable of surviving a critical utilitarian assessment.

To enable us to make use of the compelling features of a practice conception of rules and the associated notion of a differentiation of offices, we must fill in a gap in Rawls's conception. We must provide for: (i) a robust division of legislative and judicial roles, so that not every occasion for rendering particular moral judgment can be automatically transformed into an occasion for adopting a

195

new and better rule; (ii) the idea that the right can be partially defined by actually accepted, rather than hypothetically ideal, rules; (iii) a convincing connection between existing rules and the doing of good so that (a) the validity even of generally accepted rules depends on their role in advancing the good, and (b) it is rational for individual moral agents to accept the preemptive reasons that valid rules provide.

A robust division of legislative and judicial roles is provided when the moral agent thinks of himself or herself as bound by the generally accepted, justified moral rules of a social group, so that whether she or he may act under a new and putatively better rule becomes a question of whether, by publicly advocating and arguing for that new rule, one can secure its actual acceptance. Viewed in this way, there is a robust conception of shift of office: One recognizes that existing justified rules have preemptive force in defining the right, yet, since to be justified, a rule need only satisfy a baseline test of acceptability, one regards oneself as free to point out the deficiencies in accepted moral rules. Whether it is appropriate to point out such deficiencies depends on whether it would reasonably be expected to have the best consequences of various alternatives available to the agent. Whether it is right to act in violation of the existing rule while complying with the better rule, however, is not simply a matter of what would have the best consequences, but of whether the existing rule is justified.

In some cases, advocacy does not take the form of legislative advocacy, but only of the claim that prevailing rules, correctly interpreted, don't call for what people think they call for. Thus I might claim that a promise made in response to the importunate demands of a dying person is not and never was the kind of promise that is morally binding; promises made under pressure do not create obligations. In other cases, advocacy does take the form of a legislative proposal, involving the claim that existing moral rules, even as correctly interpreted, are defective. But in either case, circumstances might be extraordinary enough to warrant going beyond advocacy, making it expedient simply to refuse to comply with the existing justified rule. One would then do a moral wrong, though this wrong might be excusable, and it might even in retrospect be correctly viewed as a fortunate occurrence. In short, the robust division between roles is provided for when moral agents recognize that the question whether there *is* a valid, right-defining rule of a

196

certain sort is not merely a question of any one person's correct judgment about the rule that ideally ought to exist, but of some kind of actual agreement or consensus about a rule which is justified, even if not ideal.

When moral agents so recognize that the existence of a right-defining rule is in part a question of actual agreement, they recognize criteria that are loosely analogous to the familiar procedural rules for adopting legislation. These criteria will of necessity be vague and far rougher than their analogues in the law. Moral agents do not have a designated legislature, but they may and often do have a general understanding that in certain matters where it is important to act and judge in accordance with an agreed upon standard, what one is morally permitted to do depends on a significant degree of actual consensus. Though vague, such second-order criteria are not empty, nor do they require some mechanical counting of opinions. Further, we might have good utilitarian reasons for sharpening these criteria further. For part of the idea of a set of procedural rules for enacting legislation is to provide a clear distinction between those rules which ought on someone's view to exist and define rights and duties, and those rules which actually do define rights and duties. If some of the most important moral rules have the function of serving as public standards applying equally to all, then it will be necessary to preserve and even sharpen this distinction. We could do this, for example, if we consciously made a clearer distinction than we usually do between judgments about what is right and wrong as things stand, and judgments about what we as a community ought or ought not to start regarding to be right and wrong.

The moral reasons for respecting practices

As we have seen, Rawls's account stresses the importance of practices in giving meaning to what one is doing, allowing one's action to be described in a certain way; for example, as striking out. If we ask why actions are to be so described only in accordance with a practice, his answer would seem to be that the practice has simply been accepted, and, assuming one knows what one is doing, it no longer makes sense to ask that question: "Those engaged in a practice recognize the rules as defining it."[9] If you already

9 Rawls, 1968, p. 87.

recognize the rules as the standard that defines how particular cases are to be described, you can logically infer the answer to your question. What you have done is of course describable as having "struck out." To make use of this idea in moral thinking, however, we need to know what analogue there is to having "engaged" in a practice. Most especially, we need to know what moral reason there is for one to recognize and respect a practice. For the issue is not whether an action can be described with some technical term that only has meaning within the context of rules of a game, but whether an action is morally wrong and thus ought not to be done simply because it contravenes an existing practice.

Here we must supplement Rawls's account if an answer is to be provided. A plausible reason for treating certain moral rules and practices as partially defining the right begins with the premises that, first, each person is bound by the primary principle of doing good, and, secondly, that the most good is done through the collective recognition of right-defining rules. Given that such right-defining rules are already recognized by others, and that one can not realistically expect in all situations that ideal rules will be recognized, moral agents have objective reasons for accepting the rules that are already accepted. Unlike the playing of chess or baseball, where the playing of the game is optional and the describability of one's actions in terms of the game is optional for moral agents, the primary principle makes doing the morally wrong thing nonoptional. So in many cases, it will not be reasonable to reject the accepted rule, and one ought to recognize the preemptive reasons it provides.

9.2. BRANDT'S RIGHT-DEFINING IDEAL MORAL CODE

R. B. Brandt has recently provided, in more than one version, a sophisticated rule–utilitarian account of the right.[10] An explanation of the function of rules in his theory will be useful as a contrast with the MLM presented here.

10 My discussion here will be of his earlier (1963) "Toward a Credible Form of Utilitarianism," (in Bayles, 1968, pp. 143–86 pagination below from 1963); and idem, 1979.

The rule utilitarian, Brandt recognizes, is confronted from the start with a choice between two alternative courses that theory might take. When the rule utilitarian takes the right to be defined by a "moral rule," that rule might be taken either to refer to an accepted moral rule, or to a correct moral rule, where correctness is understood as that which best promotes the ultimate end. Brandt allows that a strong reason for adopting the first alternative is that "we shall probably all agree that the moral rules accepted in a community often do fix real obligations on members of the community." But in his view the net advantage rests finally with a modified version of the second alternative, for we do not ordinarily think that we decide moral rightness by reference to accepted rules, and the very notion itself goes counter to the whole tradition emphasizing the role of conscience in ethical reasoning.[11] The modification is designed to take account of the fact that some proposed moral codes, however desirable they might be if they were adopted by everyone, would have bad consequences if they were adopted by an insufficient number. For example, it might have the best results if children were regarded as responsible for an elderly parent who needs help. But it would be far from the best if the Hopi, who place this obligation elsewhere, were to think "that their presently recognized obligation had no standing on this account."[12] So Brandt's early version of rule utilitarianism makes room for existing moral commitments:

The modified theory, then, is this: 'An act is right if and only if it conforms with that learnable set of rules, the recognition of which as morally binding, roughly at the time of the act, by all actual people insofar as these rules are not incompatible with existing fairly decided moral commitments, would maximize intrinsic value.'[13]

Such a theory has a major disadvantage. When it takes into account "existing fairly decided moral commitments," it allows too much. Existing moral commitments may be worse than nonideal; having those rules may result in a net utilitarian loss to society. The utilitarian state of nature in which the primary principle alone reigns

11 Brandt, 1963, pp. 115–17.
12 Ibid., p. 128.
13 Ibid., p. 129.

might be better. The result of the general acceptance of these moral rules may be to impose burdensome obligations where none should be placed at all, where it would be better if people were merely to follow an act–utilitarian principle of doing the most good on a case-by-case basis. The effect of following rules that would maximize given some set of existing moral commitments is to "grandfather in" those background commitments, taking them, in effect, as right-defining simply because they are too deeply held to be changed. If we have no deeper reason than this for respecting an existing rule, our theory would indeed be open to the familiar "rule worship" charge.

In spite of these difficulties, it is clear that the rule utilitarian has good reason for giving special place in the theory to already accepted moral rules provided those rules have some utilitarian merit in the first place. For there may be significant costs associated with the transition to the new and better rule. To hold, without further qualification, that the right thing for anyone to do is that which conforms to the rules of a moral code that would be ideal if accepted is not only utopian; it is utopian in just the kind of way that a utilitarian should seek to avoid. This is particularly the case when we think of moral rules as having the function, among other things, of serving as an understood, agreed upon public standard to which people can make reference, not only in guiding their own behavior, but in criticizing behavior and in defending behavior against criticism.

What is it for a rule to have some utilitarian merit? The most plausible answer to this, I have suggested, takes as a baseline that state of affairs in which behavior is generally governed by the primary principle. If some of the rules of a generally prevailing social morality make things worse than they would be if everyone were simply to be guided by the primary principle, then the pre-vailing rules, however deeply entrenched they may be, should have no preemptive force in the reasoning of a rational utilitarian moral agent. For example, suppose that the existing moral code provides for a burdensome and disutilitarian role differentiation in the rights and duties of men and women, and that this part of the moral code is roughly independent of the rest of the moral code; that is, is not an integral part of a larger set of rules that, taken together, are utilitarianly justified. If that is the case, then the most plausible utilitarian position to take, even for a rule utilitarian, would be to

200

hold that individuals should simply do the best they can, reasoning as ordinary act utilitarians living in an imperfect society. In this way, we allow preemptive force for justified prevailing rules while not giving up utilitarian scrutiny of anything through any process of "grandfathering in."

More recently, Brandt has refined his conception of the right in the following way. His suggestion for a definition of "is morally wrong" is the meaning, "would be prohibited by any moral code which all fully rational persons would tend to support, in preference to all others or to none at all, for the society of the agent, if they expected to spend a lifetime in that society."[14] The code that a fully rational person would tend to support, Brandt explains, is

the one he will expend means to bring about; presumably one whose socialization procedures are both feasible and not too expensive; one simple enough to be understood by most people; and probably one with motivation not so strong as to guarantee conformity in the face of unlimited temptation, and so on.[15]

In considering what a fully rational person would tend to support, we are to rule as "extraneous" certain costs, like the costs to oneself in helping bring about a new code. So when considering whether a rational person would support Code C rather than Code B, one takes into account only the consequences that each code would have if it were in full operation, but with proper subjective probability attached. Thus it would appear that transition costs too would be ruled out as extraneous; they are not among the consequences of the code considered just by itself. It also seems clear from Brandt's comments about codes that have extremely small probability of being adopted, that that small probability does not stand in the way of the code's being supported. Thus one might recognize that public opinion is adamant and stands in the way of change, but still have a positive tendency to support the change. For he will recognize "that his little effort will not have noticeable effects, but that the summation of the support of many like-minded persons over a period of time presumably can have some success."[16]

14 Brandt, 1979, p. 194.
15 Ibid., pp. 189–90.
16 Ibid., p. 191.

Given this notion of a code which the rational person will support, combined with Brandt's concept of the morally wrong as that which would be prohibited by any moral code which all fully rational persons would tend to support, we have a rule utilitarianism which is in some respects practical and empirical, while in other respects oriented toward rules that ideally ought to exist. The practical and empirical orientation is evident in that proposed moral codes are to be evaluated for their learnability and efficiency in securing desirable behavior. The ideal orientation emerges in the ruling that the costs of transition to another code, whether they be costs to oneself or others, are extraneous to the question of rational support; and, because of the fact that one's tendency to support a code need be little affected by the extremely low probability that other people will support it too, this ideal orientation is then transmitted to the concept of the morally wrong.

I believe that this concept of the morally wrong, like Brandt's earlier version, also has major drawbacks. But here the problem is roughly the opposite of that of the earlier version. In the first version, the problem was that accepted rules, if they represent convictions held deeply enough, are taken uncritically for purposes of theory. In the present version, the problem is that existing rules, even if utilitarianly justified in the sense I have proposed, are not taken to define the right so long as there is a better code which arguably would obtain the support of all rational persons. However, this would undercut one of the most important functions of moral rules. In order to provide a public standard of right that applies to all, at least rough agreement about what they are is necessary. If such agreement already exists around a justified though imperfect rule, it would undercut the good of this agreement if moral agents were to adhere to Brandt's definition of the right. This damage would merely be the most obvious if, as in the example of Hopi familial obligations that Brandt discussed in his earlier article, some were to follow the existing rule while others were to follow the ideal definition. But the damage would no doubt also ensue if everyone were to follow the ideal definition; for it is most probable that there is no unique ideal moral code that would be the object of every rational person's choice.

We must have a proper grasp of the utilitarian value of the general

202

acceptance of a justified rule and then of the transition costs from one code or rule to another. To start, there is the problem that Brandt's example of the Hopi is meant to illustrate: It would not be good if some of the Hopi were to take their obligations under the prevailing code less seriously because some ideal code would not impose those same obligations. But there is another kind of cost, one arising from the fact that our moral judgments and our actions serve to communicate to others our stance toward the demands of a social morality. Suppose that on the prevailing moral code people in a particular role are obligated to do X, but that on the moral code that all rational persons would tend to support, people in that role are not obligated to do X. If I decide straightway to judge and then to act in accordance with the ideal, rationally favored code, my actions are likely to be taken by others as showing indifference or contempt for the demands of a justified code that others respect. My action may tend to be viewed as a self-arrogation of power, indicating my unwillingness to be bound by anything but the rules of an ideal code. It is not only odd, but oddly un-utilitarian, to regard these costs of transition as extraneous to the utilitarian's choice of a moral code.

Brandt's defense of his definition of "morally right" focuses on its educational value. It will serve to remind people of the rational basis of morality, and that moral rules are not taboos, heaven-sent, or whatever, but that a moral code is properly subject to change arising from rational human reflection.[17] This is certainly a plausible position for a utilitarian to take. Utilitarians have traditionally sought to remind people of the importance of scrutinizing their moral rules and, if need be, jettisoning them in favor of improved ones. But here we should be reminded that this jettisoning may also have its very significant costs. What is needed, it appears, is some distinction between the different functions of judgments about the morally right.

17 "[A]t least two beneficial educational effects would accrue. First, whenever a person used a moral term he would be reminded that morality is not a matter of conventions, taboos, or uncriticized traditions of the Establishment, as many people today tend to think, or that it is a system of laws handed down from Heaven or self-evident to the Wise, as some others think; but that it has, or can have, the status of being rationally preferred, one which deserves respect but is not something above human reflection, sensitivity, and debate." Brandt, 1979, pp. 194–5.

It is at this point in Brandt's account, I think, where something like Rawls's distinction between the different offices of respecter and legislator of practices could be put to use. We are not compelled to accept Brandt's definition of "morally right" for all contexts of moral judgment and action. Indeed, part of the costs of transition from one moral code to another – those arising from the general perception that the moral critic is self-arrogating and unwilling to follow anything less than ideal rules according to his conception of the ideal – can be avoided if the moral critic publicly recognizes a clear distinction between taking the role of critic and would-be legislator of rules, and taking the role of one bound by rules on equal terms with others.

This is a distinction that we already recognize, albeit sometimes dimly, in ordinary discussion and practice. When criticizing the prevailing moral code, we sometimes frame this criticism in general terms about what the moral code ought to be like, and how our attitudes about right and wrong ought to be changed. And we recognize the difference between lobbying in this way for changes in our moral attitudes, and proceeding in our other "office," judging and acting in particular cases. Thus, you can simultaneously recognize that your obligations, say, as a husband are for everyday purposes of decision and action pretty much as they are prescribed by the moral code, even while you also acknowledge, and publicly assert, that moral attitudes about this, and thus the code, ought to be changed. And, as I argued earlier, there are good utilitarian reasons for strengthening and sharpening this distinction. For when the distinction is observed, the costs of transition to an improved moral code will be reduced. Like people who strongly urge legislative reform even while respecting existing laws, moral agents who attempt to bring about a change in moral attitudes while acknowledging the force of the existing code indicate their willingness to be bound as equals under actually accepted rules. Recognizing this distinction, Brandt's proposal for a definition of "morally right" would work better as a definition for "ought to be generally recognized as morally right." Then, using some baseline test of minimum utilitarian acceptability of a rule or code, the new proposal for "morally right" would be something like "is permitted or required by the actually recognized rules of the society of the agent, provided the acceptance of those rules results in greater net good, for that sphere of behavior, than would the general acceptance of an act-utilitarian principle."

If moral consensus about some kind of behavior has been replaced by controversy, then the importance of maintaining the distinction between offices diminishes in at least one obvious way. For example, if it is already clear that there is no longer any generally accepted moral code about the obligations and rights of husbands toward their wives and wives toward their husbands, there will be less need to distinguish in judgment and practice between urging changes in attitudes and deciding how to act in particular cases. If consensus has evaporated, then judgment and action naturally shifts directly to the legislative. There is no longer a generally accepted rule whose force one would have reasons to acknowledge. The best that one can do in such a situation is to propose a rule, act in accordance with it and generally indicate readiness to acknowledge the force of some justified rule that stands a chance of gaining acceptance.

The main difference, then, between Brandt's concept of moral legislation and that of the MLM is that Brandt's concept seems to make no provision that would prevent individual judgments about moral right and wrong from all collapsing into questions about the moral legislation that all rational persons would choose. And, while it is true that his formulation of the concept of right in his earlier article did make provisions that would prevent this collapse, those provisions were unacceptable because they had the effect of "grandfathering in" existing moral rules simply because they are too firmly held to be dislodged. By contrast, the MLM would have the moral agent approach existing rules by first (i) asking whether an existing rule is justified, then (ii) asking whether the existing rule, interpreted in the light of its rationale, really does require or forbid the action in question; and then, assuming that the first two answers are positive, (iii) making clear what kind of judgment one is making – that is, whether legislative, as to what rules we ought to recognize, or adjudicative, as to what existing rules already require. If the answer to (i) is negative, the moral agent is to be guided by the primary principle of doing good and avoiding evil, and will need to consider, among other things, whether it would be best to propose a rule for general acceptance, or simply to do what act utilitarians always advise doing, namely, to make the best of a bad situation.

Whether rules should be conceived to be right-defining

We have seen that Brandt's concept of the right uses the idea of the rules of a social moral code in the definition of "morally right." On the earlier version, morally right action is defined as that which conforms to rules ("not incompatible" with decided moral commitments), the recognition of which would maximize intrinsic value. On the more recent version just discussed, morally wrong is defined as that which would be prohibited by any moral code which all rational persons would tend to support. Whether one adopts the first or the second version, an important question will need to be answered: Given that some rule on code C satisfies the test, and that a contemplated action X conforms to C, why should the rational moral agent conclude that X is, indeed, morally right and therefore the thing that morally ought to be done? To make this question more precise, we can distinguish within it two subquestions: (1) Why do we need a moral code that contains any right-defining rules? Why would it not be enough to think of the rules of a social moral code very much as Brandt does think of them – as not too complex, as teachable, and as rules that it is desirable for moral agents to have internalized – without thinking of them as standards by which right action is defined? We could, for example, think of Brandt's ideal social moral code as a set of generally useful strategies that at least most moral agents ought to internalize so that they will not yield to temptation and mistake, and will therefore be most likely to do the most good. (2) If moral code C satisfies the appropriate utilitarian test, and X conforms to C, should the moral agent conclude that X is morally right even if X does not maximize the good? Though the general usefulness of rules may be clear enough, their general usefulness does not by itself translate into the necessity of following the rules in those instances when it will not be useful to do so.

When we look carefully at Brandt's concept of a social moral code, it becomes clear that, in his definition of "morally right," the notion of a moral code serves mainly as a heuristic device. It is not to be taken literally as defining what an individual moral

206

agent morally may do. This becomes apparent when we realize that even if an existing social moral code were in every respect ideal from the Brandtian perspective, such that it would be supported by every rational moral agent, we still could not conclude that that code defined what is morally right for any individual. Thus Brandt sees one of the main differences between morality and law in the fact that law does define what is legally right for the individual.[18] Moreover, a social moral code, as he understands it, need not be public, and may consist of nothing more than the overlapping personal moralities of a great majority of people in a group. So if each person in a group has an intrinsic motivation for or against performing a certain type of action in a certain kind of situation as called for by rule R, then R constitutes part of a social morality in G, even though each person is motivated separately, and no one believes that behavior in accordance with R is anything that the members of G can legitimately expect of one another.[19]

It is clear that this conception of the role of a social moral code differs substantially from that of the MLM. There would seem to be no good reason for excluding the possibility that morality as well as law should contain some right-defining rules, at least if we take proper account of their utilitarian advantages. Apart from their more familiar advantages of guiding behavior and providing coordination, public, right-defining rules can provide people with a public understanding about what is right – that is, each has reason to believe that a rule R exists, R indicates to everyone that everyone has reason to believe that R exists, and R indicates to everyone that they have preemptive moral reasons for doing what R requires.[20] This public understanding, I have suggested, is itself a source of good over and above the beneficial conforming behavior it may help to secure. No doubt much of an individual's moral thinking

18 "An individual...need not regard the social code as fixing what his moral obligations really are. ... The point is that the social moral code does not define what is morally right for an individual in the way in which the law defines what is legally right for the individual." Brandt, 1979, p. 173.
19 Brandt, 1979, pp. 165–70. Brandt's conception of a social moral code comes closest to recognizing a kind of collective character when he lists disapproval of others for engaging in actions, against which one has an intrinsic motivation. But to disapprove of someone's actions does not entail the judgment that they have done something that we can legitimately expect them not to do.
20 I have adapted for my purposes Lewis's notion of something's being common knowledge in a group. See Lewis, 1969, p. 56.

is and ought to be guided by those strategies and principles which one thinks would be best for one's own case, or by standards that everyone ought to adopt for themselves, whether they actually have or not. But it would be both dogmatic and unutilitarian to suppose that a social morality, unlike law, *must* consist only of so many overlapping personal codes.

The second question has to do with an individual's reasons for conforming even to an ideal code if conformity in that case does not maximize intrinsic value. That Brandt's account leaves us with no answer to this second question can be partly attributed to the concept of a social moral code that he uses. If a social moral code is conceived to be nothing more than an overlapping set of personal moral codes, there are no rules, the point of which is to serve as the basis for a public understanding about the right. But if there are such rules, one can take the perspective of collective rationality, thinking of oneself as one would think of any arbitrarily chosen member of the group. So if the point of the rules is to constrain the reasoning of all, and if it is rational for one to take part in this collective enterprise of advancing the good, one will have sufficient reason for recognizing the preemptive force of the rules of the enterprise.

9.3. HARE ON THE LEVELS OF MORAL THINKING

R. M. Hare has recently developed a utilitarian conception of moral thinking which, because of his notion of principles that mediate between critical thinking and everyday decision, merits special attention here. Hare distinguishes between what he calls the *intuitive* and *critical* levels of moral thinking. At the intuitive level, we are properly guided by what Hare calls "prima facie principles" (hereafter, PF-principles). These correspond roughly to our everyday convictions about such things as the wrongness of lying, cheating, and killing, and the necessity of being loyal and keeping one's promises. They are more than mere rules of thumb or strategies, for unlike these latter, PF-principles "excite compunction": A moral agent following a PF-principle will have deep feelings corresponding to the intuitions the principle provides. PF-principles serve a useful purpose, guiding us where we would otherwise be likely to make mistakes or yield to the temptation to "cook" rationalizations for what we want to do. Principles that are to serve this purpose must therefore be simple and general rather than complex and specific.[21]

Though they are the principles that we must follow if we are to have the best chance of doing the right, PF-principles are not definitive of "the right act."[22] That role is played by critical principles, appeal to which must sometimes be made, especially in cases where PF-principles come into conflict. Critical moral thinking is act utilitarian "in that, in considering cases, actual or hypothetical, it can be completely specific, leaving out no feature of an act that could be alleged to be relevant." It is also rule utilitarian, but in the limited version of the rule-utilitarian doctrine which allows rules to be of unlimited specificity, and "in effect not distinguishable from act-utilitarianism."[23] It seems clear from this that Hare thinks of the right action as defined by some act–utilitarian principle, however much it may be desirable for us to guide our everyday thinking and decision by the use of PF-principles.

The differences between critical principles and prima facie principles, then, can be summarized in the following way: PF-principles are epistemologically secondary to critical principles, are general, backed by strong compunction, suitable as action guides, but not definitive of the right action. Critical thinking is epistemologically primary, uses an act–utilitarian principle of unlimited specificity, need not be backed by strong compunction (particularly where replaced in some sphere by a PF-principle), is typically deficient as an action guide or decision procedure, but is definitive of the right action. Although by and large we only need to appeal to critical thinking in cases of conflict or revision of our PF-principles, the two levels of thinking can exist side by side. When one thinks critically, as Hare's "archangel," one considers cases as an act utilitarian would; when thinking as a "prole," one reasons as a rule utilitarian.

The function and status of prima facie principles

The status of the PF-principles needs closer examination. Their status, I shall argue, is significantly different from that of generally accepted rules as conceived on the MLM. I do not wish to suggest

21 Hare, 1981, pp. 38–43.
22 Ibid., p. 38.
23 Ibid., p. 43.

that there is no place in the moral thinking of a utilitarian for principles like these, but that they do not serve to explain some of the most important, and utilitarianly necessary, aspects of our moral thinking.

Consider one of Hare's own illustrations of the function of a PF-principle: the case of marital fidelity. The principle of marital fidelity supplies people with presumably desirable reaction patterns, both in judgment and action. Though it is possible, Hare observes, to depict with verisimilitude situations in which the principle leads to unhappy results, and this may lead people to reject the principle, this rejection would not be rational unless such situations are sufficiently common to outweigh the others in which the principle is for the best.[24] This account of the moral principle of marital fidelity is unclear in at least one crucial respect. It does not distinguish between a principle which it is rational for a group collectively to adopt as an action guide that is to apply to all, and a principle which it would be rational for most people, acting as individuals, to adopt. Hare sometimes characterizes the acceptance or rejection of such a principle as a collective, or at least general, function of people in a group, and done with the purpose of applying them equally to everyone. Thus, in addition to speaking of the "acceptance by society" of a principle, or of the "public" being "persuaded" that the principle of marital fidelity ought to be rejected, he speaks also of the adoption of a "set of maxims for general use." However, at other times his formulations suggest that he is thinking of the principles that it is rational for this or that *individual* to accept or reject. Thus he speaks of it being "bad policy to question *one's* [emphasis mine] prima facie principles in situations of stress," or that a particular person may, presumably for his own part only, decide to "qualify" a principle he has accepted for a long time.[25]

Whether Hare would opt for the individual or collective conception of PF-principles, it seems clear that the rationale that he supplies for having such principles justifies only an individual conception, and not a collective one. My argument here recapitulates some of the earlier discussion of collective and individual strategies. Presumably the reason for having a PF-principle about marital fidelity is to help people to resist the obvious temptations to act in

24 Ibid., p. 48.
25 Ibid., pp. 48–51.

ways that, more often than not, are utilitarianly mistaken. Without some such principle, the temptation to "cook" rationalizations in favor of indulging oneself would lead to much unhappiness. But as I argued earlier with respect to strategies, there will be significant differences in the strengths and weaknesses that individuals exhibit, and while some will be in need of such a principle, others will not, or will need only a softened version of the principle. It is a notorious fact that some people regularly yield to a constant and almost obsessive temptation to marital infidelity. It is also a fact that there are some who are never even slightly tempted, though they may find themselves in a bad and unhappy marriage and would even be better off if they developed temptations in order to have something to yield to. So instead of suggesting that a PF-principle of marital fidelity is something that it would be rational, either for the general public to adopt, or to make equally applicable to all, or both, it would be more justified to conclude that different PF-principles should be tailored and adopted to fit different individual situations, depending upon the strengths and weaknesses of the individual in question. Though Hare often speaks of moral principles in the way that it is natural to speak of them – as principles that are somehow designed for general public use, we are left with no rationale, certainly no utilitarian rationale, for this to be the case.

This point can be approached from a different direction, starting with some observations about the role of moral indignation, blame and censure. In an earlier article, Hare distinguishes the function of PF-principles from that of rules of thumb by characterizing the former as principles which, once implanted in individuals, will be "principles which they will not be able to break without the greatest repugnance, and whose breach *by others* [emphasis mine] will arouse in them the highest indignation."[26] It is the rationality of this second part – the indignation at the actions of others – that becomes difficult to explain on Hare's account. Suppose that S is given to the average degree of temptation to be unfaithful in marriage, but that J is unlikely ever to be so inclined. S will then have good reason to adopt for himself, and to urge, for those sufficiently similar to himself, a PF-principle of fidelity, along with the repugnance toward his own infidelity that internalization of the principle would involve. J will not have good reason to adopt nearly as

26 Hare, 1982, p. 32.

strong a principle about fidelity. Perhaps it will be rational for J to have no principle one way or the other about marital fidelity. Now, it goes considerably beyond any reasons that S has for S to develop a reaction pattern of indignation toward the infidelity of *others* (like J). One reason for this is that indignation, unlike repugnance, presupposes more than strong dislike; it presupposes a judgment of wrongness or injustice. If S is to have reason for a reaction of indignation toward the infidelity of people like J, it must be because J has violated a principle of the right which correctly applies to J. But the "principle" of marital fidelity that S, and perhaps many others, had reason to adopt does not in fact apply to J. At most, it might be weakly presumed to apply to J if we knew little about J and had to assume that he was average in this respect, and that his marital infidelities were probably also wrongs. What could certainly be presumed to apply to J, given Hare's view, would be the act-utilitarian principle, for it is right-defining. That is to say, an action that does not have the best overall results of any available to the agent is not right, period. But then it is also clear that the act-utilitarian principle does not automatically condemn marital infidelity, but only those instances of marital infidelity that lead to less than the best overall results.

Although one component of a PF-principle is something like a rule of thumb – that is, a generalization to the effect that most cases of marital infidelity are also wrong on act-utilitarian grounds – can that fact afford a basis for S's indignation about J's infidelity? Again, if S has little information about J, and so makes the assumption that J is probably an average person, then there is some basis for an epistemological presumption that J's act of infidelity is also wrong. But if S knows that J is not the kind of person who is much tempted by this sort of thing, J's infidelity might well afford the opposite epistemological presumption, namely that, because J normally has such a weak desire for such things that this case of infidelity is most probably justified on act-utilitarian grounds, being the kind of unhappy situation from which J ought to extricate himself.

This line of thought can be summarized in the following way. The rational individual, recognizing that PF-principles are useful rules of thumb backed by compunction, will also recognize that the PF-principles best for him are often not the best for others. He will therefore be cautious about making the adoption of a PF-principle a matter of indignation toward others' actions, though he will recognize its function in causing desirable repugnance toward some of his own behavior. This caution will appear in the rational individual's unwillingness to become indignant about behavior unless he has good reason to believe it to be wrong by the act-utilitarian principle, for that principle is right-defining and applicable to all.

One might suggest here that as a matter of psychological fact, repugnance and indignation are inseparable. Thus given the way we human beings are, we tend also to develop moral indignation toward those actions (perhaps with the qualification that they adversely affect the interests of others) toward which we have developed repugnance; that is, that indignation rides piggy-back on ordinary, personal repugnance. So if S is rational in developing a personal repugnance toward his own marital infidelity, S's indignation at the infidelity of others will be derivatively justified as a psychologically inescapable part of the package. But this suggestion is unconvincing. As is clear from our reactions in many departments of life, we are quite capable of making a distinction between those things which we strongly dislike for our own part only, and those things which, we think, rightly arouse our indignation. Thus I personally feel repugnance at the thought of my drinking snake-blood wine or, to a lesser extent, of my eating rabbit. But I certainly don't get indignant about someone else's doing so, mainly because I would not think that I had any *reason* for indignation. Although I do not think there is anything morally wrong with these things, I also do not think that indignation is in order. No doubt the extent to which one is capable of developing reactions that respect this distinction depends on the extent to which one has developed an understanding of the difference. Perhaps more people ought to work harder to remember it in their own reactions and judgments. But the crucial point is that we are capable of making the distinction, and that the rational person adopting a PF-principle will not have reason for adding indignation to repugnance.

Because it represents moral rules for the most part as those existing or proposed rules that rational utilitarian moral agents could not reasonably object to, the function of which is to apply equally to all and partially to define the right, this set of problems does not arise for the MLM. A moral rule or principle like that of marital fidelity, if justified in the first place, will likely be justified as a public, collective moral rule for a group, and not only as a standard of behavior that it will be rational, in some particular form, for most individuals to adopt as a means of making more effective their own individual attempts to do good. If a public, collective status for the rule is justified, then it is natural to conceive of it as a rule, compliance with which is a matter of legitimate concern to everyone.

If a moral rule has this status, indignation at its breach by others is a reaction with a genuine foundation. For the rule constitutes a standard that rational individuals who seek to promote the good, and who take a collective point of view, would agree to. The point of the rule is to constrain the reasoning and actions of all, and to do so in the interest of promoting good. Further, part of the reason for having such a rule is to enable collective influence on the behavior of individuals. Thus a breach of the rule is properly seen as something in which another individual can legitimately take an interest. In this way, indignation has the foundation that simple repugnance does not need: the well-founded judgment that a standard of the right has been violated. One whose indignation is based on this kind of a judgment then invokes the authority of social collective rules. To invoke legitimate collective demands in this way would be quite impossible if the standard being violated represented nothing more than a personal rule of thumb backed by strong compunction.

The relationship between the levels

The relationship between critical and intuitive thinking, it seems, would on Hare's levels approach be especially unstable. Recall that PF-principles do not define the right, but that the critical, act-utilitarian principle does. Internalizing and following PF-principles may be instrumental in leading us to do the right things, but the right is defined independently of them. So far as knowing what the right action is, it is the rule of thumb component of a PF-principle which is useful, affording as it does an epistemological presumption that compliance will also turn out to be morally right. The compunction component itself provides no reason why something is right or wrong; it provides at most a feeling and a reaction. This sets up a tension between the way in which the disposition appears from the inside, and the way in which it appears from the outside. From the outside, such a disposition is seen as a useful

214

though sometimes flawed instrument toward achieving the right behavior and intuitions. From the inside, they are to appear as an immediate sense of what is right or wrong, as the source of moral intuitions. Moreover, they are only a part of the character of the moral person if they are viewed from the inside, noninstrumentally.[27] This problem would be eliminated if PF-principles were taken to be right-defining, at least in certain contexts, and on the assumption that certain background conditions were satisfied. Then one could appeal to objective criteria (as to whether the background conditions were in fact satisfied) in order to determine whether the critical principle or the PF-principle was right-defining. But such is not Hare's view. Whether we are to think like archangels or like proles depends at bottom on happenstance. It depends on how much we tend already to be like an archangel or like a prole: "[I]t depends on what powers of thought and character each one of us, for the time being, thinks he possesses."[28]

The PF-principles are therefore unstable, because those who adopt them will have to know that they constitute nothing more than roughly reliable guides backed by compunction. If one did not know that they are epistemologically secondary to the act-utilitarian principle, then one would not know that that critical principle is to be appealed to in cases of revision, adoption, or conflict among PF-principles. And if one does know that the act-utilitarian principle is right-defining while PF-principles are not, there will be an ever-increasing tendency simply to cut through the nonessential and go directly to the critical principle. This is especially likely when, in engaging in moral debate with others, one recognizes that the PF-principle that it is rational to adopt can vary significantly from one individual to another. Rather than inquire deeply into questions about the PF-principles that it would be rational for a person in your position to adopt (as opposed to someone in my position), why not simply carry on the debate using the act-utilitarian principle as our shared premise? The pressures in this direction are only strengthened when one realizes that, in cases of

---

27 Williams, 1985, pp. 107–8.
28 Hare, 1981, p. 45. Bernard Williams remarks that, having identified the distinction between theory and practice in psychological terms, Hare's view makes the artificial supposition that "a thorough commitment to the values of friendship and so on can merely alternate, on a timetable prescribed by calm or activity, with an alien set of reflections." Williams, 1985, p. 109.

conflict, one who employs act-utilitarian reasoning – assuming that his reasoning is otherwise correct – can always trump someone who reasons with PF-principles. The instability would then find its way into the very compunctions which form a necessary part of our acceptance of PF-principles. If we recognize the epistemologically secondary status of these principles, and tend increasingly to think of the real moral debate as taking place on act-utilitarian territory, moral persons will tend to transfer their compunction to the act-utilitarian principle itself.

The source of these difficulties about the relationship between PF-principles and critical principles lies in the fact that PF-principles do not constitute objective standards of right behavior, but psychological dispositions and beliefs that it is useful for individuals to have. On the MLM, the relationship between the levels of moral reasoning is a matter, not of psychological barrier or compunction, but of objective moral standards available to all. For example, whether it is appropriate for one to use the primary principle rather than a generally accepted moral rule depends on whether the generally accepted rule is justified in the sense explained above. It is not a matter of what powers of thought and character one happens to possess, or happens to think one possesses.

Another example is the way in which Hare's treatment of the normative force of PF-principles differs from the MLM's treatment of the normative force of a group's justified moral rules. On Hare's view, it will be a rare case indeed in which one can know that noncompliance with a familiar PF-principle (like that prohibiting killing the innocent) will maximize overall good. Examples of this are far rarer than philosophers think, and PF-principles are beneficial precisely because they give us the inhibitions and caution necessary to avoid the temptations of theory and hypothetical example. But if it is absolutely clear that compliance with a PF-principle would not maximize, then it is also clear that it is the right-defining act-utilitarian principle that should be followed, not the PF-principle. If killing one innocent person really will save several innocent persons from being killed, and that is the sum total of relevant consequences, then one ought to do as an act utilitarian would do.

On the MLM one also recognizes the many reasons for caution. Even one who follows nothing but the primary principle would have reason to be very careful about proposals to do such things as kill the innocent to save many more. In short, all of the act-

216

utilitarian cautionary strategies remain in force. But what is different about the MLM's way of conceiving of moral rules is that they can provide a further reason; that is, they can preempt the primary principle, and exclude certain considerations that would otherwise be relevant. If rational utilitarian agents would have reason to agree to certain right-defining rules, thus abdicating their title to make direct use of the primary principle, then the point of such an enterprise can be recognized by the rational person faced with such a dilemma. That certain reasons are to be excluded is then correctly understood as a truth to be apprehended, and not just a strong personal disposition to be grappled with. Thus there are, let us assume, generally accepted public rules that prohibit the taking of innocent life, and allow little or no leeway for projects where life is taken in order to save more lives. Let us assume also that there are good utilitarian reasons for incorporating this restriction in the rules. In addition to the usual cautionary reasons, then, I have further reasons for complying with the rule: I recognize the good that the rule secures and, taking the collective point of view, I recognize that my position under the rules is no different from that of any other arbitrarily chosen person.

10

Concluding observations: Summary and a look ahead

The preceding chapter's examination of some alternative consequentialist conceptions was unfortunately brief, being limited to some of the most noteworthy proposals. There are clearly many other examples of indirect consequentialism that could just as well have been usefully considered. More importantly, each of these proposals no doubt would contain ideas important to a full understanding of ethical reasoning. But at the same time, our examination of alternative conceptions does, I think, show some recurrent patterns of failure.

One such pattern of failure arises from the fact that the secondary, or intermediate, rules of the theory either are not conceived to be right-defining or, if they are, no adequate rationale is provided for our recognition of their right-defining status. Hare's account of PF-principles is an example of the former; Rawls's practice-rules an example of the latter. Thus, to consider the former kind of case, when intermediate rules are not conceived as right-defining, their status as objective standards of right behavior is compromised and unstable. This is so because, in cases of genuine conflict, the act-utilitarian formula will always take priority over a PF-principle, since the PF-principle is to be viewed as no more than a generally useful and often fallible guide to right action, while the act-utilitarian formula serves as the standard defining the rightness of actions. It is, as it were, the ultimate authority on questions of rightness. It follows that the extent to which one can dispense with the PF-principles that are useful to the masses of people depends on one's personal knowledge, skills, strengths, weaknesses, and proclivities. As we noticed, this problem is not restricted to Hare's account of PF-principles, but belongs to any conception of rules or principles that takes them to be an individual's instruments for helping one reduce mistakes, all in a program of attempting to do

218

at is right by some other standard. Thus we saw that Berger's account of rules as strategies, combined with familiar facts about individual human differences, implies that the rule that it is rational for one person to adopt will often be different from the rule that it is rational for another to employ.

A second, and more important, source of difficulty, however, flows from this very person-relativity. If moral rules are person-relative in this sense, they cannot serve functions that we commonly understand them to perform and, above all, that it is greatly beneficial to have performed. Moral rules of this kind cannot serve as objective standards of judgment and criticism, standards both applicable and available to all within an understood group. Using only person-relative rules, our moral judgments would become complicated in odd and unexpected ways, because different rules would be applicable to different people, depending on their personal characteristics and situations. Moreover, as we have seen in connection with Hare's view, the repugnance toward certain actions that comes with acceptance of a PF-principle does not provide any legitimate foundation for *indignation* when those same actions are done by others, and this too suggests that person-relative rules are insufficient to what we usually regard as one of the main functions of moral judgment. That *all* moral rules are like this does not square with phenomenological facts. I have argued that, if a moral rule is understood, not as a person-relative strategy or set of dispositions to react, but as a collectively rational rule that is independent of such personal characteristics and so applies to all, collective influence can be exercised on behavior in a manner consistent with the good of social union. This utilitarian benefit would therefore weigh in favor of the kind of rule that moral phenomenology already suggests moral rules to be.

Another recurrent pattern of failure for indirect versions of consequentialism arises from a dilemma they usually pose for the idea of maximization. On the one hand, the idea of maximization seems to be built into consequentialism from the very outset. At the least, the twin ideas that doing good constitutes the basis for morality, and that doing the most good possible is what the rational person ought therefore to do, have seemed to many to constitute the main motivation behind consequentialism. But it has not been easy to see how an indirect version of consequentialism can make use of the idea of maximization without losing the force of its main idea:

that some concept like that of a rule stands between the rightness of acts and the promotion of good. For if it be supposed that nothing less than a maximizing rule will do the job of defining the right, we must usually admit that nothing in fact exists or is likely to exist that will do the job. And if the rightness of our acts is to be measured against hypothetical rules that would be ideal, the moral guidance yielded will no doubt be ambiguous and conflicting. Further, a collapse back into act consequentialism will threaten if rules are too freely revisable. On the other hand, if we abandon or modify the idea of maximization, holding that even the rules themselves need not maximize to be right-defining, we seem to lose touch with what motivated the theory in the first place.

Faced with this dilemma, what has seemed to me to be the most plausible course is not to abandon the maximization idea, but to push it further in the background: first, by allowing collective maximization sometimes to replace individual maximization, because there are circumstances in which the public, collective recognition of restrictions on individual maximization can better serve the purpose of maximization simpliciter; secondly, by recognizing a reasonable requirement for the minimal acceptability of moral rules, such that a necessary condition for the validity of an accepted moral rule is that its acceptance constitute an improvement over the utilitarian state of nature in which everyone separately follows the primary principle; and thirdly, by the continuing obligation under the primary principle to improve rules and institutions. Now, it seems clear that these theoretical expedients do not together amount to a disguised form of act consequentialism. For they require the moral agent to take existing, justified moral rules seriously in ways that go beyond the status that such rules would have in any act-consequentialist theory. The performance of one's general obligation to improve rules and institutions, I have argued, is to be regarded as a different enterprise – to be conducted using different ground rules – from that of deciding what one's obligations are under existing rules. Moreover, the reasons for regarding it as a different enterprise with different ground rules spring from the very idea of moral rules as public, collective standards of right applying equally to all. And this conception of the two enterprises as distinguished in this way is itself, I have argued, defensible on consequentialist grounds: When people adopt and respect the distinction, they are much more likely to produce greater overall good in the long run than when they do not.

Perhaps the most vexing and recurring problem for any version of indirect consequentialism is that of providing a rationale to explain why one ought to comply with a moral rule, even a generally optimific moral rule, when doing so in that instance would not maximize overall good. For many philosophers it has seemed irrational to pass by an opportunity to maximize when maximization is, after all, conceived to be the ultimate object of action. In addition, to many of these same philosophers, it has seemed inconsistent with the idea of individual moral autonomy for the moral agent simply to exclude from moral reasoning considerations that are normally relevant and, moreover, considerations which, on the consequentialist view, are supposed to constitute the foundation of the right. It might seem to constitute a kind of deliberate blindness, an abdication of individual moral responsibility. But there need be nothing irrational in taking a collective point of view, recognizing that certain important goods can only be realized if there is a collective acknowledgement of rules that apply equally to all – of rules conceived from the outset to set a new standard of rightness rather than merely to capture some preexisting set of distinctions. Indeed, there would be something prima facie odd about an account of rationality which implies that it is irrational for individuals to acknowledge themselves as parts of collective effort to maximize, each then doing his part in respecting collectively rational limits on individual maximization.

The argument for the priority of rules made use of the idea that some important components of the good derive from a collective resolve, thus not being reducible to the good consequences of individual acts. If some find this idea to be a source of unease, perhaps it is because it seems to open up possibilities for abuse. For to speak of mutual resolve and trust, apart from the good-producing actions to which they lead, seems perilously close to the idea that group solidarity, even group exclusivity, constitutes a reason for action in and of itself. And this, the thought might run, may in turn be the first conceptual step toward totalitarian collectivism.

I can only say that the collective good of trust that I have in mind here is far too lean to support such a line of thought. The good of trust and of social union generally is important because it constitutes a basis for virtually any kind of cooperation. It is important even in societies in which people do good primarily through the immediate pursuit of their own private ends.

All of this forces us, then, to the place where consequentialism is designed to lead us: to the theory of the good. Some would claim that indirect consequentialism solves problems about the rightness of actions by pushing them back to questions about the appraisal of states of affairs. But in answer to this, one can say that, if consequentialism, direct or indirect, is correct, that is precisely where many of the questions about the right ought to be resolved. For if some kind of mystical social solidarity – some "realization of the self in the whole" – were ultimately good (and there are strong reasons for thinking it is not), then, if our fundamental duty is to do good, it would be hard indeed to avoid the implications: Maximizing this good would be part of our duty.

This shift of concern to the theory of the good does not trivialize theory so long as we are able to analyze and see the connections that various goods have to one another, and, in doing this, not to base our conclusions on a theory of the right. If the argument of this book makes even covert appeal to intuitions, therefore, it is not to moral intuitions about what is right or wrong, but to intuitions about human psychology – mutual attitudes and perceptions, and the ways in which those attitudes and perceptions, as well as the behavior that arises from them, can be altered for the better by moral rules and codes.

A case in point is the use made in this book of the notion of the good of publicity and autonomy. The conception of our reasons for action does not depend, as some versions of indirect consequentialism would make it depend, on denying or limiting publicity to moral truths. It is not as if the ordinary moral agent is to be prevented somehow from knowing what is objectively right, so that passing up an opportunity to maximize will be natural and even rational, given his limited evidence and false beliefs. On the contrary, the claim is that exclusionary reasons can be public such that the rational moral agent consciously bases actions upon them. Indeed, as I have argued, publicity plays an even more important role than that. It is necessary to realizing the good of autonomy, because we cannot be fully self-governing creatures if we deprive ourselves, or are deprived by others, of the exercise of our capacities to know what is right. So, if this claim about autonomy's value is

222

correct, any suggestion that we might do more good in the world by having systematically false beliefs about the right must take account of the tradeoff: the gain in producing external good will have to be weighed against the loss of autonomy. It is plausible to suppose – though I have not attempted to provide very much argument for the idea – that this notion of the good of moral-agent self-governance through exercise of one's normal, undiminished capacity to know the right is central to our very concept of morality, and that this is one of the main reasons why the public character of moral norms has most often simply been taken for granted rather than explicitly argued for.

A final observation concerns my most general purpose in writing this essay. I have tried to buttress the case for some version of a consequentialist account of morality. But I do not even claim that a version of consequentialism can ever be constructed that will be capable of providing a complete account of all aspects of morality. I have, rather, argued a case for an indirect consequentialism primarily in the belief that indirect consequentialism does not, or need not, deserve its current unpopularity among moral philosophers. This unpopularity, I think, has two main sources. One is a predisposition to think of justified morality almost exclusively as a converging set of individually rational rules, strategies, or traits and dispositions, rather than as a social, collectively rational instrument that requires the individual's acknowledgement and participation. This may be due to what Hart called "an excessively Protestant approach" to morality. A second may have to do with this century's bad experiences with the opposite kind of morality, one in which individual principles are conceived to be strictly subordinate to the group and its collective ideas about the good and the right. The philosopher's job, I think, is to correct the one kind of error without encouraging an opposite error. This, I would like to think, I have in some small part done in this book.

Bibliography

Adams, Robert Merrihew. 1976. "Motive Utilitarianism." *The Journal of Philosophy* 73, no. 4:467–81.

Aiken, H. D. ed. 1972. *Hume's Moral and Political Philosophy*. New York: Hafner Publishing Co.

Anscombe, G. E. M. 1958. "Modern Moral Philosophy." *Philosophy* 33, pp. 1–19, reprinted in *The Definition of Morality*. 1970. Edited by G. Wallace and A. D. M. Walker. London: Methuen & Co., Ltd.

Aquinas, St. Thomas. 1945. *The Basic Writings of Saint Thomas Aquinas*. Edited by Anton C. Pegis. New York: Random House, Inc.

Bales, R. Eugene. 1971. "Act-Utilitarianism: Account of Right-Making Characteristics or Decision-Making Procedure?" *American Philosophical Quarterly* 8, no. 3:257–65.

Baron, Marcia. 1984. "The Alleged Repugnance of Acting From Duty." *The Journal of Philosophy* 81, no. 4:197–220.

Bayles, Michael D., ed. 1968. *Contemporary Utilitarianism*. Garden City, N.Y.: Doubleday & Co.

Bell, John. 1983. *Policy Arguments in Judicial Decisions*. New York: Oxford University Press.

Berger, Fred. 1984. *Happiness, Justice, and Freedom: The Moral and Political Philosophy of John Stuart Mill*. Berkeley: University of California Press.

Brandt, R. B. 1954. *Hopi Ethics*. Chicago: University of Chicago Press.

1959. *Ethical Theory*. Englewood Cliffs, N.J.: Prentice-Hall, Inc.

1963. "Toward a Credible Form of Utilitarianism." In *Morality and the Language of Conduct*. Detroit: Wayne State University Press.

1979. *A Theory of the Good and the Right*. Oxford: Oxford University Press.

1985. "A Motivational Theory of Excuses in the Criminal Law." In *Nomos XXVII: Criminal Justice*. New York: New York University Press.

Darwall, Stephen L. 1986. "Agent-Centered Restrictions from the Inside Out." *Philosophical Studies* 50:291–319.

Dworkin, Gerald. 1988. *The Theory and Practice of Autonomy*. Cambridge University Press.

Dworkin, Ronald. 1986. *Law's Empire*. Cambridge, Mass.: Harvard University Press.

Feinberg, Joel. 1970. *Doing and Deserving*. Princeton, N.J.: Princeton University Press.

1984. *Harm to Others*. New York: Oxford University Press.

1986. *Harm to Self*. New York: Oxford University Press.

Fletcher, George. 1978. *Rethinking Criminal Law*. Boston: Little, Brown and Co.

Fontana, Biancamaria, ed. 1988. *Benjamin Constant: Political Writings*. Cambridge University Press.

Friedman, Lawrence M. 1984. *American Law: An Introduction*. New York: W. W. Norton & Co.

Griffin, James. 1986. *Well-Being: Its Meaning, Measurement and Moral Importance*. New York: Oxford University Press.

Hare, R. M. 1963. *Freedom and Reason*. New York: Oxford University Press.

1981. *Moral Thinking: Its Levels, Method and Point*. Oxford: Oxford University Press.

1982. "Ethical Theory and Utilitarianism." In *Utilitarianism and Beyond*. Edited by Amartya Sen and B. A. O. Williams. Cambridge University Press.

Hart, H. L. A. 1958. "Legal and Moral Obligation." In *Essays in Moral Philosophy*. Edited by A. I. Melden. Seattle: University of Washington Press.

1961. *The Concept of Law*. New York: Oxford University Press.

Hayek, F. A. 1967. *Studies in Philosophy, Politics and Economics*. London: Routledge & Kegan Paul.

1978. *New Studies in Philosophy, Politics, Economics and the History of Ideas*. Chicago: University of Chicago Press.

Hodgson, D. H. 1967. *Consequences of Utilitarianism*. Oxford: Oxford University Press.

Hume, David. 1888. *A Treatise of Human Nature*. Edited by L. A. Selby-Bigge. New York: Oxford University Press.

Johnson, Conrad D. 1981. "Equity: Its Scope and Its Relation to Other Objectives." In *Income Support: Conceptual and Policy Issues*. Edited by Peter G. Brown, Conrad Johnson, and Paul Vernier. Totowa, N.J.: Rowman and Littlefield.

Kagan, Shelly. 1989. *The Limits of Morality*. Oxford: The Clarendon Press.

Kavka, Gregory. 1986. *Hobbesian Moral and Political Theory*. Princeton, N.J.: Princeton University Press.

Klosko, George. 1987. "Presumptive Benefit, Fairness, and Political Obligation." *Philosophy & Public Affairs* 16, no. 3:241–59.

Lewis, David. 1969. *Convention*. Cambridge, Mass.: Harvard University Press.

Luban, David. 1988. *Lawyer's Ethics*. Princeton, N.J.: Princeton University Press.

Lyons, David. 1965. *Forms and Limits of Utilitarianism*. Cambridge University Press.

McCloskey, H. J. 1968. "An Examination of Restricted Utilitarianism." In *Contemporary Utilitarianism*. Edited by Michael D. Bayles. Garden City, N.Y.: Doubleday & Co.

Mill, John Stuart. 1956. *On Liberty*. Edited by Currin V. Shields. Indianapolis: Bobbs-Merrill Co.

226

1957. *Utilitarianism.* Edited by Oskar Piest. Indianapolis: Bobbs-Merrill Co.

Moore, G. E. 1966. *Principia Ethica.* Cambridge University Press.

Nagel, Thomas. 1979. *Mortal Questions.* Cambridge University Press.

1986. *The View from Nowhere.* New York: Oxford University Press.

Nozick, Robert. 1974. *Anarchy, State, and Utopia.* New York: Basic Books.

Parfit, Derek. 1984. *Reasons and Persons.* New York: Oxford University Press.

Postow, B. C. 1977. "Generalized Act Utilitarianism." *Analysis* 37, no. 2:49–52.

Quinn, Warren. 1989. "Actions, Intentions, and Consequences: The Doctrine of Double Effect." *Philosophy & Public Affairs* 18, no. 4:334–51.

Railton, Peter. 1984. "Alienation, Consequentialism, and the Demands of Morality." *Philosophy & Public Affairs* 13, no. 2:134–171.

Rawls, John. 1955. "Two Concepts of Rules." *Philosophical Review* 64:3–32. Reprinted in *Contemporary Utilitarianism.* Edited by Michael D. Bayles. Garden City, N. Y.: Doubleday & Co.

1971. *A Theory of Justice.* Cambridge, Mass.: Harvard University Press.

Raz, Joseph. 1975. *Practical Reason and Norms.* London: Hutchinson and Co.

1977. "Promises and Obligations." In *Law, Morality, and Society.* Edited by P. M. S. Hacker and J. Raz. New York: Oxford University Press.

1979. *The Authority of Law.* Oxford: Oxford University Press.

1985. "Authority and Justification." *Philosophy & Public Affairs* 14, no. 1:3–29.

1986. *The Morality of Freedom.* New York: Oxford University Press.

Regan, Donald. 1980. *Utilitarianism and Cooperation.* New York: Oxford University Press.

Ross, W. D.. 1930. *The Right and the Good.* New York: Oxford University Press.

Scanlon, T. M.. 1972. "A Theory of Freedom of Expression." *Philosophy & Public Affairs* 1, no. 2:204–26.

1975. "Preference and Urgency." *Journal of Philosophy* 72, no. 19:655–69.

1976. "Rawls' Theory of Justice." In *Reading Rawls.* Edited by Norman Daniels. New York: Basic Books.

1978. "Rights, Goals and Fairness." In *Public and Private Morality.* Edited by Stuart Hampshire. Cambridge University Press.

1982. "Contractualism and Utilitarianism." In *Utilitarianism and Beyond.* Edited by Amartya Sen and B. A. O. Williams. Cambridge University Press.

Scheffler, Samuel. 1982. *The Rejection of Consequentialism.* New York: Oxford University Press.

1988. *Consequentialism and Its Critics.* New York: Oxford University Press.

Schelling, Thomas. 1960. *The Strategy of Conflict.* New York: Oxford University Press.

Schoeck, Helmut. 1987. *Envy: A Theory of Social Behavior*. Indianapolis: Liberty Press.

Sen, Amartya, and B. A. O. Williams, eds. 1982. *Utilitarianism and Beyond*. Cambridge University Press.

1982a. "Rights and Agency." *Philosophy & Public Affairs* 11, no. 1:3–39.

Sidgwick, Henry. 1966. *The Methods of Ethics*, 7th ed. Reissue. London: Macmillan.

Simmons, A. John. 1979. *Moral Principles and Political Obligations*. Princeton, N.J.: Princeton University Press.

1987. "The Anarchist Position: A Reply to Klosko and Senor." *Philosophy & Public Affairs* 16, no. 3:269–79.

Slote, Michael A. 1983. *Goods and Virtues*. Oxford: The Clarendon Press.

1985a. *Common-sense Morality and Consequentialism*. London: Routledge & Kegan Paul.

1985b. "Utilitarianism, Moral Dilemmas, and Moral Cost." *American Philosophical Quarterly* 22, no. 2:161–8.

Smart, J. J. C., and B. A. O. Williams. 1973. *Utilitarianism: For and Against*. Cambridge University Press.

Sobel, Jordan Howard. 1987. "Kant's Moral Idealism." *Philosophical Studies* 52:277–87.

Stocker, Michael. 1976. "The Schizophrenia of Modern Ethical Theories." *The Journal of Philosophy* 63, no. 4:453–6.

Urmson, J. O. 1968. *The Emotive Theory of Ethics*. New York: Oxford University Press.

Williams, B. A. O.. 1967. "The Idea of Equality." In *Philosophy, Politics and Society*. 2d ser. Edited by Peter Laslett and W. G. Runciman. Oxford: Basil Blackwell.

1973. "A Critique of Utilitarianism." In *Utilitarianism: For and Against*. Edited by J. J. C. Smart and B. A. O. Williams. Cambridge University Press.

1985. *Ethics and the Limits of Philosophy*. Cambridge, Mass.: Harvard University Press.

Winston, Kenneth I., ed. 1981. *The Principles of Social Order: Selected Essays of Lon L. Fuller*. Durham, N.C.: Duke University Press.

Wong, David B. 1984. *Moral Relativity*. Berkeley and Los Angeles: University of California Press.

Index

act adequacy premise
  stated, 24–5
  see also priority of acts to rules;
    rules, surplus causal effect of
act consequentialism
  and blaming, *see* praise and blame
  defined, 1
  and MLM on conflicts, 161–3
  simplicity of, 143–4
  see also primary principle
act utilitarianism, *see* act
    consequentialism
Adams, R., 21, 92
Aiken, H., 132
Anscombe, E., xi
Aquinas, xi–xii, 109
Audubon Society, 183–4
autonomy
  definition, 101·
  good of, 6, 13–15, 222–3
  meanings of, 13–14
  see also publicity and the value of
    autonomy

Bales, R., 41, 89, 99
Baron, M., 105
Bayles, M., 5, 50, 78–9, 155, 160, 170,
    188–9
Bell, J., 119
Bentham, J., vi
Berger, F., 5, 22, 110–11, 219
blame, *see* praise and blame
Brandt, R., xii, 25, 35–7, 41, 44, 46,
    89, 96, 118, 121, 157, 170, 198–
    208
Brandt's concept of morally wrong,
    201–2
Brandt's definition of morally right,
    36, 199
  proposed revision of, 204–5
compliance with rules: argument for,
    45–6, 221

conflicts, *see* practical reasoning
conscience: person of, 157–60
conscience utilitarianism, 92
conscience worship, 92
consequentialism
  defined, 1
  indirect, 3, 218–23
  rule, 3
Constant, B., 88, 104
constraints, *see* restrictions, agent-
    centered

Darwall, S., xii, 21
deontology, 3
  see also intuitions, deontological;
    Kantian deontology; moral
    emotions, deontological
discretion, *see* primary principle
duty, *see* obligation
Dworkin, R.,. 119, 127
Dyson, E., 173

equality
  instrumental value of, 17–19, 65–6
  intrinsic to the good, 64
  see also rules, equal applicability of
excuses, *see* justifications and excuses

fairness, deontological intuitions
    about, 64
Feinberg, J., 11, 130–2, 139–40
Fletcher, G., 57, 96
Fontana, B., 88
Friedman, L., 174–5
Fuller, L., 34

good
  distribution-sensitive dimensions
    of, 13, 64
  pluralistic concept of, 10
  species ideal and, 10
good-doing, *see* primary principle

229

good-doing projects, argument for obligation of, 45–7
goods
  indispensable, 4–6, 46–7, 149–50
  optional, 46–7, 149–50
grading of wrongs, 161–2
Griffin, J., 10–11
group membership
  circumstances of, 146–51
  concept of, 39
  see also good-doing projects

Hare, R.M., xi, 15, 35, 208–18
Hare's concept of prima facie principles, 208–14
Hart, G., 176–8
Hart, H.L.A., xi, 129, 134, 223
Hayek, F., 168–9
Hopi familial obligations, 199, 202–3
Hume, D., xii, 26–9, 45, 60, 132, 165
Humean convention, 6, 43, 45, 82

indignation
  personal repugnance contrasted, 211–13
  see also Hare's concept of prima facie principles
infallible optimizer, 53–6
interests
  comparison of, 11–13
  concept of, 11
  universal, 11–13
  see also goods, indispensable
intuitions
  deontological, 59–62
  see also fairness

Johnson, C., 19
justice (individual virtue of), 6, 27–9, 34
justifications and excuses, 95–8

Kagan, S., 67, 76–7
Kant, I., xii
Kantian deontology, 17, 58–61, 99–102
Kavka, G., 46
Keynes, J., vi, 82

levels of thinking, 208–17
  see also Hare, R.M.
Lewis, D., 207
Luban, D., 70, 73
Lyons, D., 25, 193–4

McCloskey, H., 155, 160, 189
marital fidelity
  as individual versus collective strategy, 210–13
  see also Hare's concept of prima facie principles
maximization of good
  doctrine of, 2–7, 67–9, 75–6, 219–22
  reconciliation of agent-centered restrictions with, 51–8
Mercer, H., 182, 184–5
Miami Herald, 177–8, 181
Mill, J.S., xi–xii, 16, 110, 134
mistrust
  collective license as source of, 54–5, 79
  discretion as source of, 22, 32, 34–5, 42–3, 49, 79, 81–2, 85–7, 152
  and indefinite public boundaries, 34
  see also strategies, collective; trust
Moore, G.E., 102
moral emotions: deontological, 59–64
moral imperialism, 146
moral and legal obligation
  circumstances of, 136–42
  see also priority of rules
moral legislation, concept of, 7–8, 168–73, 183–5, 205–6
moral relativism, 113–14, 129–30, 146, 170

Nagel, T., 51–2, 55, 67
Nozick, R., 129

objective rightness
  contrasted with character traits, 91–5
  contrasted with decision procedures, 90–1
  magnetism of, 108–9
obligation: analysis of, 134

Parfit, D., 24, 38, 68
Piest, O., 134
Postow, B., 48
practical reasoning
  in the absence of generally accepted rules, 165–7
  and agent's relation to group's code, 146–51, 163–5
  and conflicting rules, 160–5
  and nonideal rules, 151–6

230

practices
  consensus model of, 119–23
  deeper rationale (DR-) model of,
    123–8
  see also rules
praise and blame: role of rules in, 30–2
primary principle
  act consequentialism compared,
    20–1
  defined, 20
  and discretion, 19–23
  and killing, 129–30
  motive utilitarian interpretation of,
    20–1
  as scalar principle, 20
  see also utilitarian state of nature
priority of acts to rules, 25, 66–7
  see also act adequacy premise
priority of rules
  circumstances, 83–7
  and general acceptance, 36, 44, 49,
    196–7
  see also Rawls's concept of the logi-
    cal priority of rules
privacy of candidates for public office,
    176–82
private society: social union contrasted
    with, 15–17
public accumulative harms
  defined, 130–2
  Snowy Egret, example of, 182–7
publicity
  characterizes the right, 98–100
  for circumstances of blameworthi-
    ness, 32
  and traits, 107–9
  and the value of autonomy, 100–2,
    104, 222–3

Quinn, W., 61

Railton, P., 22, 89–96, 99, 102
rationalist constructivism, 168–9
rationality: points of view of collective
    and individual, 48–51, 67–9
Rawls, J., 5, 11, 15–6, 46, 50, 188–98,
    218
Rawls's concept of the logical priority
    of rules, 188–90
Rawls's legislator/judge distinction, 5,
    50, 192–7
Raz, J., 36, 40, 136
reasons

exclusionary, 40–1, 69–75
protected, 40–1, 110, 136, 155
Regan, D., 38
restrictions
  agent-centered (ACR), 21–3, 51–8
  see also maximization of good
Ross, W.D., 83–4
rules
  as bases of mutual trust, 27–9
  as collective expressions, 54–8, 62
  coordination as function of, 27–8,
    190–2
  equal applicability of, 17–19, 64–6
  general acceptance of:
    defined, 37
    potential: defined, 39
  hypothetical ideal, 36, 49, 151–2
  justified: concept of, 38, 145–6
  moral and legal distinguished, 132–
    42
  praising and blaming role, 30–2
  preemptive status of justified, 39–
    41
  rationale of, 68–9, 79–83
  right-defining function of, 5, 30–2,
    35, 49, 77–8, 88, 190–2, 206–8,
    218–19
  strategy conception of, 5–6, 110–7
  surplus causal effect of, 6, 26–30,
    48
  of thumb, 35, 91, 111–12, 212, 214
  universality and scope of, 65, 169–
    73
  worship of, 78–83, 200
  see also strategies, collective; moral
    and legal obligation; practices;
    priority of rules

Safer, M., 177–8
Scanlon, T., 12, 34, 46, 53, 55, 129
Scheffler, S., 2, 21, 52–4, 89, 99
Schelling, T., 34
Schoeck, H., 19
Selby-Bigge, L. A., 26
self-defense, 56–7
Sen, A., 128
Sidgwick, H., 30, 92, 106
Simmons, J., 64, 151
Slote, M., xii, 2, 20, 58, 75, 94–5, 97,
    165
Smart, J., 24, 30–2, 41, 44, 78–83,
    103, 152

231

Smart's mixed strategy proposal on
  rule compliance, 44–5, 82–3,
  152
Sobel, J., 49
social union
  defined, 15–6
  good of, 15–7
software property rights, 173–6
Stocker, M., 105
strategies
  collective:
    and individual contrasted, 32–8,
      112–17, 210–14
    as public boundaries, 34–5
    supervision and control, role in,
      33–4
    see also rules
  individual
    relative to average individual,
      113–14
    relative to particular individual,
      113
    and universality, 114–15
    see also Hare's concept of prima
      facie principles

traits and motives
  as instrumental, 92
  as right defining, 92

rules of thumb contrasted, 91
  see also utilitarianism
trust
  bases of, 27–30
  kinds of, 28–9
  see also mistrust

Urmson, J., 159
utilitarian state of nature, 38, 43, 49–
  50, 144, 199, 220
utilitarianism
  conscience: defined, 92
  motive: defined, 20–1
  see also consequentialism
utility
  acceptance, 25, 194
  and blaming, 30–2
  conformity, 25, 194–5
  as reducible to that of acts, 6,
    24–5
  see also act adequacy premise; rules,
    surplus causal effect

Victoria, Queen, 183–5

Williams, B., 18, 24–6, 30, 41, 44, 73,
  103, 215
Winston, K., 34
Wong, D., 170